Gaelic-English
English-Gaelic

Gaelic-English
English-Gaelic
DICTIONARY

Gaelic-English Dictionary compiled by Dougal Buchanan
English-Gaelic Dictionary compiled by RLS Ltd

HIPPOCRENE BOOKS
New York

Hippocrene paperback edition, 1999.
Third printing, 2006.
First published in the United States of America in 1999 by
arrangement with Lomond Books, Scotland.

Gaelic-English dictionary compiled by Dougal Buchanan,
English-Gaelic dictionary compiled by RLS Ltd

© Text 1998 Geddes & Grosset Ltd,
David Dale House, New Lanark, Scotland

ISBN 0-7818-0789-1

Printed in the United States of America.

Introduction

Within its convenient coat-pocket compass, this dictionary aims to provide a generous range of vocabulary. It is designed both for the student of Gaelic and for those with a more general interest in Scotland's languages and cultures — for all, in fact, who wish to have a sample, a handy *vade mecum*, an *aide-mémoire*, of the ancient tongue.

The emphasis remains on mainstream language while touching on a wide range of activity and experience, from the traditional and rural way of life still to be found in the Highlands and Islands to some of the innovations of the later twentieth century. The Gaelic-English section also includes a significant number of common phrases and expressions and so will reward the browser as well as the searcher for a particular word.

In a publication of this size, it is not possible to include all the different inflections of the items listed or to give much help with grammar. Anyone wishing to learn the language is recommended to use this dictionary in conjunction with one or more of the printed, audio and audiovisual courses readily available in bookshops. They should also find it very useful to get in touch with the Gaelic learners' organisation, CLI, 62 High Street, Invergordon, Ross-shire IV18 0DH, e-mail cli@sol.co.uk, which runs and co-ordinates courses and support for learners and publishes a quarterly magazine.

Gaelic is a language the structure of which is markedly different from that of English. In particular, in common with the other Celtic languages, Gaelic can show grammatical change at the beginning of many words, a process known as lenition or aspiration. This involves the softening of certain initial consonants and is represented in writing by the insertion of *h* immediately after the consonant concerned. By mentally removing this *h*, the newcomer to the language will be able to identify the radical or basic form of an aspirated word, and so on coming across *mhaighdeann*, *bhaile* or *chuir*, for example, will look up *maighdeann*, *baile* and *cuir* respectively.

Format

Words are given in alphabetical order. It is not uncommon in Gaelic for words to express a variety of meanings, and in such cases the most common meaning or meanings are given. Often further meanings are given, with significant differences separated by a semicolon. In many cases, an explanatory note is inserted in brackets to help with clarification.

Abbreviations

abbrev	abbreviation	*m/f*	a noun the gender of which may change according to what it names, its case (often the genitive) or its dialect
adj	adjective		
adv	adverb		
anat	anatomy		
arith	arithmetic		
art	article	*milit*	military
coll	colloquial/collective	*mus*	music
comput	computing	*neg*	negative
conj	conjunction	*occas*	occasionally
corres	correspondence	*orthog*	orthography
derog	derogatory	*part*	particle
esp	especially	*pers*	personal
excl	exclamation	*phys*	physical
f	noun (feminine gender)	*pl*	plural
fam	familiar	*poss*	possessive
fig	figurative	*pp*	present or past participle
fin	financial	*prep*	preposition
fml	formal	*pron*	pronoun
govt	government	*refl*	reflexive
gram	grammar	*rel*	relative
imper	imperative	*relig*	religion
interrog	interrogative	*sing*	singular
lit	literature	*usu*	usually
m	noun (masculine gender)	*v*	verb
med	medical	*vulg*	vulgar

Gaelic-English Dictionary

A

a *prep* to. • *rel pron* that.

a'[1] *art* the; of the.

a'[2] *see* **ag**.

a' cnàmh na cìre chewing the cud; mulling things over.

ab *m* abbot.

abachadh *m* ripening.

abaich *adj* mature, ripe. • *v* mature, ripen.

abaichead *m* maturity, ripeness.

abaid *f* abbey.

abair *v* say.

abair amadan! *excl* what a fool!

abairt *f* phrase, expression.

àbhacas *m* mirth, ridicule.

àbhachd *f* humour.

àbhachdach *adj* amusing.

abhag *f* terrier.

abhainn *f* river.

àbhaist *f* custom, habit.

àbhaisteach *adj* usual.

a-bhàn *adv* down.

a bhon-dè *adv* day before yesterday.

a bhon-raoir *adv* night before last.

a bhon uiridh *adv* year before last.

a bhos *adv* over here, hither.

ablach *m* carcase.

abstol *m* apostle.

aca *prep pron* their.

acadamh *m* academy.

acaid *f* stabbing pain.

acainn *f* apparatus; tools.

acainneach *adj* equipped.

acair *f* anchor.

acaire *f* acre.

acarsaid *f* harbour, mooring.

ach *conj* but.

achadh *m* field.

ach a-mhàin *prep* except, apart from.

a-chaoidh *adv* always, for ever.

achd *f* (*politics*) act.

a cheana *adv* already.

a chèile *pron* each other.

a chialll *excl* good heavens!

a chionn *prep* because of.

a chionn is gu *conj* because.

achlais *f* armpit.

achlasan *m* armful.

achmhasan *m* reprimand.

a-chum *prep* for.

a-chum is gu *conj* in order that.

acraich *v* anchor, moor.

acras *m* hunger.

acrasach *adj* hungry.

actair *m* actor.

a' cur part snowing.

ad *f* hat.

adag *f* haddock.

adha *m* liver.

a dh'aindeòin *prep* in spite of.

a dh'aithghearr *adv* soon.

adhaltraiche *m* adulterer.

adhaltranas *m* adultery.

a dh' aon ghnothach *adv* expressly, deliberately.

a dh'aon rùn *adv* expressly, deliberately.

adhar *m* air, sky.

adharc *f* horn.

adharcach *adj* horned.

a dh' easbaidh *adv* lacking, needed.

a dh' ionnsaigh *prep* to, towards; against.

a dhìth *adv* lacking, required; in short supply.

adhartach *adj* progressive.

adhartas *m* progress.

adhbhar *m* cause, reason.

adhbhar-gàire *m* laughing stock.

adhbrann *f* ankle.

a dheòin no a dh'aindeòin *adv* willy-nilly.

a dh' fhad *adv* long, in length.

adhradh *m* worship.

a' dol bàs *part* dying out.

Afraga *m* Africa.

Afraganach *m/adj* African.

ag, a' *part introducing pres part.*

agad *prep pron* your (*sing*).

agaibh *prep pron* your (*pl*).

againn *prep pron* our.

agallamh *m* interview; conversation.

agam *prep pron* my.

ag eudach rithe jealous about her.

àgh *m* joy; good fortune.

agh *f* heifer.

aghaidh *f* face; nerve, cheek.

aghaidh-cholmhich *f* mask.

aghann *f* frying pan.

a ghaoil! *excl* love! dear!

àghmhor *adj* pleasant; joyful.

a ghràidh! *excl* dear! love!

agus *conj* and.

a h-uile càil everything.

a h-uile duine everyone, everybody.

a h-uile sian *f* everything.

aibidil *f* alphabet.

aibidealach *adj* alphabetical.

aice *prep pron* her.

àicheadh *m* denial.

àicheidh *v* deny.

aideachadh *m* confession.

aidich *v* confess, own up.

aifrionn *m* Mass.

aig *prep* at; in the possession of.

aig a' cheann thall *adv* in the end, eventually.

aig àmannan *adv* at times.

aig an taigh *adv* at home.

aig baile *adv* at home.

aige *prep pron* his.

àigeach *m* stallion.

aighearach *adj* cheerful, merry.

aighearachd *f* cheerfulness.

aigne *f* spirit; mind.

aig Sealbh tha brath! *excl* Heaven knows!

allbhinn f flint.

àile m air, atmosphere.

àileach adj airy.

aileag f (with art) **an aileag** hiccups.

àill f desire, will.

àilleag f jewel.

àillidh adj shining; beautiful.

aillse f cancer.

ailseag f caterpillar.

ailtire m architect.

ailtireachd f architecture.

aimbealains m ambulance.

aimhreit f disorder, trouble.

aimhreiteach adj quarrelsome.

aimsir f weather.

aimsireil adj temporal; climatic.

ain- prefix un-.

aindeòin f reluctance.

aindeònach adj reluctant.

aineach adj (gram) imperative.

aineolach air adj unfamiliar with.

aineolas m ignorance.

aingeal m angel.

ainm m name.

ainmeachadh m naming; mentioning.

ainmear m noun.

ainmeil adj famous.

ainmhidh m animal.

ainmich v name; mention.

ainmneach adj (gram) nominative.

ainneamh adj scarce, rare.

ainneart m violence.

aintighearn m tyrant, oppressor.

air prep on; about. • prep pron on him, on it (m).

air adhart adv forwards, onwards.

air a dheagh dhòigh on good form; chuffed.

air aghaidh adv forward(s).

air ais adv back; ago.

air allaban adv wandering.

air alt is gu conj so that.

air an dùthaich adv in the country.

air an spot adv on the spot.

air a phronnadh adv drunk.

air ball adv immediately.

air banais adv at a wedding.

air beulaibh prep in front of.

air bhàinidh adv mad with rage.

air bhog adv afloat.

air bholle adv furious, raging.

air bith adv any at all.

air bòrd adv aboard, on board.

air chall adv lost.

airchealladh m sacrilege.

air chois adv up and about.

air choreigin adj some or other.

air chor is gu conj so that.

air chrith adv shaking, shivering.

air chuthach adv mad; furious.

air corra-biod adv on tiptoe.

air cùl prep behind.

air cùlaibh prep behind.

air cumha is gu conj on condition that.

àird f point, promontory.

air dàir adv on heat, rutting.

àirde f height; (mus) pitch.

aire f attention.

air deireadh adv last.

air dheireadh adv lagging behind.

air dhòigh is gu conj so that; in order that.

air dòigh adv in good order.

air do shocair! excl steady on! go easy!

air dreach adv looking like.

air eagal gu conj lest; for fear that.

àireamh f number.

àireamhair m calculator.

àireamh fòn f phone number.

air èiginn adv hardly, barely; with difficulty.

air fad adv entirely, completely; all.

air falbh adv away, gone.

air feadh prep throughout, all over.

air fleòdradh adv floating.

air flod adv floating, afloat.

airgead m money; silver.

airgeadach adj well-off, monied.

airgead pòcaid m pocket-money.

airgead pronn m small change.

airgead ullamh m ready money, cash.

air lasad adv on loan.

airidh adj worthy, deserving.

àirigh f shieling.

air lomrall adv wandering; astray, erring.

air iteig adv flying, on the wing.

air leth adv apart; exceptional.

air leth-mhisg adv tipsy.

air leth-shùil adv one-eyed.

air m'aigne adv on my mind.

air m'aire adv on my mind.

air mhisg adv drunk.

air mhodh eile adv otherwise, alternatively.

air mo chùram adv on my mind; under my responsibility.

air mo sgàth adv for my sake.

àirneis f furniture.

air neo conj or else, otherwise.

air sgàth prep on account of.

air sgàth is gu conj because.

airson prep for; in favour of.
• conj in order to.

airson a reic adv sale, for.

air snàmh adj inundated, flooded.

air stailc adv on strike.

air tholseach air prep ahead of.

airtnealach adj sad, weary.

air tuaiream adv at random.

air uairean adv at times.

air uaireann adv occasionally.

air urras adv on bail.

aiseag f ferry.

aiseal f axle.

aisean m rib.

aiseirigh f resurrection; resurgence.

Aisia f (with art) **an Aisia** Asia.

Aisianach *m/adj* Asian.

aisling *f* dream; vision.

alste¹ *f* essay.

aiste² *prep pron* from her, from it (*f*).

àite *m* place.

àiteach *m* cultivation.

àiteachas *m* agriculture.

àite-coise *m* pedestrian crossing.

aiteal *m* glimpse.

aiteamh *m* thaw.

àite-còmhnaidh *m* dwelling place.

àite-fuirich *m* dwelling place.

àiteigin *m* some place or other.

àite-suidhe *m* seat, sitting place.

aithghearr *adj* short; quick; abrupt.

aithghearrachd *f* short cut. • *adv* **an aithghearrachd** swiftly, sharpish.

aithne *f* acquaintance.

aithnich *v* know, recognise.

aithreachail *adj* repentant.

aithreachas *m* repentance.

aithris *v* recite. • *m* report.

àitich *v* cultivate.

aitreabh *m* building; dwelling.

àl *m* litter, young.

àlainn *adj* lovely; fine.

a laoigh! *excl* my love! my dear!

Alba *f* Scotland.

Albais *f* Scots language.

Albannach *m/adj* Scotsman, Scot; Scottish.

alcol *m* alcohol.

allaban *m* wandering.

allaidh *adj* wild.

allt *m* stream, burn.

alt *m* joint; method; (*gram*) article.

altachadh *m* (*prayer*) grace.

altair *f* altar.

altraim *v* foster; nurse.

am¹ *poss adj* their.

am² *art* the.

àm *m* time. • *adv* **aig àmannan** at times. • **an t-àm a dh'fhalbh** the past.

a-mach *adv* out.

a-mach air a'bhus *adv* overflowing.

a-mach à seol *excl* get out!

amadan *m* fool, silly man.

amaideach *adj* foolish, silly.

amaideas *m* foolishness.

a-màireach *adv* tomorrow.

amais *v* aim; hit upon.

amaiseach *adj* accurate.

amalach *adj* complicated.

amar *m* basin; pool.

amar-ionnlaid *m* wash basin.

amar-snàmh *m* swimming pool.

am bitheantas *adv* usually, normally.

am bliadhna *adv* this year.

am broinn *prep* inside, within.

am bròn *adv* in mourning.

Ameireagaidh *f* America.

Ameireaganach *m/adj* American.

am feasd *adv* ever; for ever.

amh *adj* raw; unripe.
amhaich *f* neck; throat.
a-mhàin *adv* only.
àmhainn *f* oven.
amharas *m* suspicion.
amharasach *adj* suspicious, distrustful.
amharc *m* sight.
amhran *m* song.
am measg *prep* among.
a-muigh *adv* outside.
an[1] *art* the; of the.
an[2] *poss adj* their.
an[3] *prep* in.
an-abaich *adj* unripe; premature.
anabarrach *adj/adv* extreme(ly).
an aghaidh *prep* against.
anail *f* breath.
an ainm an àigh! *excl* in Heaven's name!
anainn *f* eaves.
an àite *prep* instead of.
a-nall *adv* over here, hither.
anam *m* soul.
ana-mhiann *m/f* lust.
an àrd *adv* up.
anart *m* linen.
anart bàis *m* shroud.
an-asgaidh *adv* free of charge.
an ath-bhliadhna *adv* next year.
an ath dhoras *m* next door.
an ath-oidhche *adv* tomorrow night.
an ceann *prep* (*of time*) in, after.
an ceann a chèile *adv* one after the other, in succession.

an ceartuair *adv* just now, presently.
an clàr a aodainn *adv* full in the face.
an coimeas ri *prep* compared to.
an coinneimh *prep* towards.
an cois *adv* near; accompanying.
an comhair *prep* in the direction of.
an comhair a chinn *adv* head first.
an comhair a thoisich *adv* frontwards.
an-còmhnaidh *adv* always, constantly.
an crochadh *adv* hanging.
an crochadh air *prep* depending on.
an cumantas *adv* commonly, normally.
an dà chuid *pron* both.
an dà là *m* changed days.
an dàn *adv* destined, ordained.
an dara cuid a no b either a or b.
an-dè *adv* yesterday.
dèideadh *m* (*with art*) **an dèideadh** toothache.
an dèidh *prep* after.
an dèidh sin? *adv* so?.
an-diugh *adv* today.
an dòlas! *excl* woe is me!
an-dràsta *adv* just now.
an-dràsta fhèin *adv* this instant.
an droch-shùil *f* the evil eye.
an ear eastern.
an-earar *adv* day after tomorrow.

an eisimeil *adv* dependent (on).

anfhann *adj* infirm.

an-fhoisell *adj* restless, uneasy.

an impis *conj* about to.

an-iochdmhor *adj* merciless, pit-iless.

an iomadh-chomhairle in a quandary.

an ìre mhath *adv* quite, fairly; just about.

an làthair *adv* present.

a-nìos *adv* up.

a-nise *adv* now.

an là roimhe *adv* the other day.

an lùib *prep* involved in/with.

anmoch *adj* late.

ann[1] *adv* there.

ann[2] *prep pron* in him; in it (*m*).

annad *prep pron* in you (*sing*).

annaibh *prep pron* in you (*pl*).

annainn *prep pron* in us.

annam *prep pron* in me.

ann an *prep* in.

ann an cabhag *adv* in a hurry.

ann an dà-rìreadh *adv* serious, in earnest.

ann an droch staid *adv* in a bad way.

ann an sheo *adv* here.

ann an shin *adv* there.

ann an shlud *adv* there, yonder.

annas *m* rarity; novelty.

annasach *adj* novel; odd.

anns a' bhad *adv* immediately.

anns a' chiad dol-a-mach in the first instance.

anns an *prep* in the.

anns an dealachadh *adv* on parting.

annta *prep pron* in them.

a-nochd *adv* tonight.

an-raoir *adv* last night.

an sàs *adv* captured; involved.

an seo *adv* here.

anshocrach *adj* uneasy.

an sin *adv* there.

an slud *adv* there, yonder.

an taca ri *prep* compared to, alongside.

an taic ri *prep* leaning on/against; in comparison with.

an taobh a-muigh *m* outside.

an taobh an ear *m* the east.

an taobh an iar *m* the west.

an taobh a-staigh *m* inside.

an taobh sear *m* the east.

an taobh siar *m* the west.

an t-Eilean Sgitheanach *m* (the Isle of) Skye.

an tòir air *prep* in pursuit of; looking for.

an toiseach *adv* at first.

an uair a *conj* when.

an uair sin *adv* then, next.

a-nuas *adv* down.

an-uiridh *adv* last year.

a-null *adv* thither; over.

a-null thairis *adv* abroad, over-seas.

an urra ri *prep* responsible for; in charge of.

aocoltach *adj* dissimilar.

aodach *m* cloth; clothes.

aodach-leapa *m* bedclothes.

aodach oidhche *m* nightclothes.

aodann *m* face; hillface.

ao-dìonach *adj* leaky.

aoibhneach *adj* glad.

aoigh *m* guest; resident.

aoigheachd *f* hospitality.

aoighell *adj* generous; hospitable.

aoir *f* satire.

aois *f* age.

aol *m* lime.

aon *adj* one.

aonach *m* moor, moorland.

aonad *m* unit.

aona deug *adj* eleventh.

aonadh *m* union.

aonadh-cèaird *m* trade union.

aonaich *v* unite, combine.

aonaran *m* hermit; loner.

aonaranach *adj* lonely; desolate.

aon chuid a no b either a or b.

aon deug *n* eleven.

aon-fhillte *adj* uncomplicated.

aon-inntinneach *adj* unanimous.

aonta *m* agreement.

aontaich *v* agree.

aosta *adj* old, aged.

aotrom *adj* light; trivial.

aotromaich *v* lighten; alleviate.

aotroman *m* bladder.

aparan *m* apron.

ar *poss adj* our.

àr *m* slaughter.

àra *f* kidney.

àrach *m* rearing, upbringing.

àrachas *m* insurance.

àradh *m* ladder.

àraich *v* raise, bring up.

àraid *adj* particular; peculiar.

àraidh *adj* particular; exceptional.

ar-a-mach *m* rebellion, rising.

aran *m* bread.

ar-aon *adv* both.

arbhar *m* corn.

àrc *f* cork.

Arcach *adj/n* Orcadian.

Arcaibh *m* Orkney.

àrdachadh *m* promotion; rise.

àrdaich *v* raise; increase.

àrdan *m* pride, arrogance.

àrdanach *adj* proud, arrogant.

àrd-doras *m* lintel.

àrd-easbaig *m* archbishop.

àrd-ìre *adj (education, etc)* higher, high-level.

àrd mo chlaiginn *adv* at the top of my voice.

àrd-ollamh *m* professor.

àrd-sgoil *f* secondary school.

àrd-ùrlar *m* stage, platform.

àrd-urram *m* honour, distinction; reverence.

a-rèir *prep* according to.

a-rèir choltais *adv* seemingly, apparently.

a-rèist *adv* in that case.

argamaid *f* argument.

a-riamh *adv* ever.

a-rithist *adv* again.

ar leam v I consider.

arm m army.

armachd f armour.

armaich v arm.

arm-lann f armoury.

arsa v say, says, said.

àrsaidh adj ancient.

àrsaidheachd f archaeology.

àrsair m archaeologist.

às prep from, out of. • prep pron from him, from it (m).

às a' cheud adv percent.

às a' chumantas adv out of the ordinary.

asad prep pron from you (sing).

asaibh prep pron from you (pl).

asaid anabaich f miscarriage.

asainn prep pron from us.

asal f ass; donkey.

asam prep pron from me.

às an amharc adv out of sight.

às an làthair adv out of sight.

às aonais prep without.

as bith cò prep whoever.

as bith cuine adv whenever.

as bith dè prep whatever.

às d'aonais without you.

à sealladh adv out of sight.

às eugmhais prep without.

asgaidh f present, gift.

a shiorraidh! excl for Heaven's sake!

às leth prep on behalf of.

às mo chiall adv out of my mind.

às mo rian adv out of my mind.

asta prep pron from them.

a-staigh adv in, inside.

astar m distance; speed.

a-steach adv in, inside.

a-steach do prep into.

as t-fhodhar adv in Autumn.

Astràilia f Australia.

Astràilianach m/adj Australian.

as ùr adv afresh; anew.

at v swell, puff up. • m swelling.

ataireachd f (of sea) swell, surge.

ath adj next.

àth¹ f kiln.

àth² m ford.

ath- prefix re-.

athair m father; progenitor.

athair-cèile m father-in-law.

athaireil adj fatherly.

athaiseach adj dilatory.

ath-aithris v repeat.

a thaobh prep concerning.

atharrachadh m change, alteration.

atharraich v change, alter.

atharrais v imitate, mimic.

ath-bheothachadh m renaissance.

ath-bheothaich v revive.

ath-chruthaich v re-create.

ath-dhìol v repay.

ath-leasachadh m redevelopment; (with art) **an t-Ath-leasachadh** the Reformation.

ath-leasaich v redevelop.

ath-nuadhachadh m renewal.

ath-nuadhaich v renew.

athraichean mpl forefathers.

ath-sgrìobh *v* rewrite.
ath-sgrùdadh *m* revision.

a thuilleadh air *prep* in addition to.

B

bac *v* prevent; obstruct.
bacach *adj* lame. • *m* lame person.
bacadh *m* prevention; obstacle.
bacan *m* hobble.
bachall *m* crozier.
bachlach *adj* curly.
bachlag *f* curl, ringlet.
bachlaich *v* curl.
bad *m* place; clump.
badan *m* thicket.
baga *m* bag; hand-bag.
bagaid *f* bunch; cluster.
bagair *v* threaten.
bagairt *f* threat.
bàgh *m* bay, cove.
bagradh *m* threat.
bàidh *f* affection; favour.
bàidheil *adj* kindly.
baidhsagal *m* bicycle.
baile *m* township, village. • *adv* **aig baile** at home.
bailead *m* ballad.
baile beag *m* village, small town.
baile mòr *m* town, city.
baile-margaid *m* market town.
baile-puirt *m* sea port.
bàillidh *m* bailiff; baillie.
b'àill leam? *adv* pardon?.
bàine *adj* whiter, whitest.

bàinead *f* whiteness.
bainne *m* milk.
bainne lom *m* skimmed milk.
bàirdse *f* barge.
bàirlinn *f* (*law*) summons.
bàirneach *f* barnacle, limpet.
baist *v* baptise, christen.
Baisteach *adj/m* Baptist.
baisteadh *m* baptism.
bàl *m* (*dance*) ball.
balach *m* boy, lad.
balachan *m* wee boy.
balbh *adj* dumb; speechless.
balbhan *m* dumb person.
balg *m* abdomen; blister.
balgair *m* fox; rogue.
balgam *m* sip; swig.
balgan *m* mushroom; toadstool.
balgan-buachair *m* edible mushroom.
ball *m* organ; member.
balla *m* wall.
bàlla *m* ball.
ball-acainn *m* tool.
ballach *adj* speckled, spotted.
ball-airm *m* weapon.
ball-àirneis *m* piece of furniture.
ballan *m* tub.
ball-aodaich *m* garment.
ball-basgaid *m* basketball.

ball-bodhaig *m* bodily organ.
ball-coise *m* football.
ball-dòbhrain *m* (*on skin*) mole.
ball-maise *m* ornament.
ball pàrlamaid *m* MP.
ballrachd *f* membership.
ball-seirce *m* beauty spot.
ball-stèidhe *m* baseball.
bàn *adj* blonde; white; blank; fallow.
bana-bhuidseach *f* witch.
bana-charaid *f* female friend or relative; (*corres*) **A Bhana-charaid** Dear Madam.
bana-chliamhainn *f* daughter-in-law.
ban-adhaltraiche *f* adulteress.
bànag *f* sea trout.
bana-ghaisgeach *f* heroine.
banail *adj* womanly, feminine.
banais *f* wedding.
Ban Albannach *f* Scotswoman.
banaltram *f* nurse.
bana-mhaighistir-sgoile *f* schoolmistress.
bana-phrionnsa *f* princess.
banarach *f* milkmaid, dairymaid.
banca *m* bank.
bancair *m* banker.
bancaireachd *f* banking.
bàn-dhearg *adj* light red.
ban-dia *f* goddess.
ban-diùc *f* duchess.
bàn-ghorm *adj* pale blue.
ban-iompaire *f* empress.
ban-leòmhann *f* lioness.

bann *m* strip; bandage.
banntach *m* hinge.
banntrach *m/f* widow(er).
ban-ogha *f* grand-daughter.
bànrigh *f* queen.
ban-rùnaire *f* (female) secretary.
baoghalta *adj* stupid.
baoghaltachd *f* stupidity.
baoit *f* (*fishing*) fly, bait.
baoiteag *f* (*fishing*) fly, bait.
baoth *adj* foolish, simple.
bàr *m* (*hotel, etc*) bar.
barail *f* opinion.
baraille *m* barrel.
bàrd *m* poet, bard.
bàrdachd *f* poetry.
bàrr *m* top; cream; crop.
Barrach *m/adj* from Barra.
barrachd *f* surplus; more. • *prep* **barrachd air** more than. • *adv* **a bharrachd** extra, in addition, **a bharrachd air sin** moreover.
barragach *adj* creamy.
Barraidh *m* Barra.
barrall *m* shoelace.
barrantas *m* pledge, guarantee.
bàrr na teangaidh *m* tip of the tongue.
bas *f* palm.
bàs *m* death.
bàsaich *v* die.
bas-bhualadh *m* applause.
basgaid *f* basket.
bàsmhor *adj* mortal; deadly.
bàsmhorachd *f* mortality.
bata *m* stick.

bàta *m* boat.

bata-coiseachd *m* walking stick.

bàt' aisig *m* ferry.

bàta-ràmh *m* rowing boat.

bàta-sàbhalaidh *m* lifeboat.

bàta-siùil *m* sailing boat.

bàta-smùide *m* steamer.

bàta-teasairginn *m* lifeboat.

bàth *v* drown; muffle.

bàthach *f* byre, cow-shed.

bathais *f* forehead; impudence.

bathar *m* goods, merchandise.

bàthte *adj* drowned.

bàt'-iasgaich fishing boat.

beach *m* bee; wasp.

beachd *m* idea; opinion.

beachdail *adj* abstract.

beachd-smaoinich, beachd-smaointich *v* meditate.

beachlann *m* beehive.

beag *adj* little, • *m* a' bheag the least bit. • *adv* beag air bheag bit by bit; **beag is beag** little by little.

beagan *adv* a bit, slightly. • *m* a little; few.

beag-nàrach *adj* shameless.

bealach *m* pass, col; detour.

bealaidh *m* broom.

Bealltainn *f* May Day, Beltane.

bean[1] *f* wife.

bean[2] *v* touch, meddle with.

bean- *prefix* woman-, female.

bean-an-taighe, bean-taighe *f* housewife; landlady.

bean-bainnse *f* bride.

bean-eiridinn *f* nurse.

bean-ghlùine *f* midwife.

beannachadh *m* beatification; greeting.

beannachd *f* blessing; regards.

beannachd leibh! *excl* goodbye!

beannaich *v* bless.

beannaich do *v* greet.

beannaichte *adj* blessed.

bean phòsda *f* married woman, Mrs.

bean ri *v* brush against.

bean-shìthe *f* fairy woman.

bean-an-taighe *see* bean-taighe.

bean-teagaisg *f* (female) teacher.

bean-uasal *f* noblewoman; (*fml*) **a Bhean-uasal!** *excl* Madam! (*corres, fml*) Dear Madam.

beàrn *f* gap; notch.

beàrna-brìde *f* dandelion.

Beàrnarach *m* Berneray person.

Beàrnaraigh *f* Berneray.

beàrr *v* shave; shear.

bearradair *m* barber.

beart *f* machine.

beartach *adj* rich, wealthy.

beartas *m* riches, wealth.

beart-fhighe *f* loom.

beatha *f* life.

beathach *m* animal.

beathach-mara *m* sea-creature.

beathaich *v* feed; maintain.

beath-eachdraidh *f* biography.

beic *f* curtsey.

Beilg *f* (*with art*) **a' Bheilg** Belgium.

Beilgeach *m/adj* Belgian.
being *f* bench.
beinn *f* ben, mountain.
Beinn Nibheis *f* Ben Nevis.
beinn-teine *f* volcano.
beir *v irreg* bear; give birth to.
beir air *v* seize; overtake.
beir air làimh air *v* shake hands with.
beirm *f* yeast.
beò *adj* alive, living.
beò-ghlacadh *m* obsession.
beòshlaint *f* livelihood.
beothaich *v* revive; liven up.
beothail *adj* lively, active.
beothalachd *f* vivacity.
beuc *m* roar, bellow. • *v* roar, bellow.
beud *m* harm, loss.
beul *m* mouth.
beul a bhi *adv* about to be.
beul-aithris *f* oral tradition.
beulchar *adj* plausible, smooth-talking.
beul-ìochdair *m* lower lip.
beul-oideachas *f* lore.
beul ri *prep* nearly.
beul-uachdair *m* upper lip.
beum *m* stroke; blow.
beum-grèine *m* sunstroke.
Beurla *f* (*often with art*) **a' Bheurla** English.
beusach *adj* modest; well-behaved.
beus-eòlas *m* ethics.
bha *past tense of v* **bith**.

bhàrr *prep* off, down from.
bha spòrs agam *v* I enjoyed myself/had fun.
Bhèineas *f* Venus.
bheir *future tense of v* **thoir**.
bho *prep* from; since.
bho àm gu àm *adv* from time to time.
bhòt *v* vote.
bho thùs *adv* originally.
bhuaibh *prep pron* from you (*pl*).
bhuainn *prep pron* from us.
bhuaipe *prep pron* from her, from it (*f*).
bhuaithe *prep pron* from him, from it (*m*).
bhuam *prep pron* from me.
bhuapa *prep pron* from them.
bhuat *prep pron* from you (*sing*).
bhur *adj* your (*pl*).
biadh *m* food; meal.
biadhlann *m* refectory, canteen.
bian *m* fur, hide.
biast *f* beast.
biastail *adj* bestial.
biath *v* feed; fodder.
bìd¹ *v* bite.
bìd² *m* chirp.
bìdeag *f* fragment, crumb.
bidse *f* bitch. • *excl* **a bhidse!** sod it!
bile¹ *f* lip, rim.
bile² *m* (*politics*) bill.
bileag *f* petal; (*commerce*) bill.
binid *f* rennet.
binn¹ *adj* sweet.

binn² *f* judgement; sentence.

binnean *m* peak.

binneas *m* sweetness.

bìoball *m* bible.

bìoballach *adj* biblical.

biodach *adj* tiny; trifling.

biodag *f* dirk, dagger.

bìog *f* chirp. • *v* cheep, chirp.

biolar *f* cress.

biona *f* bin.

biona-stùir *f* dustbin.

bior *m* point; prickle.

biorach *adj* sharp, pointed.

bioran *m* a pointed stick.

biorra-crùidein *m* kingfisher.

bior-ròstaidh *m* (*cooking*) spit.

biotais *m* beet.

bìrlinn *f* galley, birlinn.

bìth¹ *f* existence, being. • *v* be.

bìth² *f* tar, pitch.

bith- *prefix* ever-.

bith-bheò *adj* ever-living, immortal.

bith-bhuan *adj* eternal, everlasting.

bitheanta *adj* frequent, common.

bitheantas *m* frequency.

bith-eòlas *m* biology.

bithis *f* screw.

bithiseach *adj* spiral.

blais *v* taste.

blàr *m* plain; battle(field).

blas *m* flavour; accent.

blasad *m* taste.

blasad bìdh *m* bite to eat.

blasaich *v* flavour.

blasmhor *adj* full of flavour.

blasta *adj* tasty.

blàth¹ *m* bloom, blossom.

blàth² *adj* warm; affectionate.

blàthaich *v* warm.

blàth-chridheach *adj* warm-hearted.

blàths *m* warmth.

bleideag *f* flake.

bleith *v* grind, pulverise.

bleoghainn *v* milk.

bliadhna *f* year.

bliadhnach *adj* yearling.

bliadhnail *adj* annual, yearly.

bliadhna-leum *f* leap year.

bliadhna ùr *f* new year.

blian *v* sunbathe.

bloigh *f* half.

bloighd *f* fragment, splinter.

bloinigean-gàraidh *m* spinach.

blonag *f* lard.

bò *f* cow.

bò bhainne *f* milk cow.

bobhla *m* bowl.

boc *m* billy goat; roebuck.

bòc *v* swell, bloat.

bòcan *m* apparition; bogy-man.

boc-earba *m* roe-buck.

bochd *adj* poor; unfortunate; poorly.

bochdainn *f* poverty; misfortune.

bocsa *m* box.

bocsa-ciùil *m* accordion.

bocsa-fòn *m* phonebox.

bocsair *m* boxer.

bocsa-litrichean *m* letterbox.

bod *m* penis.

Bòd *m* Bute.

bodach *m* old man, old guy.

Bodach na Nollaig *m* Santa Claus.

bodach-ròcais *m* scarecrow.

bodach-sneachda *m* snowman.

bodhaig *f* body.

bodhair *v* deafen.

bodhar *adj* deaf. • *m* deaf person.

bòdhran *m* bodhran.

bodraig *v* bother, trouble.

bog[1] *adj* soft; tender. • *v* soak, steep.

bog[2] *v* bob, dip.

bogadaich *f* bouncing, bobbing.

bogaich *v* soften.

bog fliuch *adj* soaking wet.

bogha *m* bow; curve.

bogha-frois *m* rainbow.

boglach *f* bog.

bòid *f* oath; swearing.

Bòideach[‘] *m/adj* from Bute.

bòidhchead *f* beauty.

bòidheach *adj* pretty, beautiful.

boile *f* madness; frenzy.

boillsg *m* flash; gleam. • *v* flash; glitter, shine.

boillsgeach *adj* gleaming; glittering.

boinne *f* drop.

boinneag *f* droplet.

boireann *adj* female, feminine.

boireannach *m* woman, female.

boireannaich *mpl* womenfolk.

boireannta *adj* effeminate.

boiseag *f* slap; palmful.

boladh *m* smell.

bò laoigh *f* in-calf cow.

bolgan *m* bulb.

boltrach *m* smell; perfume.

boma *m* bomb.

bonaid *m/f* bonnet, cap.

bonaid bhlorach *f* Glengarry.

bonn *m* base; coin.

bonnach *m* bannock; scone.

bonnach-uighe *m* omelette.

bonn airgid *m* coin; silver medal.

bonn còmhraidh *m* chat.

bonn-cuimhne *m* medal.

bonn-dubh *m* heel.

borb *adj* wild, barbarous.

borbair *m* barber.

bòrd *m* board; table.

bòrd ceadachaidh *m* licensing board.

bòrd-dàmais *m* draught board.

bòrd-dubh *m* blackboard.

bòrd-geal *m* whiteboard.

bòrd-iarnaigidh *m* ironing board.

bòrd-sgrìobhaidh *m* desk.

bòrd slàinte *m* health board.

bòstail *adj* boastful.

botal *m* bottle.

botal teth *m* hotwater bottle.

bòtann *m* boot, wellie.

bothan *m* cottage; shebeen.

bothan àirigh *m* sheiling bothy.

bracaist *f* breakfast.

brach *v* ferment; (*boil, etc*) gather.

brachadh *m* fermentation; pus.
bradan *m* salmon.
brag *m* bang.
bragail *adj* boastful.
braich *f* malt.
braid *f* theft, thieving.
bràigh[1] *m* upper part; upland.
bràigh[2] *m* captive; hostage.
bràighdeanas *m* captivity.
braim *m* fart.
braisead *f* impetuosity.
bràiste *f* brooch.
bràmair *m* girlfriend.
branndaidh *f* brandy.
braoisg *f* grin; grimace.
braoisgeil *adj* grinning.
braon *v* drizzle. • *m* drop;.
bras *adj* hasty; bold.
brat *m* cover; mat; cloak.
bratach *m* banner, flag.
brath[1] *v* betray; inform on.
brath[2] *m* knowledge; advantage.
bràth *m* judgement; **gu bràth tuilleadh** *adv* (*with neg v*) never again.
brathadair *m* betrayer.
brathadh *m* betrayal.
bràthair *m* brother.
bràthair athar *m* uncle.
bràthair-cèile *m* brother-in-law.
bràthair-màthar *m* uncle.
brat-leapach *m* bedcover, coverlet.
brat-ùrlair *m* carpet.
breab *v* kick. • *m* kick.
breabadair *m* weaver; daddy-long-legs.

breac[1] *adj* speckled, variegated.
breac[2] *m* trout.
breacadh-seunain *m* freckles.
breacag *f* bannock.
breacan *m* plaid, tartan cloth.
breacanach *adj* tartan.
breac-bhallach *adj* freckled.
breac-òtraich *f* (*with art*) **a' bhreac-òtraich** chicken pox.
buinneach *f* (*with art*) **a' bhuinneach** diarrhoea.
brèagha *adj* fine, lovely.
Breatannach *m/adj* Briton; British.
breice *f* brick.
breicire *m* bricklayer.
brèid *m* kerchief; patch.
brèid-sholthichean *m* dishcloth.
brèige *adj* deceitful; artificial.
breisleach *m* confusion; delirium.
breislich *v* talk irrationally.
breith[1] *f* birth.
breith[2] *f* decision; sentence.
breith anabaich *f* abortion.
breithnich *v* judge; assess.
breug *f* lie.
breugach *adj* lying.
breugaire *m* liar.
breug-riochd *m* disguise.
breun *adj* putrid, corrupt.
briathar *m* term.
briathran *mpl* statements, words.
briathran teicneolach *mpl* technical terms.
brìb *v* bribe. • *f* bribe.

brìgh *f* meaning; essence; energy.
brìghmhor *adj* pithy; energetic.
briogais *f* trousers, breeches.
briosgaid *f* biscuit.
bris *v* break, smash.
briseadh *m* break, fracture.
briseadh-cridhe *m* heartbreak.
briseadh-dùil *m* disappointment.
briseadh-là *m* daybreak.
brisg *adj* crisp; brittle.
briste *adj* broken, smashed.
britheamh *m* judge.
broc *m* badger.
brochan *m* porridge.
brod *v* drive on; encourage. • *m* goad, prod.
bròg *f* shoe, boot.
broilleach *m* bosom, chest.
broinn *f* interior.
bròn *m* sadness, sorrow.
brònach *adj* sad, sorrowful.
brosnachadh *m* encouragement.
brosnachail *adj* encouraging.
brosnaich *v* encourage; arouse.
brot *m* soup, broth.
broth *m* rash.
brù *f* womb; belly; bulge.
bruach *f* (*river, etc*) bank.
bruadair *v* dream.
bruadar *m* dream.
brùchd *v* burst out; belch. • *m* belch.
brù-dhearg *m* robin.
bruich *v* cook; boil. • *adj* cooked; boiled.
bruichell *adj* sultry.

brùid *m* brute; beast.
brùidealachd *f* brutality.
brùideil *adj* brutal.
bruidhinn *v* talk, speak. • *f* talk, talking.
bruidhinn ri *v* talk to.
bruidhneach *adj* talkative, chatty.
bruis *f* brush.
bruis-aodaich *f* clothes brush.
bruis-fhiaclan *f* toothbrush.
bruisig *v* brush.
brùite *adj* bruised; oppressed.
brùth *v* bruise; shove.
bruthach *m/f* bank, slope.
bruthainneach *adj* sultry.
bu *v* was; were; would be.
buachaille *m* cowherd.
buachailleachd *f* cattle herding.
buachaillich *v* herd cattle.
buachar *m* cowdung.
buadh *f* quality, virtue.
buadhair *m* adjective.
buadhmhor *adj* effective; successful.
bualc *f* wick.
buaidh *f* victory; success; influence.
buail *v* hit.
buail a-steach *v* call in, drop in.
buail bas *v* applaud.
buaile *f* sheepfold.
buailteach *adj* liable, apt to.
buain *f* reaping, harvest(ing).
buair *v* upset; tempt.
buaireadh *m* temptation.

buaireas *m* anxiety; confusion.
buaireasach *adj* troublesome.
bualadh *m* blow.
buan *adj* lasting, durable.
buannachd *f* profit, advantage.
buannaich *v* win.
buar *m* herd.
bucaid *f* bucket.
bucas *m* box.
bu chiatach orm *v* I should.
bu chòir dhomh *v* I ought, I should.
bugair *m* bugar.
buideal *m* bottle.
buidhe *adj* yellow; lucky.
buidheach *adj* thankful, grateful.
buidheachas *m* gratitude.
buidheagan *f* yolk.
buidheann *m/f* group; firm.
buidheann-cluich *m* playgroup.
buidheann-obrach *m* working party.
buidheann òigridh *m/f* youth club/group.
buidheann-strì *m* pressure group.
buidhe-ruadh *adj* auburn.
buidhinn *v* win.
buidhre *f* deafness.
buidseach *m/f* wizard.
bùidsear *m* butcher.
buige *f* softness; moistness.
buil *f* consequence; conclusion.
buileach *adv* completely, quite.
buileann *f* loaf.

builgean *f* bubble.
builgeanach *adj* bubbly.
builich air *v* bestow upon.
buill a' chuirp *mpl* parts of the body.
buille *f* blow; emphasis; (*mus*) beat.
buille cridhe *f* heartbeat.
buill-ghineamhain *mpl* genitals.
buin do *v* belong to; be related to.
buinnig *v* win.
buin ri *v* interfere with.
buinteanas *m* links, relationship.
buirbe *f* barbarity, wildness.
bumailear *m* oaf; no-user.
bun *m* base, bottom, foot.
bunait *f* foundation, fundamentals.
bunaiteach *adj* stable; fundamental(ist).
bunasach *adj* radical.
bun-dealain *m* power point.
bun-os-cionn *adv* upside down.
bun-sgoil *f* primary school.
buntàta *m* potato(es).
buntàta pronn *m* mashed potato(es).
bùrach *m* mess, guddle.
bùrn *m* water.
burraidh *m* fool, blockhead.
bus[1] *m* bus.
bus[2] *m* mouth; grimace, pout.
bùth *f* shop.
bùth-chungaidh *f* pharmacist's.
bùth-eisg *f* fish shop.

C

cab *f* gob.
cabach *adj* talkative.
cabadaich *f* chatter.
cabaireachd *f* chatter.
càball *m* cable.
cabar *m* rafter, pole; caber.
cabar-droma *m* ridge pole.
cabar-fèidh *m* deer's antlers.
cabhag *f* haste.
cabhagach *adj* hurried, hasty.
cabhlach *m* fleet.
cabhsair *m* pavement, causeway.
cabstair *m* horse's bit.
cac *v* defecate. • *m* excrement.
càch *pron* other people, the others.
càch-a-chèile *pron* each other.
cadal *m* sleep.
cadalach *adj* sleepy.
cafaidh *m/f* café.
cagailt *f* hearth, fireside.
cagainn *v* chew.
cagair *v* whisper.
cagar *m* whisper; secret.
caibe *m* spade; mattock.
caibeal *m* chapel.
caibideil *m/f* chapter.
caibideil a h-aon chapter one.
caidil *v* sleep.
caidil gu math! *excl* sleep well!
càil¹ *f* desire; appetite.
càil² *m* thing.
cailc *f* chalk.

cailleag *f* girl, lassie.
cailin *f* girl.
caill *v* lose; miss.
caill do rian *v* go out of your mind.
cailleach *f* old woman; wifie; hag.
cailleach dhubh *f* nun.
cailleach-oidhche *f* owl.
caill mùn *v* wet oneself.
caillte *adj* lost.
caillteach *adj* ruinous.
càil sam bith *m* anything at all.
càin¹ *v* scold.
càin² *f* tax.
cainb *f* hemp.
caineal *m* cinnamon.
cainnt *f* speech, language.
caiptean *m* captain, skipper.
càir *v* repair.
càirdeach do related to.
càirdean *mpl* friends; relations.
càirdeas *m* friendship; kinship.
càirdeas fola *m* blood relationship.
càirdeil *adj* friendly.
càirdineal *m* cardinal.
càireas *m* (*in mouth*) gum(s).
cairgein *m* carrageen.
cairt¹ *v* tan (leather); muck out.
cairt² *f* card; chart.
cairt³ *f* cart.
cairt-bhòrd *m* cardboard.

cairt-chluiche *f* playing card.

cairteal *m* quarter.

cairteal na h-uarach *m* quarter hour.

cairt-iùll *f* navigation chart.

cairt-Nollaig *f* Xmas card.

cairt-phuist *f* postcard.

càise *m* cheese.

caise *f* abruptness; impetuosity.

caisg *v* abate; prevent.

Càisg *f* (*with art*) **a' Chàisg** Easter.

caismeachd *f* alarm; march.

caisteal *m* castle.

càite? *interrog adv* where?

caith *v* wear; spend; consume; waste.

caitheamh *m* (*with art*) **a' chaitheamh** tuberculosis.

caithte *adj* worn-out; consumed.

caithteach *adj* wasteful.

Caitligeach *m/adj* Catholic.

càl *m* cabbage, kale.

cala *m* harbour.

càl-colaig *m* cauliflower.

calg *m* prickle.

calg-dhìreach *adv* completely.

calg-dhìreach an aghaidh *adv* dead against.

call *m* loss; waste.

calla *adj* tame, domesticated.

callaich *v* tame, domesticate.

callaid *f* fence; hedge.

calltainn *m* hazel.

calma *adj* stout; sturdy.

calman *m* dove, pigeon.

calpa[1] *m* (*leg*) calf.

calpa[2] *m* (*fin*) capital.

cam *adj* bent, curved.

camacasach *adj* bow-legged.

camag *f* curl, ringlet; bracket.

camagach *adj* curled, curly.

caman *m* shinty stick.

camanachd *f* shinty.

camara *m* camera.

camas *m* bay.

càmhal *m* camel.

camhanach *f* dawn, twilight.

campa *m* camp.

campaich *v* camp.

can *v* say.

cana *m* tin, can.

canabhas *m* canvas.

canach *m/f* bog cotton.

cànain *f* language, tongue.

can air *v* say for.

cànan *m* language, tongue.

cànanach *adj* linguistic.

canastair *m* tin, can, canister.

Canèidianach *m/adj* Canadian.

can ri *v* call.

caochail *v* change, alter; die.

caochladh *m* change, alteration.

caochlaideach *adj* changeable, fickle.

caog *v* blink; wink.

caogad *m* fifty.

caoidh *v* lament, weep; mourn.

caol *adj* narrow; thin. • *m* strait, kyle.

caolan *m* gut, intestine.

caol an droma *m* small of the back.

caol an dùirn *m* wrist.

caolas *m* strait, kyle(s).

Caolas Bòideach *m* Kyles of Bute.

caol na coise *m* ankle.

caol-shràid *f* vennel, alley.

caon *adj* wily.

caomh *adj* dear, beloved.

caomhain *v* save, economise.

caora *f* sheep, ewe.

caorann *f* rowan.

car[1] *m* turn; stroll; trick. • *as adv* a bit, somewhat.

car[2] *prep* during, for.

càr *f* car.

carabhaidh *m* boyfriend.

carach *adj* wily; unreliable.

carachd *f* wrestling.

caractar *m* (*play, etc*) character.

càradh *m* repair; state, condition.

caraich *v* move.

càraich *v* repair.

caraiche *m* wrestler.

caraid[1] *m* friend, relative; (*corres*) **A Charaid** Dear Sir; **A Chàirdean** Dear Sirs.

càraid[2] *f* pair; twins.

càraid phòsda *f* married couple.

car a' mhuiltein *m* somersault.

caran *adv* a bit, slightly.

carbad *m* vehicle; carriage; craft.

carbad-eiridinn *m* ambulance.

cargu *m* cargo.

càrn *v* pile up; accumulate. • *m* heap; cairn; hill.

càrnaid *f* carnation.

càrnan *m* cockroach.

càrn-cuimhne *m* monument.

càrr *f* dandruff.

carragh *m* rock; stone pillar.

carraig *f* rock.

carson? *interrog adv* why?

carson a chiall? *excl* why on earth?

cartadh *m* mucking out.

carthannas *m* kindness; charity.

cas[1] *f* foot; leg; handle.

cas[2] *adj* steep; impetuous;.

càs *m* difficulty, predicament.

casad *m* cough.

casadaich *v* cough.

casa-gobhlach air *prep* astride.

casaid *f* complaint; accusation.

cas-chrom *f* foot-plough.

casgadh *m* prevention.

casgair *v* slay, massacre.

casgairt *f* slaughter, butchery.

casgan *m* brake.

casg-gineamhainn *m* contraception; contraceptive.

cas-lom *adj* barefoot, barelegged.

cas-ruisgte *adj* barefoot, barelegged.

cas toisich *f* foreleg.

cat *m* cat.

cat fiadhaich *m* wildcat.

cath *m* battle; warfare.

càth *f* chaff.

cathadh *m* snowdrift.

cathag *f* jackdaw.

cathair *f* chair; city.

cathair-chuibhle *f* wheelchair.

cathair-eaglais *f* cathedral.

cath-bhuidheann *f* batallion.

cead *m* permission; permit, licence.

ceadach *adj* tolerant.

ceadachail *adj* permissive.

ceadaich *v* permit, allow.

ceadaichte *adj* allowed.

cead-dol-thairis *m* passport.

cead dràibhidh *m* driving licence.

cead telebhisein *m* television licence.

ceàird *f* trade, craft.

cealg *f* deceit; hypocrisy.

cealgach *adj* deceitful; hypocritical.

cealgair *m* deceiver, cheat; hypocrite.

cealla *f* (*biol*) cell.

ceanalta *adj* pretty, comely.

ceangail *v* tie; join.

ceangal *m* connection; bond.

ceann *m* head; end.

ceannach, ceannachd *m* purchase, buying; trading.

ceannaich *v* buy.

ceannaich air dhàil *v* buy on credit.

ceannaiche *m* purchaser; merchant.

ceannard *m* leader; chief.

ceann-bliadhna *m* birthday.

ceann-cinnidh *m* clan chief.

ceann daoraich *m* hangover.

ceann-feadhna *m* clan chief.

ceann goirt *m* sore head, headache.

ceann-làidir *adj* headstrong.

ceann-pholan *m* tadpole.

ceann-ruisgte *adj* bareheaded.

ceannsaich *v* conquer; control; tame.

ceannsal *m* authority.

ceannsalach *adj* authoritative.

ceann-simid *m* tadpole.

ceann-suidhe *m* president.

ceann-uidhe *m* destination.

ceap[1] *m* block; lump.

ceap[2] *m* cap.

ceapach *m* (garden) plot, bed.

ceapaire *m* sandwich.

cearb *f* rag; defect.

cearbach *adj* clumsy; ragged.

cearc *f* hen.

cearcall *m* circle, ring.

ceàrd *m* tinker, smith.

ceàrdach *f* smithy.

ceàrd-airgid *m* silversmith.

ceàrd-copair *m* coppersmith.

ceàrn *m* corner; district.

ceàrnach *adj* square.

ceàrnag *f* square.

ceàrr *adj* wrong; left.

ceàrraiche *m* gambler.

ceart *adj* correct; just; same.

ceartachadh *m* correction; marking.

ceartaich *v* correct; put right.

ceartas *m* justice.

ceart gu leòr *adv* right enough; okay!

ceart-mheadhan *m* dead centre.

ceart-uillinn *f* right angle.

ceasnachadh *m* questioning; questionnaire.

ceasnaich *v* question; interrogate.

ceathach *m* mist.

ceathrad *m* forty.

ceathramh *adj* fourth. • *m* quarter.

ceathrar *m* foursome.

cèic *f* cake.

cèidse *f* cage.

ceil (air) *v* hide, conceal (from).

cèile *m/f* spouse; counterpart.

cèilidh *m/f* visit; ceilidh.

ceilir *v* sing sweetly, warble.

ceilp *f* kelp.

Ceilteach *m/adj* Celt; Celtic.

ceimig *f* chemical substance.

ceimigeachd *f* chemistry.

ceimigear *m* chemist.

cèin *adj* foreign; faraway.

cèir *f* wax.

cèir-chluaise *f* ear wax.

cèis *f* frame; envelope.

cèiseag *f* cassette.

ceist *f* question; problem; point.

ceisteachan *m* questionnaire.

ceistear *m* questioner; question master.

Cèitean *m* (*with art*) **an Cèitean** May.

ceithir *m/adj* four.

ceò *m* mist; haze; smoke.

ceòl *m* music.

ceòl beag *m* light music for the pipes.

ceòlmhor *adj* musical; melodious.

ceòl mòr *m* classical pipe music, pibroch.

ceòthach *adj* misty.

ceud *m* hundred.

ceudameatair *m* centimetre.

ceudamh *adj* hundredth.

ceud mìle fàilte! *excl* a hundred thousand welcomes!

ceudna *adj* same.

ceud taing! *excl* many thanks! thanks a lot!

ceum *m* step; pace; degree.

ceum air ceum *adv* step by step.

ceumnachadh *m* graduation.

ceumnaich *v* graduate.

ceus[1] *v* crucify.

ceus[2] *m* suitcase.

ceusadh *m* crucifixion.

cha, chan *part negating the clause or sentence.*

cha bheir mi ho-ro-gheallaidh air . . . I don't give a toss for . . .

cha b'urrainn dhomh gun . . . I couldn't help.

chaidh *past tense of v* **rach.**

chaidh agam air *v* I managed it.

cha mhòr *adv* nearly.

cha mhòr nach *conj* almost.

chan *see* **cha.**

chan fhad' thuige! it won't be long!

chan longnadh e! no wonder!

cha ruig thu leas . . . v you don't need to.

chì *future tense of v* **faic.**

chleachd mi v I used to.

cho *adv* so, as.

cho luath is . . . *conj* as soon as . . .

cho math sin *adv* that good, as good as that.

chuala *past tense of v* **cluinn.**

chuca *prep pron* to them.

chugad *prep pron* to you (*sing*).

chugaibh *prep pron* to you (*pl*).

chugainn *prep pron* to us.

chugam *prep pron* to me.

chuice *prep pron* to her, to it (*f*).

chuige *prep pron* to him, to it (*m*).

chun *prep* to, towards, up to.

chun a seo *adv* up to now, so far.

chunnaic *past tense of v* **faic.**

ciad *adj* (*with art*) **a' chiad**. the first.

ciad-fhuasladh *m* first aid.

ciall *f* sense(s); meaning.

ciallach *adj* sensible.

ciallaich *v* mean.

ciamar? *interrog adv* how?

cia mheud? *interrog adv* how many? how much?

cian *adj* distant; long. • *m* distance; remoteness.

cianail *adj* sad.

cianalach *adj* homesick.

cianalas *m* sadness.

ciar *adj* dark; swarthy; dun.

clatach *adj* pleasant; attractive.

cidhe *m* quay.

cidsin *m* kitchen.

cileagram *m* kilogram.

cilemeatair *m* kilometre.

cill *f* cell; church; kirkyard.

cineal *m* race; species.

cinn *v* grow; multiply.

cinneadail *adj* clannish.

cinneadh *m* clan; people; surname.

cinneas *m* growth.

cinne-daona *m* (*with art*) **an cinne-daona** mankind.

cinnt *f* certainty.

cinnteach *adj* certain; confident.

ciobair *m* shepherd.

cioch *f* breast.

ciochag *f* valve.

clomach *m* prisoner; detainee.

clon *m* lack; desire.

clonta *m* guilt; guilty action.

clontach *adj* guilty. • *m* guilty person; offender.

clontaich *v* commit an offence.

clora *f* (*fam*) sheep.

clorram *m* disability, handicap.

clorramach *adj* disabled, handicapped. • *m* disabled person; (*pl with art*) **na clorramaich** the disabled.

clotach *adj* left-handed.

cipean *m* stake; tether post.

cìr *v* comb. • *f* comb; cud.

cìrean *m* (*of hen, etc*) comb, crest.

cìr-mheala *f* honeycomb.

cìs f tax; taxation.
cìs-chusbainn f customs duty.
cìs-cinn f poll tax.
cìs olghreachd f inheritance tax.
ciste f (furniture) chest.
ciste-chàir f car boot.
ciste-laighe f coffin.
ciste-urrais f trust fund.
clùb m cube.
clùbach adj cubic.
clùbhran m drizzle, shower.
cludha f queue.
clùin adj gentle; quiet; calm.
clùineas m calm, calmness.
clùinich v quieten, calm down.
clùraig v (bacon, etc) cure.
clùrr v hurt; torture.
clùrrte adj hurt, injured.
clabar-snàimh m flipper.
clabhstair m cloister.
clach v stone. • f stone; (fam) testicle.
clachach adj stony.
clachair m (stone-)mason.
clachan m village; kirktown; kirkyard.
clach-bhalg f (toy, etc) rattle.
clach culmhne f memorial, monument.
clach-ghràin f granite.
clach-mheallain f hailstone.
Clach na Cineamhainn f the Stone of Destiny.
clach sùla f eyeball.
clach uasal f precious stone.
cladach m shore, beach.

cladh m kirkyard, cemetry.
cladhaich v dig.
cladhaire m coward.
cladhaireach adj cowardly.
clag m bell.
clagarsaich f clinking; rattling.
clag-rabhaidh m alarm bell.
claidheamh m sword.
claidheamhair m swordsman.
claidheamh caol m rapier.
claigeann m skull.
clàimhean m latch.
clais f ditch; furrow.
claisdeachd f hearing.
claisneachd f hearing.
clamhan m buzzard.
clann f children; clan.
clann-nighean f (collective) girls.
claoidh v exhaust; vex.
claoidhte adj exhausted.
claon v incline; go astray; pervert. • adj awry; oblique; perverse.
claonadh m slant, slope; squint; perversion.
clàr m board; table; record.
clàraich v record.
clàr-amais m index.
clàr-aodainn m brow, forehead.
clàr-dùthcha m map.
clàr-fhiacail f incisor.
clàr-gnothaich m agenda.
clàr-innsidh m table of contents.
clàr-oideachais m curriculum.
clàrsach f harp; Celtic harp, clarsach.

clàrsair *m* harper.

clàr-tìde *m* timetable.

clas *m* class.

clasaigeach *adj* classical.

cleachd *v* use; accustom.

cleachdadh *m* habit; practice.

cleachdte ri *adj* accustomed to, used to.

cleas *m* feat; trick.

cleasachd *f* conjuring; juggling.

cleasaiche *m* actor; comic; conjurer.

cleas-chluich *f* comic film/play.

clèir *f* clergy; Presbytery.

clèireach *m* clergyman; clerk. • *m/adj* Presbyterian.

clèireachail *adj* clerical.

cleoc *m* clock.

cleòc *m* cloak.

clì *adj* left.

cliabh *m* pannier; creel; (*anat*) chest.

cliamhainn *m* son-in-law.

cliath *v* (*agric*) harrow. • *f* grate; bars; harrow.

cliathaich *f* side, flank.

cliath-theine *f* fire grate.

cliath-uinneig *f* window bars.

clìomaid *f* climate.

clis *adj* nimble.

cliseachd *f* nimbleness, agility.

clisg *v* start, jump; startle.

clisgeach *adj* jumpy, on edge; timid.

clisgeadh *f* start, fright.

clisgear *m* exclamation.

clisg-phuing *f* exclamation mark.

cliù *m* fame; reputation.

cliùiteach *adj* famous, celebrated.

cliùthaich *v* praise.

clò[1] *m* cloth; tweed.

clò[2] *m* print; printing press.

clòbha *f* clove.

clobha *m* tongs.

clòbhar *m* clover.

clobhsa *m* (*in tenement, etc*) close.

clò-bhuail *v* print.

clò-bhuailte *adj* printed.

clò-bhualadair *m* printer(s).

clò-bhualadh *m* printing; publication.

clò-chadal *m* doze, dozing.

clochar *m* convent.

clogaid *f* helmet.

clòimh *f* wool.

clòimhteachan *m* eiderdown.

Clò Mòr na Hearadh *m* Harris Tweed.

closach *f* carcase.

clòsaid *f* closet.

clò-sgrìobh *v* type.

clò-sgrìobhadair *m* typewriter.

clò-sgrìobhadh *m* typing; typescript.

clò-sgrìobhaiche *m* typist.

cluain *f* meadow, pasture.

cluaineas *m* retirement.

cluaran *m* thistle.

cluas *f* ear; handle.

cluasag *f* pillow.

cluas-fhail *f* earring.

club *m* club.

clùd *m* rag; cloth.

cluich *m* play; game. • *v* play.

cluich-bùird *m* board game.

cluicheadair *m* player; actor.

cluinn *v* hear.

cnag *v* crunch; bang, knock. • *f* bang, knock.

cnag-aodaich *f* clothes peg.

cnag-dealain *f* electric plug.

cnag na cùise *f* the crux of the matter.

cnàlmh *m* bone.

cnàlmh an droma *m* the spine, the backbone.

cnàlmheach *m* skeleton.

cnàlmhseag *f* acne; blackhead.

cnàlmh-silnnein *f* shoulder-blade.

cnàlmh uga *m* collarbone.

cnàmh *v* chew; digest.

cnàmh *m* potato blight.

cnàmhach *adj* bony.

cnàmh a' chìr *v* chew the cud.

cnap *m* block; lump, knob.

cnapach *adj* lumpy, nobbly.

cnap-starra *m* stumbling block.

cnatan *m* (*often with art*) cold, **tha an cnatan orm** I have a cold; **an cnatan mòr** *m* influenza.

cnead *m* groan.

cnèadaich *v* caress; stroke.

cneutag *f* small ball, puck.

cnò *f* nut.

cnoc *m* hill.

cnocach *adj* hilly.

cnocan *m* hillock.

cnò challtainne *m* hazelnut.

cnò Fhrangach *m* walnut.

cnò-thalmhainn *m* peanut.

cnuas *v* chew; ponder.

cnuimh-thalmhainn *f* earthworm.

co- *prefix* co-.

cò? *interrog pron* who? which?

co aca *conj* whether.

co-aimsireil *adj* contemporary.

cò air bith? *interrog pron* whoever?

co-alta *m/f* foster brother/sister.

cò am fear? which one?.

co-aoiseach *m/adj* contemporary.

co-aontaich *v* agree.

cò às? *adv* where from?

cobhair *f* help; relief.

cobhair orm! *excl* help! help me!

cobhar *m* foam.

cobhartach *m/f* plunder; prey.

co-bhuail *v* collide.

còc *m* (*fuel*) coke.

còcaire *m* cook, chef.

còcaireachd *f* cookery.

cochall *m* husk; hood.

co-cheangail *v* tie together; connect.

co-cheangailte *adj* linked together.

co-chomann *m* commune; co-operative.

co-chòrd v agree mutually.

co-chothrom m balance, equilibrium.

co-chruinnich v assemble.

co-chruinneachadh m assembly; collection.

còco m cocoa.

co-dhèanta adj put together.

co dhlubh conj whether.

co-dhlubh, co-dhlù adv anyway; at least.

co-dhlùthaich v condense.

co-dhùin v conclude; end.

co-dhùnadh m conclusion; end.

co-èlgneachadh m compulsion.

co-èlgnich v compel.

cofaidh m coffee.

co-fharpais f competition.

co-fharpaiseach m competitor.

co-fhlaitheachd f republic; republicanism.

co-fhlaitheas m commonwealth.

co-fhoghar m consonant.

co-fhreagair v match; correspond.

co-fhulangach adj sympathetic.

co-fhulangas m sympathy.

cofhurtachd f consolation; comfort.

cofhurtaich v comfort, console.

cofhurtail adj comfortable.

cò fon ghrèin'... ? who on earth ... ?

cogadh m war; warfare.

cogais f conscience.

co-ghin v mate, copulate.

co-ghineadh m mating, copulation.

co-ghnìomhair m adverb.

coibhneas m kindness, kindliness.

coibhneil adj kind, kindly.

coidse f coach.

còig m/adj five.

còigeamh adj fifth.

còignear m fivesome.

coigreach m foreigner; stranger.

coileach m (fowl) cock.

coileach-gaoithe m weathercock.

coilean v accomplish; complete.

coileanta adj completed; perfect.

coilear m collar.

coill f guilt; sin.

coille f wood.

coilleag f cockle.

coillear m forestry worker; woodcutter.

coille mhòr f forest.

colmeas f comparison; like(s) of. • v compare, liken.

colmeasach adj comparable.

colmh- prefix co-.

colmheach adj foreign; unfamiliar. • m foreigner; stranger.

colmhead v watch; look.

colmhead air v look at.

colmhead ri v expect.

colmhearsnach m neighbour.

colmhearsnachd f neighbourhood.

colmheatailt f alloy.

coimhlion v accomplish; complete.

coimisean m commission.

coimpiutair, coimpiutar m computer.

coineanach m rabbit.

còinneach f moss.

coinneal f candle.

coinneamh f meeting.

coinnich v congregate.

coinnich ri v meet.

coinnleir m candlestick.

co-ionann adj identical, the same.

còir f obligation; right; justice.
• adj decent; worthy; kindly.

coirbte adj corrupt.

coirce m oats.

coire[1] f wrong; blame.

coire[2] m kettle; cauldron; corrie.

coireach adj guilty; responsible.
• m guilty person; offender.

coirich v blame.

còir-slighe f right of way.

coiseachd f walking.

coisich v walk.

coisiche m walker, pedestrian.

coisinn v win; earn.

còisir f choir.

còisir-chiùil f choir.

coisrig v consecrate; devote.

coitcheann adj common, communal; general, universal.

coithional adj congregation.

coitich v urge.

co-labhairt f conference.

co-là-breith m birthday.

cola-deug m fortnight.

colaiste f college.

colann f body.

colbh m column.

Colla m Coll.

Collach m/adj from Coll.

collaidh adj sensual, carnal.

coltach adj likely.

coltach ri prep like.

coltaich ri v compare to.

coltas m appearance.

com m bosom, chest area.

coma adj indifferent; unconcerned.

coma co-dhiubh adj quite indifferent.

comain f obligation.

coma leat! excl never mind! don't worry!

comanachadh m Communion.

comanaich v take Communion.

comanaiche m communicant.

comann m association; club, society.

comann eachdraidh m history society.

comar f confluence.

comas m ability; faculty.

comasach adj able.

comasach air capable of.

comas inntinn m mental ability.

comataidh f committee.

combaist f compass.

comh- prefix co-.

comhachag f owl.

comhair f direction.

comhairle *f* advice; council.
comhairleach *m* adviser.
comhairlich *v* advise.
comhairliche *m* councillor.
comharrachadh *m* marking, correction.
comharradh *m* mark; sign; symbol.
comharradh-ceiste *m* question mark.
comharradh-rathaid *m* road sign.
comharradh-stiùiridh *m* landmark.
comharraich *v* mark, correct.
comhart *m* (*of dog*) bark.
comhartaich *v* (*of dog*) bark.
còmhdach *m* cover, covering.
còmhdaich *v* cover.
còmhdaichte *adj* covered.
còmhdhail *f* congress, conference.
co-mheasgaich *v* intermix, mix; amalgate; mingle.
co mheud? *interrog adv* how much? how many?
còmhla[1] *adv* together.
còmhla[2] *m/f* door.
còmhlan *m* band; company.
còmhlan-ciùil *m* (*mus*) band, group.
còmhla ri *prep* with, along with.
còmhnaich *v* live, dwell.
còmhnaidh *f* dwelling.
còmhnard *adj* level; smooth. • *m* plain; level ground.

còmhradh *m* conversation, talk.
còmhradh beag *m* chat.
còmhrag *f* combat; conflict.
còmhrag-dithis *f* duel.
còmhraiteach *adj* talkative, chatty.
còmhstri *f* strife; competition.
com-pàirtich *v* take part.
companach *m* companion; pal.
companaidh *m/f* firm, company.
companas *m* companionship.
comraich *f* sanctuary.
còn *m* cone.
conaire *f* rosary.
conaltrach *adj* social; sociable.
conaltradh *m* conversation; company.
conasg *m* gorse, whins.
conastabal *m* constable.
connadh *m* fuel.
connadh-làmhaich *m* munitions.
connlach *f* straw.
connrag *f* consonant.
connsachail *adj* quarrelsome; argumentative.
connsaich *v* argue, quarrel.
connspaid *f* dispute; controversy; wrangling.
connspaideach *adj* disputatious; controversial.
conntraigh *f* neap tide.
consal *m* consul.
consan *m* consonant.
co-obrachadh *m* co-operation; co-operative.

co-obraich *v* co-operate.

co-ogha *m* cousin.

co-oibrich *v* work together.

co-oibriche *m* fellow worker.

cop *m* foam, froth.

copach *adj* frothy, foaming.

copag *f* dock, docken.

copan *m* cup.

copar *m* copper.

co-phòitear *m* drinking companion.

cor *m* state, condition.

còraichean daonna *fpl* human rights.

còrcair *adj* purple.

corcais *f* cork.

còrd[1] *v* agree.

còrd[2] *m* cord.

còrdadh *m* agreement, understanding.

còrd ri *v* please.

còrn *m* drinking horn; corn.

Còrn *f (with art)* **a' Chòrn** Cornwall.

Còrnach *m/adj* Cornishman; Cornish.

còrnair *m* corner.

corp *m* body; corpse.

corpailear *m* corporal.

corp-làidir *adj* able-bodied.

corporra *adj* bodily, corporal.

còrr *adj (number)* odd. • *m (with art)* **an còrr** the rest, everything else; anything else.

corra *adj* odd, occasional.

corrag *f* finger.

corra-ghritheach *f* heron.

corran *m* sickle.

còrr is *prep* more than.

còs *m* hollow.

còsach *adj* hollow.

cosamhlachd *f* parable.

cosg *v* cost; spend; waste. • *m* cost; waste.

cosgail *adj* costly.

cosgais *f* cost.

cosgaisean siubhail *fpl* travel costs.

co-sheirm *f* harmony.

co-shìnte *adj* parallel.

cosnadh *m* earning; employment; work.

costa *m* coast.

còta *m* coat.

còta-bàn *m* petticoat.

còta-leapa *m* dressing gown, housecoat.

còta mòr *m* overcoat.

cotan *m* cotton.

cothrom *adj (number)* even. • *m* chance, opportunity; balance.

cothromach *adj* fair; decent.

cothromaich *v* weigh; balance.

cothrom na Feinne *m* fair chance.

co-thuit *v* coincide.

co-thuiteamas *m* coincidence.

cràbhach *adj* devout, pious.

cràdh *m* pain; anguish.

craiceann *m* skin.

cràidh *v* pain; torment.

cràidhteach *adj* grievous, painful.

cràin *f* sow.

crann *m* mast; plough; crane; bolt; tree; (*with art*) **an Crann** the Saltire, St Andrew's Cross; **an Crann-Ceusaidh** Christ's Cross.

crannag *f* pulpit; milk churn; crannog.

crannchur *m* drawing lots; fate.

crann-fìona *m* vine.

crann-sgaoilidh *m* transmitter; TV mast.

crann-sneachda *m* snowplough.

crann-tarsainn *m* crossbar.

craobh *f* tree.

craobh-sgaoil *v* diffuse; broadcast.

craos *m* maw; gluttony.

craosach *adj* gluttonous.

craosaire *m* glutton.

crasg *f* crutch (for walking).

crasgag *f* starfish.

crath *v* shake, tremble; brandish.

creach *v* plunder; ruin. • *f* ruination; plunder.

creachan *m* scallop.

crèadh *f* clay.

crèadhadair *m* potter.

crèadhadaireachd *f* pottery.

creag *f* crag; hill.

creagach *adj* craggy.

creamh *m* garlic.

creamh-gàrraidh *m* leek.

creapan *m* stool.

creathall *f* cradle.

creid *v* believe; think, consider.

creideamh *m* belief; trust; religion.

creideas *m* trust.

creim *v* nibble.

crèis *f* grease, fat.

crèiseach *adj* greasy, fatty.

creithleag *f* cleg, horsefly.

creud *f* creed.

creutair *m* creature.

creutair bochd *m* poor soul.

criadh *f* clay.

criathar *m* sieve, riddle.

criathraich *v* sieve, riddle.

cridhe *m* heart; courage.

cridhealas *m* heartiness; conviviality.

cridheil *adj* hearty; jovial.

crìoch *f* end; boundary.

Crìochan Shasainn the Borders.

crìochnach *adj* finite.

crìochnaich *v* finish.

crìochnaichte *adj* finished.

criomag *f* bit; crumb; (*pl*) **criomagan** bits and pieces, odds and ends.

crìon *v* wither; dry up. • *adj* tiny; petty; withered.

crioplach *m* cripple.

crios *m* belt.

Crìosdachd *f* Christendom.

Crìosdaidh *m* Christian.

Crìosdaidheachd *f* Christianity.

Crìosdail *adj* Christian.

Crìosdalachd *f* Christian-ness.

criostal *m* crystal.

cripleach *m* cripple.

crith *v* tremble, shiver. • *f* trembling, shivering.

critheanach *adj* shaky; scary.

crith-thalmhainn *f* earthquake.

crò *m* cattle pen, fold.

croch *v* hang.

crochadair *m* hangman; hanger.

crochadh *m* hanging.

crochte *adj* hung; hanged.

crodh *m* cattle, livestock.

crodh-bhainne *m* dairy cows.

crodh-dàra *m* breeding cattle.

crodh-eadraidh *m* milk cows.

crò-dhearg *adj* crimson.

cròg *f* paw; fist.

cròic *f* antler.

croich *f* gallows. • *excl* **X na croiche!** damned X! bloody X!

crois *f* cross; crucifix.

crois rathaid *f* crossroads.

croit[1] *f* croft.

croit[2] *f* (*on back*) hump.

croitear *m* crofter.

croitse *f* (*for walking*) crutch.

crom *v* bend, incline; descend, climb down. • *adj* bent, crooked; curved.

cromag *f* hook; comma; cromag, crook.

cromagan turrach *fpl* inverted commas.

crom air *v* set to.

crom-chasach *adj* bandy-legged.

cron *m* harm; fault.

cronaich *v* chide, scold.

cronail *adj* harmful, hurtful.

crònan *m* humming; murmuring; buzzing; (*stags*) belling.

crò snàthaid *m* eye of needle.

crosta *adj* cross; naughty.

crotach *adj* hump-backed.

crotal *m* lichen.

cruach *v* heap, stack. • *f* heap; rick.

cruachann *f* hip.

cruadal *m* hardship; hardihood.

cruadalach *adj* difficult; hardy.

cruadhaich *v* harden; solidify.

cruaidh *f* steel. • *adj* hard; harsh; hardy.

cruaidh-chàs *m* emergency; tight corner.

cruaidh-chridheach *adj* hard-hearted.

cruan *m* enamel.

cruas *m* hardness; harshness; toughness.

crùb *v* crouch; cringe; crawl.

crùbach *adj* lame. • *m* lame person.

crùbag *f* crab.

crùban *m* crouch, squat.

crùdh *v* (*horse*) shoe.

crudha *m* horseshoe.

cruinn *adj* round; accurate; assembled.

cruinne *m/f* sphere, globe; (*with art*) **an cruinne** the earth, the globe.

cruinneachadh *m* gathering, assembly; collection.

cruinne-cè *m/f* (*with art*) **an cruinne-cè** the world.

cruinn-eòlas *m* geography.

cruinnich *v* gather, assemble; (*fruit, etc*) pick.

cruinn-leum *m* standing jump.

crùisgean *m* oil lamp, cruisie.

cruit[1] *f* croft.

cruit[2] *f* harp.

cruit-chòrda *f* harpsichord.

cruitear *m* harper.

cruitheachd *f* creation; (*with art*) **a' Chruitheachd** the world; the universe, Creation.

cruithear *m* creator; (*with art*) **an Cruithear** God, the Creator.

Cruithneach *m/adj* Pict; Pictish.

cruithneachd *f* wheat.

crùn *v* crown. • *m* crown.

crùnadh *m* crowning, coronation.

cruth *m* shape; figure; appearance.

cruthaich *v* create.

cù *m* dog.

cuach *f* bowl, quaich.

cuagach *adj* bent; limping.

cuaille *m* club, cudgel.

cuairt *f* circuit; stroll; trip.

cuan *m* sea, ocean; **an Cuan Sgìth** the Little Minch; **an Cuan Siar** the Atlantic Ocean.

cuaraidh *m* quarry.

cuaran *m* sandal.

cuartaich *v* surround; enclose.

cùbaid *f* pulpit.

cubhaidh *adj* fitting.

cùbhraidh *adj* sweet, fragrant.

cucair *f* cooker.

cù-chaorach *m* sheepdog.

cùdainn *f* large tub.

cudthrom *m* weight; importance; stress.

cudthromach *adj* weighty, important.

cugullach *adj* unsteady; dodgy; unreliable.

cuibhle *f* wheel.

cuibhle-stiùiridh *f* steering wheel.

cuibhreach *m* chain.

cuibhreann *m* portion; allowance.

cuibhreann-ciorraim *m* disability allowance.

cuibhrich *v* chain.

cuibhrig *f* quilt, coverlet.

cuid *f* share; part. • *pron* some.

cuid-aodaich *f* clothes, clothing.

cuideachadh *m* help.

cuideachail *adj* helpful.

cuideachd[1] *f* company; companions.

cuideachd[2] *adv* too, also.

cuideachdail *adj* sociable, fond of company.

cuideigin *m/f* someone, somebody.

cuide ri *prep* with, along with.

cuidhteag *f* whiting.

cuidhteas *m* receipt; riddance.

cuidich *v* help, assist.

cuid oidhche *f* night's lodging.

cùil *f* corner, nook.

cuilbheart *f* trick; stratagem.

cuilc *f* reed; cane.

cùil-chumhang *f* tight corner, fix.

cuilc Innseanach *f* bamboo.

culleag *f* fly, house-fly.

cuilean *m* puppy; cub.

cuimhne *f* memory; remembrance.

cuimhneachan *m* memorial; memorandum.

cuimhneachan-cogaidh *m* war memorial.

cuimhnich *v* remember.

cuimir *adj* succinct; neat; shapely.

Cuimreach *m/adj* Welshman; Welsh.

Cuimrigh *f* (*with art*) **a' Chuimrigh** Wales.

cuimsich *v* aim.

cuine? *interrog adv* when?

cuing *f* yoke; (*with art*) **a' chuing** *f* asthma.

cuinneag *f* bucket; milking pail.

cuinnean *m* nostril.

culp *v* whip. • *f* whip.

cuir *v* put; send; (*seed, etc*) sow, plant.

cuir a dh'iarraidh *v* send for.

cuir air *v* light, turn/switch on; put on, don.

cuir air an spàrr *v* save; stow away.

cuir air an teine *v* light the fire.

cuir air ath là *v* defer, put off.

cuir air bhonn *v* found, set up.

cuir air chois *v* found, set up.

cuir air dòigh *v* organise; put right.

cuir air earalas *v* forewarn, alert.

cuir air flod *v* float; launch.

cuir air leth *v* put aside; save.

cuir air meidh *v* balance.

cuir air mheomhair *v* commit to memory.

cuir air snàmh *v* inundate, flood.

cuir aithne air *v* get to know.

cuir a-mach *v* bring up, vomit.

cuir am bogadh *v* steep.

cuir am fad *v* lengthen, make longer.

cuir an cèill *v* express, put into words.

cuir an clò *v* print; publish.

cuir an cràdh *v* torture.

cuir an eanchainn à *v* brain.

cuir an geall gu *v* bet that.

cuir an òrdugh *v* put in order.

cuir an sàs *v* capture; arrest.

cuir an suarachas *v* belittle, disparage.

cuir an tairgse *v* make available.

cuir an teagamh *v* cast doubt upon.

cuir às an teine *v* put the fire out.

cuir às do *v* abolish; kill.

cuir às mo leth. *v* accuse me of.

cuir bacadh air *v* obstruct; prevent.

cuir bun-os-cionn *v* upend, overturn.

cuir bus air *v* grimace, pout.

cuir cabhag air *v* rush, hurry.

cuir car de *v* move.

cuir ceart *v* correct, put right.

cuir cèilidh air *v* go to see, visit.

cuir cleas air *v* play a trick/joke on.

cuir clisgeadh air *v* startle.

cuir coire air *v* blame, lay blame on.

cuir crainn *v* toss coin.

cuir crìoch air *v* complete, finish.

cuir dàil air *v* delay.

cuir dath air *v* colour.

cuir dheth *v* turn/switch off; doff, take off; talk away, jabber on.

cuir do talc orm/rium *v* lean on me; depend on me.

cuir dragh air *v* worry; bother, trouble.

cuireadh *m* invitation.

cuir eagal air *v* frighten.

cuir earbsa ann *v* put trust in, rely on.

cuir eòlas air *v* get to know.

cuir fàilte air *v* welcome.

cuir fios do *v* let know, inform.

cuir fodha *v* sink, scuttle.

cuir fon cholll *v* outlaw.

cuir geall *v* place a bet.

cuir gruaim air *v* frown, scowl.

cuir gu feum *v* use, utilise.

cuir impidh air *v* persuade, urge.

cuir longantas air *v* amaze, astound.

cuir luach air *v* value; evaluate.

cuirm *f* feast, banquet.

cuir ma sgaoil *v* set free.

cuirm-bainnse *f* wedding reception.

cuirm-chnuic *f* picnic.

cuirmeach *adj* festive.

cuir meal an naidheachd air *v* congratulate.

cuir mo chùl ri *v* turn my back on.

cuir mùlg air *v* frown, scowl.

cuir oillt air *v* terrify; horrify.

cuir rian air *v* put in order, organise.

cuir romham *v* make up my mind, resolve (to).

cuir smùid *v* smoke, emit smoke.

cuir seachad *v* pass, spend.

cuir sneachd *v* snow.

cuir stad air *v* put a stop/end to.

cuir suim ann *v* take an interest in.

cùirt *f* court.

cùirtean *m* curtain.

cùirteil *adj* courteous; courtly.

cuir thairis *v* overflow.

cuir thar a chèile *v* set at loggerheads.

cuir timcheall *v* send/pass round.

cùirt-lagha *f* law court.

cuir urram air *v* honour.

cùls *f* matter, business; (*pl*) **cùlsean** things, matters.

cùls-bheachd *f* abstraction, abstract idea.

cùisear *m* (*gram*) subject.

cùis-ghràin f abomination.

cùis lagha f lawsuit.

cuisle f vein; pipe.

cuislean m flute.

cuisle-chinn f aorta.

cuisle-chlùil f flute.

cuisle-mhòr f artery.

cùl m nape; hair of head; back.

cùlaibh m back part. • adv **cùlaibh air beulaibh** back to front; vice versa.

culaidh f garment; suit of clothes; butt, object.

culaidh-cholmheach f fancy dress.

culaidh-fharmaid f object of envy.

cularan m cucumber.

cùl-chàin v slander.

cùl-chàineadh m slander, backbiting.

cullach m boar.

cùl-mhùtaire m smuggler.

cùl-mhùtaireachd f smuggling.

cùl na h-amhaich f the back of the neck.

cùl na làimh m the back of the hand.

cultar, cultur m culture.

cum v shape, form.

cùm v keep.

cumadh m shape, form.

cùm air v continue, go on. • excl **cùm ort!** keep at it! on you go!

cùm air ais v hold back, delay.

cùm a-mach v assert, claim.

cuman m bucket; milking pail.

cumanta adj common, ordinary.

cumantas m usualness, normality.

cùm às an làthair v keep away; keep out of sight.

cùm caismeachd ri v keep time to.

cùm faire v keep watch/guard.

cumha¹ f lament, elegy.

cumha² m stipulation, condition.

cumhach adj conditional.

cumhachd m/f power; might; (electric) power.

cumhachdach adj powerful; mighty.

cumhachd tuinne m wave power.

cumhang adj narrow.

cùmhnant m covenant; contract.

cùm ris! excl stick at it! keep it up!

cùm smachd air v keep control of.

cùm suas v maintain, support.

cùm sùil air v keep an eye on.

cùm taic ri v support.

cùm taobh ri v side with, favour.

cunbhalach adj even, regular; steady.

cungaidh f materials; ingredients.

cungaidh-leighis f medicine, drug.

cunnart m danger, risk.

cunnartach adj dangerous, risky.

cùnnradh *m* contract; deal.
cùnnt *v* count.
cùnntas *m* counting; *(finance)* account; narration; score.
cùnntasachd *f* accountancy.
cùnntasair *m* accountant.
cuntair *m* (*shop, etc*) counter.
cùp *m* cup.
cupa *m* cup.
cuplachadh *m* copulation, mating.
cuplaich *v* couple, copulate.
cùpon *m* coupon, voucher.
cur *m* placing; sending.
curach *f* coracle.
curach Innseanach *f* canoe.
curaidh *m* hero.
cùram *m* care; responsibility.

cùramach *adj* careful; prone to worry.
cur na mara *m* seasickness.
curran *m* carrot.
currcag *f* lapwing.
cùrsa *m* course.
cur-seachad *m* hobby, pastime.
cùrtair *m* curtain.
cus *m* excess, too much.
cusbainn *f* (*tax*) customs.
cusp *f* chilblain.
cuspair *m* subject, topic; (*gram*) object.
cut *v* gut.
cutair *m* fish-gutter.
cuthach *m* madness; rage.
cuthag *f* cuckoo.

D

dà *n/adj* two.
dachaigh *f* home.
dà-chànanach *adj* bilingual.
dad *f* thing, anything.
dadaidh *m* dad, daddy.
dadam *m* atom; tiny piece.
dà-dheug *n/adj* twelve.
dad ort! *excl* never mind! don't worry!
dag *m* pistol.
dail *f* meadow; dale.
dàil *f* delay.
dàimh *m/f* relationship, ties.
dàimheach *adj* relative.

daingeann *adj* firm, solid.
daingneach *f* fort; stronghold.
daingnich *v* fortify; consolidate; confirm.
dàir *m* rutting, heat.
dall *v* blind. • *adj* blind. • *m* blind man.
dàmais *f* draughts.
damh *m* stag.
dàmhair *f* rutting; (*with art*) an Dàmhair October.
damhan-allaidh *m* spider.
dàn¹ *m* fate, destiny.
dàn² *m* poem; song.

dàna *adj* daring; impudent; arrogant.

dànachd *f* poetry, verse.

danns *v* dance.

dannsa *m* dance.

dannsadh *m* dancing.

dannsair *m* dancer.

dàn spioradail *m* hymn.

daoimean *m* diamond.

daoine *mpl* people; kinsfolk.

daoine mòra *mpl* big shots, bigwigs.

daoine-sìth *mpl* fairyfolk.

daolag *f* beetle.

daolag-bhreac-dhearg *f* ladybird.

daonna *adj* human.

daonnan *adv* always, constantly.

daor *adj* dear, expensive.

daorach *f* drunkenness; spree.

daorachail *adj* intoxicating.

daorsa *f* captivity.

dara *adj* second; one.

darach *m* oak.

dara-deug *adj* twelfth.

dàrna *adj* second.

dà-sheaghach *adj* ambiguous.

dàta *m* data.

dath *v* colour; dye. • *m* colour; dye.

dath-bhacadh *m* colour bar.

dath-dhall *adj* colour-blind.

dathte *adj* coloured; dyed.

dà uair *adv* twice.

de *prep* of; from; made of.

dè *pron* what, what?

deacair *adj* hard, difficult.

deachd *v* dictate.

deachdadh *m* dictation.

deachdaire *m* dictator.

deagh *adj* good. • *adv* well.

deagh-bheusan *f* morals.

deagh-chrìtheach *adj* good-hearted.

deagh-tholl *f* good will.

dealachadh *m* parting.

dealachadh-pòsaidh *m* divorce, separation.

dealaich *v* part; separate; (*elec*) insulate.

dealan *m* electricity.

dealanach *m* lightning.

dealanaich *v* electrify.

dealanair *m* electrician.

dealan-dè *m* butterfly.

dealasach *adj* eager, zealous.

dealbh *m/f* picture; painting; shape. • *v* picture; design; construct.

dealbh-chluich *m/f* play.

dealbh-chumadh *m/f* plan, diagram.

dealbh-èibhinn *m/f* cartoon.

dealg *f* prickle, thorn; pin.

deàlrach *adj* shining, shiny.

deàlraich *v* shine, flash, glitter.

dealt *m/f* dew.

dè am fonn? (*fam*) how are you?

deamhais *m* shears.

deamhan *m* demon.

dèan *v* do; make.

dèan a' chùis *v* suffice, do the job/trick.

dèan a' chùis air *v* manage; defeat.

dèanadach *adj* industrious, active.

dèan adhradh *v* worship.

dèan altachadh *v* say grace.

dèan an gnothach *v* be just the job, do the trick.

dèan bàidh do *v* do a favour for.

dèan beic *v* curtsey.

dèan braoisg *v* grin; grimace.

dèan breug *v* lie, tell a lie.

dèan bruadar *v* dream.

dèan cabhag *v* hurry, make haste.

dèan cadal *v* sleep.

dèan casad *v* cough.

dèan casaid air *v* accuse; make a complaint against.

dèan cnead *v* groan.

dèan coimeas eadar *v* compare.

dèan còmhradh *v* talk, converse.

dèan cron air *v* harm, injure.

dèan crùban *v* crouch, squat.

dè an dòigh? (*fam*) how're you doing?.

dèan dragh *v* worry oneself.

dèan dragh do *v* cause worry to.

dèan dùrdail *v* coo.

dèan faire *v* be on guard.

dèan faite-gàire *v* smile.

dèan fanaid air *v* mock, ridicule.

dèan faoighe *v* beg.

dèan fead *v* whistle.

dèan feum *v* come in handy.

dèan feum do *v* do good to; be useful to.

dèan foill air *v* cheat.

dèan gàirdeachas *v* rejoice.

dèan gàire *v* laugh.

dèan gràgail *v* caw, croak.

dèan imrich *v* move house.

dèan iolach *v* shout.

dèan iomradh air *v* mention.

dèan malairt *v* trade, do business.

dèan mèirle *v* steal.

dèan miodal (do) *v* flatter, fawn (on).

dèan mo dhìcheall *v* do my utmost.

dèan mùn *v* urinate.

deanntag *f* nettle.

dèan oilbheum (do) *v* give offence (to).

dè an rud? what?

dèan sèisd air *v* besiege.

dèan sgairt *v* yell.

dèan sodal do *v* fawn on, butter up.

dèan sreothart *v* sneeze.

dèan stad *v* stop, call a halt.

dèan sùgradh *v* make merry, sport.

dèan suidhe! *excl* sit down! take a seat!

dèan sùil bheag ri *v* wink at.

dèan suiridhe ri *v* court.

dèan tàir air *v* despise, disparage.

dèan tarcais air *v* despise.

dèan ulfhart *v* howl.

dèan ùrnaigh ri *v* pray to.

dearbh *adj* same. • *v* prove; test.

dearbhadh *m* proof; test, trial.

dearc *f* berry.

dearcag *f* berry.

dearg *adj* red; (*fam*) utter.

deargad *f* flea.

deargann *f* flea.

deargnaich *v* redden.

dearmad *m* neglect, negligence; omission.

dearmadach *adj* negligent; neglectful.

dearmaid *v* omit, neglect (to do something).

deàrrs *v* shine.

deas *f* south. • *adj* south; right(-hand); ready; finished; active.

deasachadh *m* preparation; editing.

deasaich *v* prepare; edit.

deasaich biadh *v* cook.

deasbad *m* discussion, debate.

deasg *m* desk.

deas-ghnàth *m* ceremony.

dè a tha dhìth air? what does he require?

dè a tha a' dol?, dè tha dol? *excl* (*fam*) what's doing?

dè a tha thu ris? *excl* what are you up to?

de chlòimh *adj* woollen.

de chois *adv* on foot.

de dh' fhad *adv* long, in length.

dè do bheachd? what do you think?

dè do chor? *excl* (*fam*) how're you doing?

dè fon ghrèin'? *excl* what on earth?

deich *n/adj* ten.

deichead *m* decade.

deicheamh *adj* tenth.

deichnear *m/f* ten (people).

dèideadh *m* (*with art*) **an dèideadh** toothache.

dèideag *f* pebble; toy.

dèidheil air *adj* fond of, keen on.

deigh *f* ice.

dèile *f* board, plank.

dèilig ri *v* deal with, handle.

deimhinne *adj* sure, certain.

dèine *f* eagerness; fervour.

dèirc *f* charity, alms.

dèirceach *m* beggar. • *adj* charitable.

deireadh *m* end.

deireannach *adj* last, final.

deisciobal *m* disciple.

deise *f* suit (of clothes).

deiseil *adj* ready; finished; clockwise; sunwise; handy.

dè na tha e? how much is it?

deò *f* (*with art*) **an deò** the breath of life.

deoch *f* drink; booze.

deoch-làidir *f* alcohol; alcoholic drink.

deoch-an dorais *f* parting drink.

deoch-slàinte *f* (*drink*) toast.

deoghail *v* suck; absorb.

deòin *f* consent; willingness.

deònach *adj* willing.

deònach air prepared to.

dè tha dol? *see* **dè a tha a' dol?**

deuchainn *f* examination, test; trying time.

deuchainn-lann *m* laboratory.

deudach *adj* dental.

deug *suffix* -teen.

deugaire *m* teenager.

deur *m* tear, teardrop.

dh', dha (*for* **do**) *prep* to.

dhà *prep pron* to him; for him; to it; for it (*m*).

dhachaigh *adv* home(wards).

dhaibh *prep pron* to them; for them.

dheth[1] *adv* off.

dheth[2] *prep pron* of him; off him; of it; off it (*m*).

dhì *prep pron* of her; off her; of it; off it (*f*).

dhibh *prep pron* of you; off you (*pl*).

dhinn *prep pron* of us; off us.

dhìom *prep pron* of me; off me.

dhìot *prep pron* of you; off you (*sing*).

dhith *prep pron* to her; for her; to it; for it (*f*).

dhiubh *prep pron* of them; off them.

dhomh *prep pron* to me; for me.

dhuibh *prep pron* to you; for you (*pl*).

dhuine! dhuine! *excl* oh dear! oh dear!

dhuinn *prep pron* to us; for us.

dhut *prep pron* to you; for you (*sing*).

dia *m* god.

diabhal *m* devil.

diabhlaidh *adj* devilish, fiendish.

diadhachd *f* godhead; godliness; theology.

diadhaidh *adj* pious, godly.

diallaid *f* saddle.

dian *adj* eager; fierce; intense.

dian-ruith *f* headlong rush.

Diardaoin *m* Thursday.

dias *f* ear of corn.

dibhearsan *m* fun; entertainment.

dìblidh *adj* abject.

dìcheall *m* diligence, application.

dìcheallach *adj* diligent; hard-working.

dì-cheannaich *v* behead.

Diciadain *m* Wednesday.

Didòmhnaich *m* Sunday.

dìg *f* ditch.

Dihaoine *m* Friday.

dìle *f* heavy rain; flood.

dìleab *f* legacy.

dìleas *adj* faithful, trusty.

dìle bhàthte *f* downpour.

Diluain *m* Monday.

Dimàirt *m* Tuesday.

dìmeas *m* disrespect; contempt.

dìnichean *npl* jeans.

dinn *v* stuff, cram.

dìnnear *f* dinner.

diobair *v* desert, abandon.

diobhair *v* vomit, sick up.

diochuimhne *f* forgetfulness; oblivion.

diochuimhneach *adj* forgetful.

diochuimhnich *v* forget.

diofar *f* difference; importance.

diofarach *adj* different.

diogail *v* tickle.

diogalach *adj* ticklish.

dioghail *v* repay; take revenge.

dioghaltas *m* revenge.

dioghras *m* zeal; enthusiasm.

diolain *adj* bastard, illegitimate.

diomb *m* indignation; displeasure.

diombach *adj* out of sorts; indignant.

diombuan *adj* transient, fleeting.

diomhain *adj* vain; idle.

diomhair *adj* secret.

diomhanas *m* vanity, futility.

dion *v* protect, shelter. • *m* protection, shelter.

dionach *adj* sheltering; safe; wind and watertight.

diorrasach *adj* keen; tenacious.

diosail *m* diesel.

diosgail *m/f* creaking; crunching.

diosgan *m/f* grating; squeaking.

diosgo *m* disco.

direach *adj* straight; upright; just.

direach! *excl* quite!, just so!, exactly!

direadh *m* ascent; climbing.

dirich[1] *v* straighten.

dirich[2] *v* climb.

Disathairne *m* Saturday.

disne *m/f* dice.

dit *v* condemn, sentence.

diteadh *m* condemnation; sentence.

dith *m* lack, want.

dithean *m* flower.

dithis *f* two, twosome, pair.

dithreabh *f* desert, wilderness.

diùc *m* duke.

diùid *adj* shy, timid.

diùlt *v* refuse; disown.

diù nan the worst of..

Diùra *f* Jura.

Diùrach *m/adj* from Jura.

dleasdanas *m* duty.

dligh *f* right, due.

dligheach *adj* rightful, legitimate.

dlùth *adj* near; dense.

dlùthaich *v* draw near, approach.

dlùths *m* density.

do[1] *poss adj* your (*sing*).

do[2] *prep* to; into; for.

do- prefix un-, in-, im-.

dòbhran *m* otter.

do bhrìgh *prep* because of.

dòchas *m* hope.

do-dhèanta *adj* impossible.

dòigh *m* way, manner; condition.

dòigh-beatha *m* lifestyle, way of life.

dòighean *mpl* customs; manners.

dòighell *adj* proper; in good order.

dòll *m* dole.

doille *f* blindness.

doilleir *adj* dark; gloomy.

doilleirich *v* darken; obscure.

doimhne *f* (*with art*) **an doimhne** the deep.

doimhneachd f depth.

doimhnich v deepen.

doinnean f storm, tempest.

doirbh adj hard, difficult.

doire m/f grove, thicket, copse.

dòirt v pour; shed; flow.

do-labhairt adj unspeakable.

dolair m dollar.

dol-a-mach m behaviour, conduct.

dòlas m grief.

dol-às m way out, escape.

dol fodha na grèine m sunset.

dòmhail adj crowded; dense.

domhainn adj deep; profound.

domhan m (with art) **an Domhan** the Universe.

dona adj bad; naughty.

donas m badness, evil; (with art) **an Donas** the Devil.

donn adj brown; brown-haired.

donnal m howl.

donnalaich f howling.

doras m door.

dorcha adj dark.

dorchadas m darkness.

dòrlach m fistful, handful.

dòrn m fist.

dòrtadh-fala m bloodshed.

dos[1] m bush.

dos[2] m bagpipe drone.

dotair m doctor.

doth v singe, scorch.

drabasda adj obscene.

dràbhail adj grotty.

drabhair m drawer.

dràc m drake.

dragh m trouble, bother; worry.

draghail adj worrying; annoying.

dràibh v (car, etc) drive.

dràibhear m driver.

drama m dram.

dràma m drama.

dranndan m snarl(ing), growl(ing).

draoidh m druid; magician.

draoidheachd f wizardry, magic.

draoidheil adj magic, magical.

draosda adj smutty, lewd.

draosdachd f smut, lewdness.

drathais fpl underpants; pants, knickers.

dreach m appearance, aspect; complexion.

dreag f meteor.

dreallag f (child's) swing.

drèana f drain, drainage ditch.

dreasa f dress.

dreasair m dresser.

dreathan-donn m wren.

dreuchd f occupation, profession.

dreuchdail adj professional.

driamlach m/f fishing line.

drile f drill, auger.

drioftair m (fishing) drifter.

drip f bustle, state of being busy.

dripeil adj busy.

dris f bramble; brier.

drithleann m sparkle, flash.

driùchd f dew.

dròbh m cattle drove.

dròbhair m cattle-drover.

droch *adj* bad.

drochaid *f* bridge.

droch-bheart *f* vice; evil deed.

droch bheus *f* bad manners.

droch chainnt *f* bad language, swearing.

droch chòrdadh *m* disagreement, bad terms.

droch-ionnsaigh *f* physical assault.

droch isean *m* brat, naughty child.

droch nàdarrach *adj* ill-natured, ill-tempered.

droga *f* drug; *pl* **drogaichean** (*illegal, etc*) drugs.

drùdhag *f* drop; sip.

druid *f* starling.

drùidh *v* soak, penetrate (to skin).

drùidh air *v* affect, make an impression on.

druim *m* back; ridge.

drùis *f* lust, lechery.

drùlseach *adj* lustful, lecherous.

druma *f* drum.

duals *f* wages; reward; award.

dual[1] *m* character; birthright.

dual[2] *m* curl, lock; plait.

dualaich *v* curl; twist, plait.

dual-chainnt *f* dialect.

dualchas *m* hereditary character.

dualtach *adj* inherent, natural; **dualtach a bhith** inclined to be.

duan *m* poem, song.

duanag *f* song, ditty.

dùballte *adj* double; dual.

dubh *v* blacken. • *m* black; ink. • *adj* black; dark-haired.

dubhach *adj* gloomy; in a bad mood.

dubhadh *m* eclipse.

dubhag *f* kidney.

dubhaigeann *m* abyss, the deep.

dubhan *m* hook.

dubhar *m* shade.

dubh às *v* erase; blot out.

dubh-dhonn *adj* dark brown.

dubh-ghorm *adj* dark blue.

Dùbhlachd *f* (*with art*) **an Dùbhlachd** December.

dùbhlan *m* challenge.

dubh-nota *m* (*mus*) crochet.

dùblaich *v* double.

dùdag *f* bugle.

duibhre *f* dusk.

dùil[1] *f* hope; expectation.

dùil[2] *f* created being; element.

duileasg *m* dulse.

duilgheadas *m* difficulty; problem.

duilgheadasan sòisealta *mpl* social problems.

duilich *adj* hard, difficult; unfortunate. • *excl* **tha mi duilich!** I'm sorry!

duilleach *m* foliage.

duilleachan *m* leaflet.

duilleag *f* leaf; page, sheet.

dùin *v* shut, close.

duine *m* man; person; human being; husband. • *pron* someone; **duine sam bith** anyone at all.

duinealas *m* manliness; decisiveness.

duine cloinne *m* child.

duineil *adj* manly; decisive; mannish.

duine lag-chùlseach *m* stick-in-the-mud.

duine-uasal *m* gentleman; nobleman.

dùinte *adj* closed, shut; introvert.

dùisg *v* wake, awaken.

Duitseach *m/adj* Dutch person; Dutch.

dùn *m* heap; castle; hill fort; conical hill.

dùnan *m* small hill; dung heap.

dùr *adj* stubborn; dour.

dùrachd *f* seriousness; sincerity; greeting.

dùrachdach *adj* serious, earnest.

dùraig *v* dare.

durcan *m* pine cone, fir cone.

dùrdall *f* cooing.

dùsal *m* slumber, snooze.

dusan *m* dozen.

dùsgadh *m* awakening.

duslach *m* dust.

dust *m* dust.

dustach *adj* dusty.

dustair *m* duster.

dùthaich *f* country; homeland; countryside.

dùthchas *m* cultural inheritance.

dùthchasach *adj* native, indigenous.

E

e *pron* he; him; it (*m*).

eabar *m* mud, mire.

Eabhra *f* Hebrew (language).

Eabhrach *m/adj* Hebrew.

eacarsaich *f* exercise.

each *m* horse.

each-aibhne *m* hippopotamus.

eachdraiche *m* historian.

eachdraidh *f* history.

eachdraidheil *adj* historical.

each-oibre *m* workhorse.

each-uisge *m* water-horse, kelpie.

eaconamachd *f* economics.

eaconamaidh *m* economy.

eaconamair *m* economist.

Eadailt *f* (*with art*) **an Eadailt** Italy.

Eadailteach *m/adj* Italian.

eadar *prep* between; among; both.

eadaraibh *prep pron* between you; among you.

eadarainn *prep pron* between us; among us.

eadar-dhà-lionn *adv* undecided; between two stools.

eadar-dhealachadh *m* difference; distinction.

eadar-dhealaich *v* differentiate; distinguish.

eadar-dhealaichte *adj* different; distinct, separate.

eadar-nàlseanta *adj* international.

eadar-sholas *m* twilight.

eadar-theangachadh *m* translation.

eadar-theangaich *v* translate.

eadhon *adv* even.

eadradh *m* milking.

eag *f* nick, notch.

eagal *m* fear, fright; **eagal mo bheatha** the fright of my life.

eagalach *adj* prone to fear; terrible, dreadful. • *adv* terribly, dreadfully.

eaglais *f* church; (*with art*) **an Eaglais Shaor** the Free Church; **Eaglais na h-Alba** the Church of Scotland.

eala *f* swan.

èalaidh *v* creep; sneak away.

ealain *f* art; **Comhairle nan Ealain an Albainn** the Scottish Arts Council.

ealanta *adj* artistic.

eallach *m* load, burden.

ealta *f* (*birds*) flock.

ealtainn *f* razor.

eanchainn *f* brain.

eanraich *f* soup, broth.

ear *f* east.

ear air *prep* east of.

earalachadh *m* exhortation.

earalaich *v* exhort; caution.

Earranta *adj* (*company*) Limited, Ltd.

earb[1] *v* trust.

earb[2] *f* roe-deer.

earb à *v* trust in.

earball *m* tail.

earbsa *f* trust; confidence; reliance.

earbsach *adj* trusting; trustworthy.

eàrlas *m* (*financial*) advance.

earrach *m* spring; **as t-earrach** in spring.

earrann *f* part, section; piece.

eas *m* waterfall.

eas- prefix in-, dis-, un-.

easag *f* pheasant.

easaonta *f* disagreement; dissent.

easbalg *m* bishop.

Easbalgeach *m/adj* Episcopalian. • *adj* episcopal.

easbhaidh *f* lack, want, need.

easbhaldheach *adj* needy; needful, lacking.

eascaraid *m* foe.

èasgaidh *adj* active; willing; **èasgaidh a dhèanamh** willing/keen to do it.

easgann *f* eel.

eas-ùmhall *adj* disobedient, insubordinate.

eas-urramach *adj* dishonourable.

eathar *m/f* rowing boat.

eatorra *prep pron* between them; among them.

èibhinn *adj* funny, amusing.

èibhleag *f* ember.

èideadh *m* dress, garb; uniform.

eidheann *f* ivy.

èifeachdach *adj* effective; efficient.

eigh *f* ice.

èigh *v* shout, call. • *f* shout, cry.

eighe *f* (*tool*) file.

-eigin *suffix* some-.

èiginn *f* difficulty; trouble; need; violence.

Eilbheis *f* (*with art*) **an Eilbheis** Switzerland.

Eilbheiseach *n/adj* Swiss.

èildear *m* church elder.

eile *adj* other; another.

eilean *m* island.

eileanach *m* islander.

Eilean a' Cheò *m* (*nickname*) Skye.

Eilean I *m* Iona.

Eilean Luing *m* Luing.

Eilean Ruma *m* (the Isle of) Rum.

eilid *f* hind.

eilthireach *m* foreigner; exile.

einnsean *m* engine.

einnsean-smàlaidh *m* fire engine.

Eipheit *f* (*with art*) **an Eipheit** Egypt.

Eipheiteach *m/adj* Egyptian.

eireachdail *adj* elegant; handsome.

eireag *f* pullet.

Eireannach *m/adj* Irishman; Irish.

Eirinn *f* Ireland.

èirich *v* rise, get up; rebel.

èirich do *v* happen to, befall, become of.

eiridinn *m* nursing.

eiridnich *v* nurse, tend.

èirig *f* ransom.

èirigh na grèine *f* sunrise.

eirmseach *adj* witty.

èisd (ri) *v* listen (to).

eisimealachd *f* dependence.

eisimelleach *adj* dependent.

eisimpleir *m* example.

eist! *excl* hush! be quiet!

eitean *m* kernel; core.

eòlach *adj* knowledgeable; acquainted.

eòlach air *adv* familiar with.

eòlaiche *m* expert.

eòlas *m* knowledge; acquaintance.

eòlas-leighis *m* (*science of*) medicine.

eòrna *m* barley.

Eòrpa *f* Europe; (*with art*) **an Roinn Eòrpa** *m* Europe.

Eòrpach *m/adj* European.

esan *pron* (*emphatic form of* **e**) he; him.

eu- prefix un-, dis-, -less.

euchd *m* feat; achievement.

eucoir *f* crime.

eucoireach *m* criminal.

eu-coltach *adj* dissimilar; unlikely.

eud *m* jealousy; zeal.

eudach *adj* jealous; zealous.

eudail *f* treasure; **m'eudail!** my dear!

eu-dòchas *m* hopelessness.

eun *m* bird, fowl.

eun-àir *m* bird of prey.

eun-eòlas *m* ornithology.

eun-mara *m* seabird.

eun-uisge *m* waterfowl.

euslaint *f* illness, ill-health.

euslainteach *adj* ill, unhealthy.
• *m* invalid; patient.

F

fàbhar *m* favour.

fabhra *m* eyelash; eyelid.

facal *m* word; saying.

fa chomhair *prep* opposite; in front of.

faclach *adj* wordy, verbose.

faclair *m* dictionary.

faclaireachd *f* lexicology; lexicography.

fad *m* length; the whole, all the.

fada *adj* long; tall. • *adv* far, much.

fada air falbh *adv* faraway, distant.

fadachd *f* longing; nostalgia; impatience; boredom.

fadalach *adj* late; tedious; long drawn out.

fada nas fheàrr much/far better.

fad an là *adv* all day, the whole day.

fada 'nur comain much obliged to you.

fad às *adj* remote, distant; (*person*) withdrawn.

fàd mònach *m* a single peat.

fad na h-oidhche *adv* all night.

fad na h-ùine *adv* all the time, constantly.

fad-shaoghalach *adv* long-lived.

fad-shaoghalachd *f* longevity.

fàg *v* leave; abandon.

faic *v* see.

faiceall *f* care, caution.

faiceallach *adj* careful, cautious.

faiche *f* meadow, grass park.

faicsinneach *adj* visible; conspicuous.

failde *f* length.

fàidh *m* prophet, seer.

fàidheadaireachd *f* prophecy.

faigh *v* get, obtain; find.

faigh air. *v* get to., manage to..

faigh air adhart *v* get on, progress.

faigh a-mach *v* find out, discover.

faigh bàs *v* die, get killed.

faigh cron do *v* blame.

faigh cuidhteas de v get rid/shot of.

faigh do sheise v meet your match.

falghean m vagina.

faigh fàire air v spot, catch sight of.

faigh lorg air v track down, locate.

faigh muin v have sex, copulate.

faighneach adj inquisitive, enquiring.

faighnich v ask, enquire.

faigh seachad air v get over.

faigh seòl air v contrive to, manege to.

failc v bathe.

failleas m shadow; reflection.

failleasach adj shadowy.

faillean m eardrum.

fàillig v fail.

fàilliginn f failing, fault; blemish; failure.

failmean m kneecap.

fail-mhuc f pigsty.

fàilte f welcome.• excl **fàilte oirbh!** welcome to you! you're welcome!

fàilteach adj welcoming; hospitable.

fàilteachail adj welcoming; hospitable.

fàiltich v welcome.

faing f sheepfold, fank.

fàinne m/f (finger) ring.

fàinne-pòsaidh f wedding ring.

fàinne-solais f halo.

faire f guard; watch.

fàire f horizon, skyline.

faireachdainn f sensation; emotion, feeling.

fàireag f gland.

fairge f (in songs, etc) sea, ocean.

fairich v feel; smell.

fairtlich air v get the better of, defeat; baffle.

faisg adj near, close.

fàisg v squeeze; wring.

faisge f nearness, closeness.

fàisneachd f prophecy.

faite-gàire f smile.

faitheam m hem.

faitich v smile.

fàl m hedge; verge.

falach m hiding, concealment.

falachd f feud.

falach-fead m hide-and-seek.

falaich v hide.

falaichte adj hidden, concealed.

falamh adj empty.

falamhachd, falmhachd f emptiness; void.

falbh v leave, go away.

falbh a dh'larraidh v go to fetch/ get.

fa leth adv separate; apart.

fallain adj sound, healthy; wholesome; able-bodied.

fallas m sweat; **tha fallas orm** I'm sweating.

fallasach adj sweaty.

fallsa adj false, deceitful.

falmadair *m* helm.

falmhachd *see* **falamhachd.**

falmhaich *v* empty.

falt *m* (*of head*) hair.

famh *m/f* (*animal*) mole.

famhair *m* giant.

fan *v* wait; stay.

fanaid *f* mockery, ridicule.

fan aig *v* lodge with.

fan air *v* wait for.

fànas *m* space; void.

fànas-long *f* spaceship.

fa-near dhomh *adv* on my mind, in my thoughts.

fann *adj* weak, faint.

fannaich *v* weaken.

fanntaig *v* faint, swoon.

faobhar *m* (*of blade*) edge.

faobharaich *v* sharpen.

faochadh *m* relief, respite.

faochag *f* whelk, winkle.

faod *v* can, may, might.

faoighe *f* begging, cadging.

faoilleag *f* seagull.

faoilidh *adj* hospitable; generous; frank.

Faoilteach *m* (*with art*) **am Faoilteach** January.

faoin *adj* silly, foolish; empty-headed; futile.

faoineas *m* silliness, vacuity; futility.

faoinsgeul *m* myth, legend.

faoisid *f* confession.

faoisidich *v* confess.

faol *m* wolf.

faothachadh *m* *same as* **faochadh.**

faothaich *v* relieve, alleviate.

far *prep* from, down from.

far a *conj* where.

faradh *m* (*rail, etc*) fare.

fàradh *m* ladder.

far-ainm *m* nickname.

faram *m* loud noise.

faramach *adj* loud, noisy.

farchluais *f* eavesdropping.

fàrdach *f* house; dwelling, lodging.

farmad *m* envy.

farpais *m* competition.

farpaiseach *m* competitor.

farranaich *v* tease.

farsaing *adj* wide, broad.

farsaingeachd *f* width, breadth; area.

farspag *f* black-backed gull.

fàs[1] *v* grow; become.

fàs[2] *adj* waste, uncultivated; barren.

fàsach *m/f* desert, wilderness; deserted place.

fàsaich *v* empty; depopulate.

fàsail *adj* desolate.

fasan *m* fashion.

fasanta *adj* fashionable.

fasgach *adj* sheltered; sheltering.

fasgadh *m* shelter, protection.

fasgain *v* winnow.

fa sgaoil *adv* free, at liberty.

fastaich *v* hire, employ.

fastaidhear *m* employer.

fàth *m* cause; reason; opportunity.

fathann *m* rumour.

feabhas *m* improvement; excellence.

feachd *f* army.

fead *v* whistle. • *f* (*noise*) whistle.

feadag *f* (*instrument*) whistle; plover.

feadalreachd *f* whistling; playing a whistle.

feadan *m* chanter; pipe, tube, spout.

feadhainn *f* some; (*with art*) **an fheadhainn** those, the ones.

feagal *m* fear, fright.

feàirrde *adj* better.

fealladh *m* foul; foul play.

fealla-dhà *f* joke, jest.

feall-falach *m* ambush.

feallsanach *m* philosopher.

feallsanachd *f* philosophy.

feamainn *f* seaweed. • *v* manure (*usu with seaweed*).

feannag *f* crow; ridge; lazybed.

feannag ghlas *f* hooded crow.

feanntag *f* nettle.

feansa *f* fence.

fear *m* man; one.

fearail *adj* manly.

fearalachd *f* manliness.

fear-allabain *m* wanderer.

fearann *m* ground, land.

fear-bainnse *m* bridegroom.

fear-brèige *m* puppet.

fear-ceàirde *m* craftsman.

fear-ceuma *m* graduate.

fear-cinnidh *m* clansman, fellow clansman.

fear-ciùil *m* musician.

fear-deasachaidh *m* editor.

fear-ealain *m* artist.

fear-faire *m* guard.

fear-fianais *m* witness.

fear-foille *m* cheat.

fear-fòirneart *m* oppressor.

fear-fuadain *m* wanderer; exile.

fearg *f* anger.

feargach *adj* angry.

fear-giùlain *m* carrier, bearer.

fear-ionnsaigh *m* assailant, attacker.

fear-labhairt *m* speaker; spokesman.

fear lagha *m* lawyer, solicitor.

feàrna *f* alder.

fear-naidheachd *m* journalist.

feàrr *adj* better; best.

fear-reic *m* salesman.

fear-riaghlaidh *m* manager; administrator.

fear seach fear in turn; one by one.

fear-siubhail *m* traveller.

fear-stiùiridh *m* director.

feart *f* attention, heed; quality, characteristic.

fear-taice *m* supporter; patron, backer.

fear-tomhais *m* surveyor.

feasgar *m* afternoon; evening. • *adv* in the afternoon/evening, p.m.

fèath *m/f* (*weather*) calm.

fèlchear *m* debtor.

fèlle, fèlleadh, fèlle beag *m* kilt.

fèlll *f* feast, festival, fair; sale, market.

Fèlll Brìde *f* (*with art*) an Fhèlll Brìde Candlemas.

fèln¹, fhèln *refl pron* self; own.

fèln² *m* (*with art*) am fèln the ego, the self.

fèln-eachdraidh *f* autobiography.

fèlnealachd *f* selfishness.

fèlneil *adj* selfish.

fèln-moladh *m* conceit.

fèln-rlaghladh *m* self-government.

fèln-spèls *f* conceit, self-regard.

fèls, fèlsd, fèlst *f* festival; feast, banquet.

feith *v* wait; stay.

fèlth¹ *f* muscle; sinew; vein.

fèlth² *f* bog, marsh.

feòll *f* meat; flesh.

feòladair *m* butcher.

feòll-mulce *f* pork.

feòrag *f* squirrel.

feòralch *v* ask, enquire.

feuch, flach *v* try, attempt; try out, test.

feuch deuchainn *v* sit an exam.

feudall *f* treasure.

feum *v* must, have to; need. • *m* need; use, usefulness, good.

feumach *adj* needy, in need.

feumall *adj* useful, handy; necessary.

feur *m* grass; hay.

feurach *adj* grassy.

feuralch *v* graze.

feusag *f* beard.

feusgan *m* mussel.

fhad Is a *conj* while, as long as.

fhathast *adv* yet; still.

fhèln¹ refl *pron* same as fèln¹.

fhèln² *adv* even.

fhualr past tense of *v* falgh.

flabhras *m* fever.

flacall *f* tooth; *pl* flaclan-fuadain false teeth, dentures.

flach¹ *adj* worth, worthwhile; of value.

flach² *m* value, worth; debt.

flach³ see feuch.

flachl *excl* lo! behold!

flachall *adj* worthy, respectable; valuable.

flaclach *adj* toothed, toothy; dental.

flaclaire *m* dentist.

flaclan-fuadain see flacall.

fladh *m* deer.

fladhalch *adj* wild; angry, furious.

flal *adj* generous; hospitable; tolerant.

flamh *adj* hue, tint; complexion; expression; fear.

flamh-ghàlre *m* smile.

flanals *f* evidence, testimony.

flar *adj* bent; slanting; squinting; cunning.

flar *v* bend, curve; slant; squint.

fiaradh *m* slant; squint.

fiar-shùlleach *adj* squint-eyed.

fichead *m* twenty, a score.

ficheadamh *adj* twentieth.

fìdeag *f* (*instrument*) whistle.

fìdheall *f* fiddle, violin.

fìdhlear *m* fiddler, violinist.

fidir *v* appreciate, comprehend.

fìge *f* fig.

figear *m* (*numerical*) figure.

figh *v* weave; knit.

fighe *f* weaving; knitting.

figheachan *m* pigtail, pony-tail.

figheadair *m* weaver; knitter.

fighte *adj* woven; knitted.

fileanta *adj* eloquent, articulate; fluent.

fileantach *m* native speaker; fluent speaker.

filidh *m* poet.

fill *v* fold; pleat; plait.

filleadh *m* fold; pleat; plait.

fillte *adj* folded; pleated; plaited.

film *m* film.

fine *f* clan; tribe.

fiodh *m* wood, timber.

fìogais *f* fig.

fìolan-gòbhlach *m* earwig.

fìon *m* wine.

fìonan *m* vine.

fìon-dearc *f* grape.

fìon-geur *m* vinegar.

fionn[1] *v* flay.

fionn[2] *adj* white.

fionnach *adj* hairy; rough, shaggy.

fionnadh *m* (*animal*) hair.

fionnalreachd *f* coolness.

fionnan-feòir *m* grass-hopper.

fionnar *adj* cool, fresh; cold, offhand.

fionnaraich *v* cool; refrigerate.

fionnsgeul *m* legend.

fìor[1] *adj* real; genuine.

fìor[2] *adv* very.

fìor-uisge *m* pure water.

fios *m* knowledge; information; word, message, news.

fiosaiche *m* prophet, seer; fortune teller.

fiosrach *adj* well-informed.

fiosrachadh *m* information.

Fir Chlis *mpl* (*with art*) **na Fir Chlis** the Northern Lights, Aurora Borealis.

fireann *adj* masculine, male.

fireannach *m* man; male.

fireannach *adj* truthful.

fìreanta *adj* same as **fireann**.

fìrinn *f* truth.

fitheach *m* raven.

fiù *m* worth, value. • *adj* worth.

fiù agus/is *adv* even.

fiùdalach *adj* feudal.

flanainn *f* flannel.

flath *m* king, prince; ruler.

fleadh *m* feast, banquet.

fleasgach *m* youth, stripling; bachelor.

fleisg *f* (*elec*) flex.

fleòdradh *m* floating; buoyancy.

fliuch *v* wet. • *adj* wet.

flùr¹ *m* flower.

flùr² *m* flour.

flùranach *adj* flowery.

fo *prep* under, beneath, below; affected by.

fo-aodach *m* underwear.

fo bhlàth *adv* in bloom.

fo bhròn *adv* sad, sorrowful.

fo chasaid *adv* accused.

fo chomain *adv* obliged.

fo chùram *adv* anxious; preoccupied.

fòd, fòid *f* (single) peat; sod; clod of earth.

fodar *m* fodder.

fodha *prep pron* under him, under it (*m*).

fodhad *prep pron* under you (*sing*).

fodhaibh *prep pron* under you (*pl*).

fodhainn *prep pron* under us.

fodham *prep pron* under me.

fo-dhearg *adj* infra-red.

fo dhìmeas *adv* despised.

fòdhpa *prep pron* under them.

fo eagal *adv* afraid.

fo fhiachaibh *adv* obliged, under an obligation.

fògair *v* banish, exile; drive out.

foghain *v* suffice, do, be enough.
• *excl* **fòghnaidh!** that will do!

foghar *m* autumn; harvest.

fo gheasaibh *adv* spellbound, enchanted.

foghlaim *v* educate.

foghlaimte *adj* educated, learned.

foghlam *m* education; scholarship.

fòghnadh *m* sufficiency.

fòghnan *m* thistle.

fo ghruaim *adv* gloomy; grumpy, in ill-humour.

fògrach *m* exile; fugitive; refugee.

fògradh *m* exile, banishment.

fòid *see* **fòd**.

foldhpe *prep pron* under her, under it (*f*).

foighidinn *f* patience.

foighidneach *adj* patient.

foileag *f* pancake.

foill *f* deceit; fraud, deception; cheating.

foilleil *adj* deceitful; fraudulent.

foillsich *v* publish.

foillsichear *m* publisher.

fo imcheist *adv* anxious; perplexed.

fo iomagain *adv* anxious, troubled.

fo longnadh *adv* amazed; abashed.

foinne *m* wart.

foirfe *adj* perfect; full-grown.

foirfeach *m* (church) elder.

foirmeil *adj* formal.

fòirneart *m* violence, force; oppression.

fois *f* rest, ease, leisure; peace.

fo-lèine *f* vest.

follais *f* evidentness, obviousness; clarity; openness.

follaiseach *adj* evident, clear; public.

fo-mhothachail *adj* subconscious.

fo mhulad *adv* sad.

fòn *v* telephone. • *f* telephone.

fònaig *v* telephone.

fo nàire *adv* ashamed.

fonn *m* tune; mood, state of mind.

fonnmhor *adj* tuneful, melodious.

for *m* attention; notice; concern.

fo-rathad *m* underpass.

forc *f* fork.

forladh *m* (*army, etc*) leave.

forsair *m* forester, forestry worker.

fortan *m* fortune; luck. • *excl* **fortan leat!** good luck!

for-thalla *m* foyer.

fosgail *v* open.

fosgailte *adj* open, opened; frank.

fosgladh *m* opening, gap; opportunity.

fo smachd *adj* under subjection.

fo smalan *adv* gloomy, melancholy.

fo-thiotalan *mpl* subtitles.

fo uallach *adv* under stress.

fradharc *m* eyesight; sight, view.

Fraingis *m* (*with art*) **an Fhraingis** French (language).

Frangach *m/adj* Frenchman; French.

fraoch *m* heather, heath, ling.

fraoidhneas *m* fringe.

fras *v* rain lightly, shower. • *f* shower; seed.

frasair *m* (*bathroom*) shower.

freagair *v* answer, reply; suit.

freagairt *f* answer, reply.

freagarrach *adj* suitable.

frèam *m* frame, framework.

freasdail *v* serve, wait on.

freiceadan *m* watch; guard; (*with art*) **am Freiceadan Dubh** the Black Watch.

freiceadan-oirthire *m* coastguard.

freumh *m* root.

frìde *f* corpuscle; insect.

frids *m* refrigerator, fridge.

frioghan *m* bristle.

frionasach *adj* worried; upset; vexing, niggling.

frìth *f* moorland; deer forest.

frith-ainm *m* nickname.

frithealadh *m* attendance, service.

frithearra *adj* touchy; peevish.

frithell *v* serve, wait on.

frith-rathad *m* footpath; track.

froca *m* frock.

fuachd *f* cold, coldness; (*with art*) **am fuachd** a/the cold.

fuadach *m* banishment; driving away; *pl* (*with art*) **na Fuadaichean** (*hist*) the Highland Clearances.

fuadachadh *m* same as **fuadach**.

fuadaich *v* banish; drive away.

fuadain *adj* artificial, false.

fuadan *m* wandering; exile.

fuaigh *v* sew; stitch; seam.

fuaigheal *m* sewing; stitching; seaming.

fuaighell *v* sew; stitch.

fuaighte *adj* sewn; stitched.

fuaim *m/f* noise; sound.

fuaimneach *adj* noisy.

fuaimneachadh *m* pronunciation.

fuaimnich *v* pronounce.

fuaimreag *f* vowel.

fuaim-thonn *m* sound wave.

fual *m* urine.

fuar *adj* cold.

fuaradair *m* refrigerator.

fuaraich *v* cool, chill.

fuaraidh *adj* (*lit and fig*) cool, chilly.

fuaran *m* spring, well.

fuasgail *v* release; untie; disentangle; solve.

fuasgladh *m* solution; absolution.

fuath *f* hatred, loathing.

fuathach *adj* hateful, detestable.

fuathaich *v* hate, loathe, detest.

fùdar *m* powder.

fùdaraich *v* powder.

fuidheall *m* relic; remainder.

fuighleach *m* rubbish, refuse.

full *f* blood.

fulling *v* suffer; bear, put up with.

full-mìos *f* menstruation, period.

fullteach *adj* bloody, gory.

fulltean *m* (*single*) hair.

fuin *v* bake; knead.

fuineadair *m* baker.

fuirich *v* stay; live, dwell; wait; **fuirich aig X** lodge with X. • *excl* **fuirich ort!** hang on! wait a minute! **fuirich orm . . .** let me see now . . .

fùirneis *f* furnace.

fulang *m* suffering; endurance, hardiness.

fulangach *adj* hardy; long-suffering; passive.

fulmair *m* fulmar.

furachail *adj* watchful; observant; **furachail air** on the watch for.

furan *m* welcome, hospitality.

furasda *adj* easy.

furm *m* form, bench.

furtachd *f* relief; consolation, solace.

furtaich *v* console, comfort.

G

gabh v take; capture; perform.

gàbhadh m danger, peril.

gabh a' ghrian v sunbathe.

gàbhaidh adj dangerous, perilous.

gabhail m/f lease; course; reception, welcome.

gabh air v make for.

gabh air do shocair v take things easily.

gabh air màl v rent.

gabhaltach adj infectious.

gabhaltas m tenancy; rented holding.

gabh an cùram be converted, become devout.

gabh beachd v form an opinion.

gabh brath air v take advantage of.

gabh cead (de) v take one's leave (of).

gabh cuairt v take a stroll; take a trip.

gabh d'anail! take a rest/breather!

gabh eagal v become afraid, take fright.

gabh fois v take a rest/break.

gabh gnothach ri v interfere with/in; get involved in.

gabh grèim air v take hold of, seize.

gabh iongantas v be amazed.

gabh mo leisgeul! excl excuse me!

gabh mo thaobh v take my side.

gabh nàire v be/feel ashamed.

gabh os làimh v undertake, take on.

gabh pàirt v participate.

gabh ri v accept.

gabh sealbh air v take possession of.

gabh smùid v (fam) get drunk.

gabh socair v take one's ease.

gabh suim v care.

gabh truas de v take pity on.

gabh ùidh ann v take an interest in.

gach adj each, every.

gach aon adj every single.

gach uile adj each and every.

gad m supple stick, switch.

gadaiche m thief.

gagach adj stammering, stuttering.

Gaidheal m Gael; Highlander; Gaelic speaker.

Gaidhealach adj Highland.

Gaidhealtachd f (with art) **a' Ghaidhealtachd** the Highlands.

Gàidhlig f (also with art) **Gàidhlig/a' Ghàidhlig** Gaelic (language).

gal v weep, cry.

gailbheach adj stormy.

gailleiridh m art gallery.

gailleann f storm, tempest.

gainmheach f sand.

gainne f scarcity.

gainnead m scarcity.

gàir v laugh.

gàir m cry; outcry.

gairbhe f roughness; wildness.

gairbhead m roughness; wildness.

gàirdeachas m joy; rejoicing.

gàirdean m arm.

gàireachdainn f laughing, laughter.

gairm v cry; call; crow. • f cry;
call; cock-crow.

gairm-chogaidh f war-cry.

gairmeach adj (gram) vocative.

gàirnealair m gardener.

gàirnealaireachd f gardening.

gaisge f bravery, heroism.

gaisgeach m hero; champion.

gaisgeil adj brave, heroic.

gal m crying, weeping.

galan m gallon.

galar m disease.

Gall m Lowlander; non-Gael.

galla f bitch.

gallan m standing stone.

Gallda adj Lowland.

Galldachd f (with art) a' Ghall-
dachd the Lowlands.

gàmag f octave.

gamhainn m stirk.

gamhlas m malice, ill-will.

gamhlasach adj malevolent,
spiteful.

gann adj scarce, scant, rare.

gaoid f blemish, defect.

gaoir f (of anguish) cry.

gaoisid f animal hair; horsehair.

gaol m love. • excl a ghaoil! darling! (my) love!

gaolach adj loving; beloved.

gaoth f wind; (with art) a' gha-
oth wind, flatulence.

gaothach adj windy; flatulent.

gàradh see **gàrradh**.

garbh adj rough; harsh; coarse.
• adv (fam) very, terribly.

garg adj fierce; unruly.

gàrradh, gàradh m wall, stone
wall; garden.

gartan m garter.

gas f stalk; shoot.

gasda adj handsome; splendid;
(fam) great.

gath m barb; sting; spear; beam.

gath-grèine f sunbeam.

ge conj though.

gèadh m/f goose.

geal adj white. • m white part of
anything.

gealach f moon.

gealach-an-abachaidh f harvest
moon.

gealagan m egg white.

gealaich v whiten.

gealbhonn m sparrow.

geall v promise, pledge. • m bet,
wager; promise.

gealladh *m* promise.

gealladh-pòsaidh *m* engagement, betrothal.

gealltanach *adj* promising.

gealtach *adj* cowardly; fearful.

gealtaire *m* coward.

geama *m* game, match.

geamair *m* gamekeeper.

geamhradh *m* winter.

gean *m* mood, frame of mind.

geanmnachd *f* chastity.

geanmnaidh *adj* chaste.

geansaidh *m* jersey, jumper.

gèar *f (engine)* gear.

gearain *v* complain, grumble.

gearan *m* complaining; complaint.

gearanach *adj* complaining, querulous.

gearastan *m* garrison; *(with art)* **An Gearastan** Fort William.

Gearmailt *f (with art)* **a' Ghearmailt** Germany.

Gearmailteach *m/adj* German.

Gearmailteis *f (with art)* **a' Ghearmailtis** German (language).

geàrr[1] *v* cut; castrate. • *adj* short.

geàrr[2] *f* hare.

gearradh *m* cut; *pl* **gearraidhean** *(financial)* cuts.

Gearran *m (with art)* **an Gearran** February.

gearran *m* gelding; pony, garron.

geàrr-shealladh *m* short-sightedness.

geas *f* enchantment, spell.

geata *m* gate.

ge b'e cò *pron* whoever.

ged a *conj* though, although.

ged-thà *adv* though.

gèile *m* gale.

gèill *v* yield, surrender.

geimheal *m* fetter, shackle.

geimhlich *v* fetter, shackle.

geinn *m* chunk; wedge.

geir *f* suet; fat.

gèire *f* sharpness; bitterness.

geòcach *adj* greedy, gluttonous.

geòcaire *m* glutton.

geòcaireachd *f* greed, gluttony.

geodha *m/f* cove, narrow bay.

geòla *f* yawl, small boat.

geòlas *m* geology.

ge-tà *adv* though.

geug *f* branch.

geum *m* bellow; bellowing; lowing. • *v* bellow; low.

geur *adj* sharp; bitter; sarcastic.

geuraich *v* sharpen.

geur-chùiseach *adj* smart, shrewd.

gheibh *future tense of v* **faigh**.

giall *f* jaw.

gibht *f* gift.

Giblean *m (with art)* **an Giblean** April.

Giblinn *f (with art)* **a' Ghiblinn** April.

gidheadh *adv* nevertheless.

gilb *f* chisel.

gile *f* whiteness.

gilead *m* whiteness.

gille *m* boy, lad; young man.

gille-brìghde *m* oyster-catcher.

gin¹ *v* beget; conceive; breed.

gin² *pron* any; (*with neg v*) none.

gineal progeny; race.

ginealach *m* generation.

gineamhainn *m* conception; breeding.

ginideach *adj* (*gram*) genitive.

giodar *m* sewage.

giodhar *m* (*engine*) gear.

giomach *m* lobster.

gioma-goc *m* piggy-back.

gionach *adj* keen, ambitious; greedy.

gionaiche *f* greed: ambition.

giorrachadh *m* shortening; curtailment; abbreviation.

giorrad *m* shortness.

giorraich *v* shorten; abbreviate; curtail.

gìosg *v* gnash.

giùlain *v* carry.

giùlan *m* carrying; carriage; behaviour.

giùran *m* (*of fish*) gill.

gluthas *m* (*wood and tree*) pine, fir tree.

glac¹ *f* small valley; hollow; palm of hand.

glac² *v* catch, trap; grasp; apprehend.

glacte *adj* captured, trapped.

glagadaich *f* clattering; rattling.

glaine *f* cleanliness.

glainne *f* glass.

glainneachan *fpl* glasses, spectacles.

glais *v* lock.

glaiste *adj* locked.

glam, glamh *v* gobble, devour.

glan *v* clean, cleanse. • *adj* clean; (*fam*) fine, grand.

glaodh¹ *v* call, shout, yell. • *m* call, shout, yell.

glaodh² *v* glue. • *m* glue.

glaodhan *m* paste; pulp.

glas¹ *f* lock.

glas² *adj* grey; green.

glas-làmh *f* handcuff.

glasraich *f* vegetable(s), greens.

glè *adv* very.

gleac *v* struggle; wrestle. • *m* struggle; wrestling.

gleacadair *m* wrestler.

gleadhar *m* uproar.

gleadhraich *f* clamour, din.

gleann *m* glen, valley.

glèidh *v* keep; save; conserve.

glèidhteachas *m* conservation.

Glèidhteachas Nàdair *m* Nature Conservancy.

glè mhath *adv/adj* very good; very well.

gleoc *m* clock.

gleus *v* get ready; put in trim; adjust; (*mus*) tune. • *m/f* condition, trim; mood; (*mus*) tuning.

gleusda *adj* ready; handy; in good trim; in good humour; (*mus*) tuned.

glic *adj* wise; clever; sensible.

gllog *m* (*sound*) drip, dripping.

gllongartaich *m* clinking, jingling.

gloc *v* cackle.

glocail *f* cackle, cackling.

gloinne *f* glass.

gloinneachan *fpl* glasses, spectacles.

glòir *m* glory; fame.

glòirich *v* glorify.

glòir-mhiann *m/f* ambition.

glòrmhor *adj* glorious.

gluais *v* move; touch, affect.

gluasad *m* movement; gait; emotional arousal.

gluasadach *adj* capable of moving.

glug *m* gurgling; gulping.

glugan *m* gurgling.

glug caolnidh *m* sob.

glumag *f* pool (*in burn, etc*); puddle.

glùn *m/f* knee.

gnàth, gnàths *m* custom; habit.

gnàthach *adj* customary, normal.

gnàthaich *v* use; accustom; behave towards, treat.

gnè *f* kind; species; gender.

gnìomh *m* act, action.

gnìomhach *adj* active; enterprising; hardworking.

gnìomhachas *m* industry; business; industriousness.

gnìomhaiche *m* executive.

gnìomhair *m* verb.

gnog *v* knock; nod.

gnothach *m* business; matter, affair; errand.

gnù *adj* surly, sullen.

gnùis *f* face; complexion; expression.

gob *m* beak, bill; (*fam*) gob; point.

gobach *adj* prattling, chattering.

gobaireachd *f* prattle, prattling.

gobha *m* blacksmith.

gobhal *m* fork; (*anat*) crotch.

gobhal-gleusaidh *m* tuning fork.

gobhar *m/f* goat.

gobhlach *adj* forked.

gobhlag[1] *f* pitch-fork, hay-fork.

gobhlag[2] *f* earwig.

gobhlan-gaoithe *m* swallow.

goc *m* tap; stopcock.

gogail *f* cackling; clucking.

goid *v* steal, thieve. • *f* stealing, thieving.

goil *v* boil; seethe.

goile *f* stomach.

goileach *adj* boiling.

goileam *m* prattle, tittle-tattle.

goireas *m* resource, facility; (*pl*) **goireasan** public conveniences.

goireasach *adj* handy, convenient.

goireasan see **goireas**.

goirid *adj* short; brief.

goirt *adj* painful, sore; sour; bitter; severe.

goirtich *v* hurt.

goistidh *m* godfather; sponsor; gossip.

gòrach *adj* stupid; foolish, daft.

gòralche *f* stupidity; foolishness.

gorm *adj* blue; green.

gort *f* famine; starvation.

gràbhall *v* engrave.

grad *adj* sudden; alert; agile.

gràdh *m* love. • *excl* **a ghràidh!** love! dear!

gràdhach *adj* loving, affectionate.

graf *m* graph.

gràg *m* croak, caw.

gràgall *f* croaking, cawing.

gràin *f* hatred; loathing, disgust; **tha gràin agam air** I hate him/ it.

gràineag *f* hedgehog.

gràinell *adj* hateful, abominable, loathsome.

gràinne *f* (*single*) grain (*of corn*).

gràinnean *m* grain (*of sugar, etc*).

gràisg *f* (*derog*) crowd; mob.

gràisgell *adj* uncouth, yobbish.

gram *m* gram(me).

gramall *adj* persistent.

gràmar *m* grammar.

gràmarach *adj* grammatical.

gràn *m* cereal; (*coll*) grain.

granaidh *f* granny.

grànda, grànnda *adj* ugly.

gràpa *m* (*agricultural*) fork.

gràs *m* grace; graciousness.

gràsmhor *adj* gracious.

greadhnach *adj* gorgeous; magnificent.

greallach *f* entrails, innards.

greannach *adj* ill-tempered.

greannmhor *adj* cheerful, joyful.

greas *v* hurry, urge on. • *excl* **greas ort!** hurry up!

grèata *m* grate; grating.

greideal *f* griddle.

Grèig *f* (*with art*) **a' Ghrèig** Greece.

greigh *f* herd; flock; (*of horses*) stud.

greigheach *adj* gregarious.

grèim *m* grip, grasp, hold; (*med*) stitch.

grèim bìdh *m* bite to eat.

grèim-cluaise *m* earache.

grèimeil *adj* resolute.

grèimich ri/air *v* seize, grasp.

grèimire *m* (*table*) fork.

grèis *f* while, time.

grèis *f* needlework, embroidery (*i.e. the activity, see* **obair-ghrèise**).

grèiseag *f* short while.

Greugach *m/adj* Greek person; Greek.

Greugais *f* (*with art*) **a' Ghreugais** Greek (language).

greusaiche *m* shoemaker, cobbler.

grian *f* sun.

grinn *adj* elegant, fine; neat; accurate.

grinneal *m* gravel; (*of sea, etc*) bottom.

grinneas *m* elegance; fineness; neatness.

grìogag *f* bead.

Grioglachan *m* (*with art*) **an Grioglachan** the Pleiades.

Griomasach *m/adj* from Grimsay.

Griomasaigh *m* Grimsay.

griòs *m* (*cookery*) grill.

griosaich *v* (*food*) grill.

griùlach *f* (*with art*) **a' ghriùlach** measles.

grod *v* rot, putrefy. • *adj* rotten, rotted, putrid.

grodach *adj* grotty.

grodach-colmhead *adj* (*fam*) grotty-looking.

grodadh *m* rot, putrefaction.

gròiseid *f* gooseberry.

grosair *m* grocer.

gruag *f* (head of) hair.

gruagach *f* maid, girl, young woman.

gruagaire *m* hairdresser.

gruag-bhrèige *f* wig.

gruaidh *f* cheek.

gruaim *f* gloom, melancholy; scowl; sulkiness; grumpiness.

gruamach *adj* gloomy; morose; sulking; grumpy.

grùdair *m* brewer.

grùdaireachd *f* brewing.

grùid *f* lees, dregs, grounds; sediment.

grunn *m* crowd; many, lots of.

grunnd *m* base; sea-bed.

grùnsgal *m* growl, growling.

gruth *m* curd(s); crowdie.

grùthan *m* (*usu animal*) liver.

gu[1] *prefix introducing an adverb.*

gu[2] see **gus**.

gual *m* coal.

gualan *m* carbon.

gualann, gualainn *f* shoulder. *f* shoulder.

gual-fhodha *m* charcoal.

guanach *adj* giddy, scatter-brained; coquettish.

guanag *f* scatter-brained girl; coquettish girl.

gu bochd *adv* poorly.

gu bràth *adv* ever; for ever.

gu bràth tuilleadh *adv* (*with neg v*) nevermore.

gu bulleach *adv* entirely.

gucag *f* (*botany*) bud; bubble.

gucag-uighe *f* egg-cup.

gu chùl *adv* through and through.

gu dè? *pron* what?, whatever?.

gu dearbh *adv* indeed; definitely.

gu dearbh fhèin *adv* extremely.

gu diofair *adv* of importance.

gu dubh dona *adv* absolutely terribly.

guga *m* young gannet, young solan goose.

gu grad *adv* suddenly; shortly.

gu h-aon sgeulach *adv* unanimously.

gu h-àrald, gu h-àraidh *adv* especially, particularly.

gu h-iomlan *adv* fully, absolutely.

guidh *v* beg, beseech; pray.

guidhe *m/f* plea, entreaty; prayer.

gull *v* weep, cry.

guilbneach *m* curlew.

guin *v* sting. • *m* sting.

guineach *adj* sharp; acerbic; wounding.

guir *v* hatch.

guirean *m* pimple, spot.

gul *m* crying, weeping.

gu lèir *adv* entire, entirely.

gu leòr *adv* enough, plenty.

. . . gu leth *adv* . . . and a half.

gum, gun *conj* that.

gu mì-fhortanach *adv* unfortunately.

gu minig *adv* often.

gun¹ *see* **gum**.

gun² *prep* without.

gùn *m* gown.

gun bhuannachd *adv* fruitless.

gun chadal *adv* sleepless.

gun chaomhnadh *adv* unsparingly.

gun chiall *adv* senseless; meaningless.

gun chùnntas *adv* countless, innumerable.

gun dòchas *adv* hopeless.

gun fheum *adv* useless.

gun fhios do X without X's knowledge.

gun fhios nach *conj* lest, in case.

gun fhiù *adv* worthless.

gun ghluasad *adv* still, motionless.

gun luach *adj* worthless.

gun mheang *adj* flawless.

gunna *m* gun.

gunnair *m* gunner.

gun nàire *adv* shameless.

gun obair *adv* unemployed.

gùn-oidhche *m* nightgown.

gun sgillinn ruadh *adv* (stony) broke.

gun smior *adj* spineless, wet.

gun teagamh *adv* doubtless, without a doubt.

gun tomhas *adj* incalculable, immeasurable.

gun uiread is *adv* without so much as.

gurraban *m* crouch, crouching position.

gu ruige *prep* up to, as far as; until.

gu ruige an seo *adv* this far; so far, up to now.

gus, gu *conj* to, in order to. • *prep* to, towards, up to; until.

gus bhith . . . about to (be) . . .; **gus bhith 'falbh** about to leave.

gu sealladh orm! *excl* my goodness!

gu sealladh sealbh oirnn! *excl* Heaven preserve us!

gu sìorraidh *adv* for ever.

gu sìorraidh bràth *adv* for ever and ever.

gu sònraichte *adv* especially, particularly.

guth *m* voice; news, word; mention; **gun guth air X** not to mention X.

gu tur *adv* completely, totally, entirely.

H

hàidraidean *m* hydrogen.
halò *excl* hello/hullo.
heactair *m* hectare.
Hearach *m/adj* from Harris.
Hearadh *f* (*with art*) na Hearadh Harris.

heileacoptair, heileacoptar *m* helicopter.
Hiort *f* St Kilda.
Hiortach *m/adj* St Kildan.
ho-ro-gheallaidh *m* party, knees-up, hoolie.

I

I *pron* she, her, it (*f*).
iad *pron* they, them.
iadh-shlat *f* honeysuckle.
iadsan *pron* (*emphatic*) they, them.
iall *f* thong; dog's leash; strap; strop.
iall bròige *f* shoe-lace.
ialtag *f* (*creature*) bat.
iar *f* west.
iar-[1] *prefix* under-, deputy-; iar-stiùiriche *m* deputy director.
iar-[2] *prefix* post-; iar-cheumaiche *m* postgraduate.
iar air *prep* west of.
iarann *m* iron.
iargalt, iargalta *adj* churlish, surly.
iarla *m* earl.
iarmad *m* remnant.
iarmailt *f* (*with art*) an iarmailt the firmament, the heavens.
iarnaich *v* iron.

iar-ogha *m* great-grandchild.
iarr *v* want; ask for; invite.
iarrtas *m* request; demand; (*job, etc*) application.
iasad *m* borrowing; loan.
iasg *m* fish.
iasgach *m* (*deep-sea, etc*) fishing; angling.
iasgaich *v* fish.
iasgair *m* fisherman; angler.
iath *v* surround; enclose.
idir *adv usu with neg* (not) at all.
ifrinn *f* hell.
ifrinneach *adj* hellish, infernal.
Ìle *f* Islay.
Ìleach *m/adj* from Islay.
ìm *m* butter.
imcheist *f* anxiety, perplexity, dilemma. • *adv* an imcheist in a dilemma, perplexed.
imcheisteach *adj* worried; worrying.
imich *v* depart, go.

imleag *f* navel.

imlich *v* lick, lap. • *f* lick; licking.

impidh *m* persuasion, urging.

impidheach *adj* persuasive.

impireil *adj* imperial.

impireileas *f* imperialism.

imrich *v* move house. • *f* moving house, flitting.

inbhe *f* rank; level; adulthood.

inbheach *adj* adult. • *m* adult, grown-up.

inbheil *adj* high-ranking.

inbhir *m* confluence; (*of watercourse*) mouth.

inc *m* ink.

ine *f* toenail, fingernail; claw, talon.

inneal *m* machine; implement.

innealach *adj* mechanical.

inneal-ciùil *m* musical instrument.

inneal-clàir *m* record-player.

inneal-nighe *m* washing machine.

inneal-smàlaidh *m* fire extinguisher.

innean *m* anvil.

innear *f* dung, manure.

innidh *f* bowels; intestines.

innis[1] *v* tell, inform; (*story, etc*) recount.

innis[2] *f* island; haugh, inch.

innis breug *v* lie, tell a lie.

Innis Tìle *m* Iceland.

innleachd *f* device; inventiveness; intelligence; artfulness; stratagem.

innleachdach *adj* inventive; resourceful; intelligent; cunning.

innleadair *m* engineer, mechanic.

innleadair-dealain *m* electrical engineer.

innleadaireachd *f* engineering.

innleadair-thogalach *m* civil engineer.

innlich *v* invent, devise; plot.

innseachan *mpl* (*with art*) **na h-Innseachan** India; the Indies.

innseanach *m/adj* Indian.

innte *prep pron* in her, in it (*f*).

inntinn *f* mind, intellect.

inntinneach *adj* interesting; mental, intellectual.

inntrig *v* (*building, etc*) enter.

iobair *v* (*relig*) sacrifice, offer up.

iobairt *f* (*relig*) sacrifice, offering.

ìoc *v* pay. • *m* payment.

iochd *f* compassion, mercy.

iochdar *m* bottom, base.

iochdarach *adj* lower; inferior; subordinate.

iochdaran *m* inferior, subordinate; subject.

iochdaranachd *f* inferiority.

iochdmhor *adj* compassionate, merciful.

iocshlàint *f* medicine, remedy.

iodhal *m* idol.

iodhlann *f* stack-yard.

iolach *f* shout.

iolaire *f* eagle.

iolaire bhuidhe *f* golden eagle.

iolra *m/adj* (*gram*) plural.

ioma- *prefix* multi-.

iomadach *adj* many (a).

iomadach uair *adv* often, many a time.

iomadh *adj adv* many (a).

iomadh-fhillte *adj* complex, complicated; manifold.

iomagain *f* anxiety, worry.

iomagaineach *adj* anxious; worrying.

iomain *v* drive on (*esp livestock*); propel; play shinty. • *f* shinty.

iomair *v* (*boat*) row.

iomair an aon ràmh co-operate, pull together.

iomall *m* edge, periphery; limit; verge; rim.

iomall a' bhaile *m* suburbs.

iomallach *adj* remote, isolated; marginal.

iomchaidh *adj* suitable; decent, proper.

iomchair *v* carry, transport.

iomhaigh *f* image; likeness; idol.

iomlaid *f* exchange, barter; (*money*) change.

iomlan *adj* complete, full, absolute.

iomnaidh *f* solicitude.

iompachadh *m* conversion.

iompachan *m* convert, neophyte.

iompaich *v* persuade; (*relig*) convert.

iompaire *m* emperor.

iompaireachd *f* empire.

iomradh *m* mention; report.

iomraiteach *adj* celebrated; notorious.

iomrall *m* mistake; going astray.

iomrallach *adj* mistaken, erroneous.

iomramh *m* rowing.

ion- *prefix indicating* able to, worthy of.

ionad *m* place, spot; centre.

ionadail *adj* local.

ionad-cosnaidh *m* job centre.

ionad-latha *m* day centre.

ionad-margaid, ionad-margaidh *m* marketplace.

ionad-obrach *m* job centre.

ionad-slàinte *m* health centre.

ionad-stiùiridh *m* management centre.

ionaltair *v* graze.

ionaltradh *m* grazing, pasture.

ionann, ionnan *adj* alike, identical.

ion-dhèanta *adj* feasible, possible.

iongantach *adj* strange; surprising; marvellous.

iongantas *m* surprise, amazement; phenomenon, amazing thing.

iongna *f* toenail, fingernail; claw, talon.

iongnadh *m* amazement.

ion-ithe *adj* eatable, edible.

ionmhainn *adj* dear, beloved.

ionmhas *m* treasure; finance.

ionmhasair *m* treasurer.

ionmholta *adj* praiseworthy.

ionnan *see* **ionann**.

ionndrainn *v* miss, long for.

ionnlad *m* washing, ablutions.

ionnlaid *v* wash, bathe.

ionnsachadh *m* learning.

ionnsaich *v* learn, study.

ionnsaichte *adj* educated; trained.

ionnsaigh *m/f* attack, assault; attempt.

ionnsramaid, ionnstramaid *f* instrument.

ionracas *m* honesty; justice; righteousness.

ionraic *adj* honest; just; righteous.

iorghail *f* tumult.

iorghaileach *adj* tumultuous.

ioronas *m* irony.

ioronta *adj* ironic.

losa *m* Jesus.

ìosal, ìseal *adj* low; lowly; humble; (*voice, etc*) quiet.

ioslamach *adj* Islamic.

iotmhor *adj* (*land, etc*) parched; very thirsty.

ìre *f* degree, level; stage.

iriosal *adj* low, lowly; humble.

irioslachd *f* humility; lowliness.

irioslaich *v* humble; humiliate.

iris *f* magazine, periodical.

is[1] *v* am, is, are.

is[2] (*for* **agus**) *conj* and.

is beag orm X *v* I don't like X.

isbean *m* sausage.

is caomh leam X *v* I like X.

is ciar leam X *v* I take a dim view of X.

is cubhaidh dhomh *v* it befits me.

is dòcha! maybe!

is dòcha gun *conj* perhaps.

is duilich leam *v* I find it hard to.

is duilich sin! *excl* that's a shame!

ise *pron* (*emphatic*) she, her.

ìseal *adj* same as **ìosal**.

isean *m* chick; baby animal.

is e do bheatha! *excl* you're welcome!

is e sin a'cheist! that's the question/point!

is e sin a' chùis! that's the point!

is fheàirrde mi X *v* I'm better for X, X is good for me.

is fheàrr leam X *v* I prefer X.

is fheudar dhomh *v* I must, I have to.

is leisg dhomh. *v* I hesitate to.

ìslich *v* become lower; demote.

is math leam X *v* I find X good.

is math sin! *excl* smashing!

is miann leam *v* I wish.

is mòr am beud e! *excl* it's a great pity!

isneach *f* rifle.

Israel *f* Israel.

Israelach *m/adj* Israeli, Israelite.

ist! *excl* hush! be quiet!

is toigh leam X *v* I like X.

is truagh e/sin! *excl* it's/that's a pity.

is urrainn dhomh *v* I can.

ite *f* feather; plumage; fin.

iteach *adj* feathered.

iteachan *m* bobbin, spool.

iteag *f* small feather; flying, flight.

iteagach *adj* feathered.

itealaich *v* fly.

itealan *m* aeroplane, aircraft.

iteileag *f* kite.

ith *v* eat.

iubhar *m* yew.

iuchair *f* key; **iuchair-gnìomha** *f* (*IT*) function key.

iuchar *m* (*with art*) **an t-iuchar** July.

Iùdhach *m/adj* Jew; Jewish.

iùll-tharraing *f* magnetism.

iùll-tharraingeach *adj* magnetic.

iutharn, iutharna *f* hell.

L

là *m* day.

là a' bhràtha *m* judgement day.

labhair *v* speak, talk.

labhairt *f* speech, speaking.

là-breith *m* birthday.

lach *f* (*bird*) duck.

lachdann *adj* dun, tawny; khaki; swarthy.

ladar *m* ladle, scoop.

ladarna *adj* bold; shameless.

ladhar *m* hoof.

lag¹ *adj* weak, feeble.

lag² *m/f* hollow; pit.

lagaich *v* weaken.

lag-chùlseach *adj* unenterprising.

lagh *m* law.

laghach *adj* nice; kind.

laghail *adj* lawful, legal.

laghairt *m/f* lizard.

Laideann *f* Latin (language).

Laidinneach *adj* Latin.

làidir *adj* strong; potent.

laigh *v* lie (down); (*plane, etc*) land; subside

laighe *m/f* recumbent position.

laighe na grèine *m/f* sunset.

laigse *f* weakness; infirmity; faint.

làimhsich *v* touch, handle; wield.

lainnir *f* glint, sparkle; radiance.

lainnireach *adj* sparkling; radiant.

làir *f* mare.

làithean-saora *mpl* holidays.

làitheil *adj* daily; everyday.

là-luain *m* doomsday.

làmh *f* hand; handle.

làmhainn *f* glove.

làmh an uachdair *m* the upper hand.

làmh-lèigh *m* surgeon.

làmh-sgrìobhadh *m* handwriting; manuscript.

làmhthuagh *f* hatchet, chopper.

lampa *m/f* lamp.

làn *adj* full. • *adv* fully. • *m* one's fill.

Là na Sàbaid *m* Sunday, the Sabbath.

làn beòil *m* mouthful.

làn-chinnteach *adj* completely certain, convinced.

làn-chumhachd *m* absolute power.

làn-chumhachdach *adj* all-powerful.

làn dùirn *m* handful, fistful.

làn-fhada *adj/adv* full-length.

langa *f* (*fish*) ling.

langanaich *v* (*animals*) bellow; low.

langasaid *f* sofa, couch.

làn-mara *m* high tide.

làn mo bhroinn de. *m* (*fam*) my bellyful of.

lann *f* blade; (*fish*) scale; enclosure; repository.

lanntair *m* lantern.

là no latheigin *adv* some day or other, one fine day.

làn spàine *m* spoonful.

laoch *m* hero; warrior.

laochan *m* wee boy, wee hero.

laogh *m* calf.

laoidh *m/f* poem; hymn.

laoigh-fheòil *f* veal.

làr *m* ground, floor.

làrach *f* trace, mark; ruin; site.

làrna-mhàireach *m* the morrow, the next day.

las *v* set alight; blaze; (*fig*) light up.

lasadair *m* match (*for striking*).

lasaich *v* loosen; soothe.

lasair *f* flame(s); flash.

lasgan *m* outburst; (*of anger, etc*) fit.

lasrach *adj* flaming; blazing.

lastalg *fl/adj* elastic.

latha *m* day.

latha-fèille *m* holiday, feastday.

làthair *f* presence; sight, view.

latheigin *m* some day.

là-trasg *m* fast day.

le (*before art* **leis**) *prep* with; by; belonging to.

leabaidh *f* bed.

leabhar *m* book.

leabharlann *f* library.

leabhar-latha *m* diary, journal.

leabhra, leabhrachan *m* booklet; brochure.

leac *f* (*rock*) slab, ledge.

leacag *f* tile.

leac teallaich *f* hearthstone.

leac uaighe *f* gravestone.

leac-ùrlair *f* paving stone.

leag *v* fell; demolish; (*carpet, etc*) lay; (*window, etc*) lower.

leag càin air *v* tax, subject to taxation.

leag gu làr *v* raze (*to ground*).

leagh *v* melt, thaw; dissolve.

leam *prep pron* with/by me.

leamhalch *v* exasperate; plague.

leamhach *adj* insipid.

leamhan *m* elm.

lean *v* follow; continue; understand. • *excl* **lean ort!** keep going! **. . . a leanas** the following . . .

leanaball *adj* childish, silly; infantile.

leanaban *m* baby; small child.

leanabh *m* baby; infant; child.

leanallteach *adj* continuous, incessant.

leann *m* beer, ale.

leannan *m* lover; sweetheart, boyfriend, girlfriend.

leannanachd *f* courting, courtship.

leannra *m* sauce.

leantalnneach *adj* continuous; persevering; lasting.

leas *m* benefit, advantage; improvement; **cha leig thu leas . . .** you don't need to . . .

leasachadh *m* improvement; development.

leasalch *v* improve; develop.

leasan *m* lesson.

leat *prep pron* with/by you (*sing*).

leatha *prep pron* with/by her, with/by it (*f*).

leathad *m* slope, hillside.

leathann *adj* broad, wide.

leathar *m* leather.

le chèile *adv* together; both.

le deagh dhùrachd (*corres*) with compliments.

le dùrachd (*corres*) yours sincerely.

le foill *adv* fraudulently.

leibh *prep pron* with/by you (*pl*).

leig *v* let, allow; leave to; let out, utter; (*weapon*) fire.

leig air *v* pretend; give away.

leig air dhearmad *v* neglect.

leig anall *v* take a breather.

leig às *v* let off/out.

leig braim *v* fart.

leig brùchd *v* belch.

leig cnead *v* groan.

leig de *v* give up, cease.

leig fead *v* whistle.

leigheas *m* cure, remedy.

leighis *v* cure, heal.

leig le *v* leave alone, let be.

leig leas *see* **leas**.

leig ma sgaoll *v* free.

leig 'na thelne *v* set on fire.

leig osna, leig osnadh *v* heave/breathe a sigh.

leig seachad *v* give up, relinquish.

lèine *f* shirt.

leinn *prep pron* with/by us.

lèir *adj* visible; evident; **is lèir dhomh (gu)** (*fml*) it's clear to me (that).

lèirmheas *m* (*book, etc*) review.

lèirsinn *f* sight; perceptiveness.

lèirsinneach *adj* visible; perceptive.

leis¹ *f* thigh.

leis² *prep pron* with/by him, with/by it (*m*).

leis a' bhruthaich *adv* with the slope.

leis an t-sruth *adv* downstream.

leis a sin, leis sin *adv* whereupon, at that.

leisg *adj* lazy; reluctant. • *f* laziness.

leis gach deagh dhùrachd (*corres*) with best wishes.

leisge *f* laziness.

leisgeadair *m* lazy person, lazybones.

leisgeul *m* excuse; pretext.

leis sin *see* **leis a sin**.

leiteis *f* lettuce.

leitheach *adv* half, semi-.

leitheach-slighe *adv* halfway.

leithid (de) *f* the like(s) (of); **a leithid de . . .** such a . . .

leitir *f* slope, hillside.

Leòdhasach *m/adj* Lewisman; from Lewis.

leòghann *m* lion.

leòinteach *m* casualty, victim; *pl* (*with art*) **na leòintich** the injured; the wounded.

leòman *m* moth.

leòn *v* wound; hurt; injure. • *m* wound; hurt; injury.

leònte *adj* wounded; hurt; injured.

leòr *f* enough, sufficiency; **mo leòr de . . .** my fill of . . .

leotha *prep pron* with/by them.

le sùrd *adv* with a will.

leth *m* half; side; **sia gu leth** six and a half; **leth-** one of a pair.

leth-asal *f* mule.

lethbhreac *m* (*book, etc*) copy, reproduction; match.

lethcheann *m* cheek; side of head.

leth-cheud *m* fifty.

leth-chuid *f* half.

leth-fhuar *adj* lukewarm.

leth shean *adj* middle-aged.

le tuiteamas *adv* by accident, by chance.

leud *m* breadth, width.

leudaich *v* widen; extend.

leudaichte *adj* widened; flattened.

leug *f* jewel.

leugh *v* read.

leum *v* jump, leap; (*nose*) bleed. • *m* jump, leap.

leum-sròine *m* nosebleed.

leum-uisge *m* waterfall.

le ur cead by your leave.

leus *m* light; ray of light; torch; blister.

liagh *f* ladle, scoop.

liath *v* make or become grey. • *adj* grey.

liath-reothadh *m* frost, hoar frost.

libhrig *v* (*goods, etc*) deliver.

lide *m* syllable.

lighiche *m* doctor, physician.

lili, lilidh f lily.

linig v line.

linn m age, period; generation; century; (pl with art) **na Linntean Dorcha** the Dark Ages.

linne f pool; waterfall.

liomaid f lemon.

liomh v polish, shine. • f polish, gloss.

liomharra adj polished, glossy.

lion¹ v fill; (tide) come in.

lion² m net; web.• m flax, lint.

lion damhain-allaidh m cobweb.

lionmhor adj numerous; abundant.

lionn m liquid.

lionsa f lens.

liopard m leopard.

lios m/f garden; enclosure.

Liosach m/adj from Lismore.

liosda adj boring.

Lios Mòr m Lismore.

liosta f list.

liotair m litre.

lip f lip.

lite f porridge.

litir f letter.

litreachadh m spelling.

litreachas m literature.

litrich v spell.

liùdhag f doll.

liut f knack.

lobh v rot, decay.

lobhadh m rot, putrefaction.

lobhar m leper.

lobht, lobhta m flat; storey; loft.

locair m/f (tool) plane.

lòcast m locust.

loch m loch, lake.

lochan m small loch, pond.

lochd m fault; harm.

lochdach adj harmful.

Lochlann f Norway; Scandinavia.

Lochlannach m/adj Norseman; Norse; Norwegian; Scandinavian; Viking.

lòchran m lamp, lantern.

lof m/f loaf.

loidhne f line.

loingeas m shipping; fleet; navy.

lòinidh m/f (with art) **an lòinidh** rheumatism.

loisg v burn; (gun) fire.

loisgte adj burnt.

lòistear m lodger.

lòistinn m lodging(s), digs; accommodation.

lom v strip; shave; shear; mow. • adj bare; bleak; thin.

lomadair m shearer.

loma-làn adj full to the brim.

lomnochd adj naked.

lòn¹ m food, provisions.

lòn² m pool; puddle; meadow.

lònaid f lane.

lon-dubh m blackbird.

long f ship.

long-bhriseadh m shipwreck.

long-chogaidh f warship, battleship.

lorg v find; track down, trace. • f vestige; footprint; track.

los *m* purpose, intention. • *conj* **los gu, los gun** in order that.

lòsan *m* pane.

losgadh-bràghad *m* heartburn.

losgann *m* frog.

lot¹ *f* croft; piece of land.

lot² *v* wound. • *m* wound.

loth *f* filly.

luach *m* worth, value.

luachachadh *m* valuation.

luachaich *v* evaluate, value.

luachair *f* rushes.

luachmhor *adj* valuable, precious.

luadhadh *m* (*cloth*) waulking, fulling.

lualdh¹ *v* praise. • *m* praise; beloved person. • *excl* **a lualdh!** my love! (my) darling!

lualdh² *v* (*cloth*) waulk, full.

luaisg *v* rock, sway, toss.

luaithre, luath *f* ash(es).

luas, luaths *m* speed; agility.

luath¹ *adj* fast, quick.

luath² *f same as* **luaithre**.

luathaich *v* accelerate; hurry on.

luaths *m same as* **luas**.

luath-thrèana *f* express (train).

lùb *v* bend; bow. • *f* bend; loop.

lùbach *adj* bending; winding; flexible.

lùb a' ghlùin *v* kneel, pray.

luch *f* mouse.

lùchairt *f* palace.

luchd¹ *m* cargo.

luchd² *m* people.

luchdalch *v* load.

luchd-càraidh *m* repairers.

luchd-ciùll *m* musicians.

luchd-eòlais *m* acquaintances.

luchd-frithealaidh *m* attendants.

luchdmhor *adj* capacious.

luchd-obrach *m* workers; workforce.

luchd-polleataics *m* politicians.

luchd-siubhail *m* (*coll*) travellers.

luchd-stiùiridh *m* managers, management.

luchd-turais *m* (*coll*) tourists.

luchraban *m* dwarf, midget.

Lucsamburg *m* Luxembourg.

Lucsamburgach *m/adj* from Luxembourg.

lùdag *f* little finger; hinge.

lugha *comp adj* smaller, smallest.

lùghdachadh *m* reduction; abatement.

lùghdaich *v* lessen; shrink; abate.

lulbh *m/f* herb; plant; weed.

lulbh-eòlas *m* botany.

lulbhre *f* leprosy.

luideach *adj* shabby, scruffy.

luideag *f* rag.

luidhear *m* funnel, chimney.

Luinn *f* Luing.

Luinneach *m/adj* from Luing.

luinneag *f* song, ditty.

Lùnasdal *m* (*with art*) **an Lùnasdal** August; **Là Lùnasdail** Lammas Day.

lurach *adj* pretty; nice; beloved.

lurgann *f* shin.

lus *m* herb; plant; weed.

lùth, lùths *m* power of movement; energy.

lùthmhor *adj* strong; agile; energetic.

lùths *m same as* **lùth**.

M

ma *conj* if.

màb *v* revile, vilify.

mac *m* son; **mac bràthair, mac piuthar** *m* nephew.

mac-an-aba *m* ring finger.

mac an donais! *excl* damn it!

mac an duine *m* humanity, humankind.

macanta *adj* meek, submissive.

machair *m/f* machair; plain; (*with art*) **a' Mhachair Ghallda** the Lowlands.

machlag *f* womb, uterus.

mac-meanmna *m* imagination.

mac-meanmnach *adj* imaginary; imaginative.

mac-na-bracha *m* (*nickname*) whisky.

mac-samhail *m* equal, match; likeness.

mac-talla *m* echo.

madadh *m* dog.

madadh-allaidh *m* wolf.

madadh ruadh *m* fox.

madainn *f* morning. • *adv* **sa' mhadainn** a.m.

ma dh'fhaoidte *adv/conj* maybe, perhaps.

mag (air) *v* mock, make fun (of).

màg *f* paw.

magadh *m* mockery.

magail *adj* mocking, jeering.

magairle *m/f* testicle.

maghar *m* fly, bait.

maide *m* wood, timber; stick; **maide-droma** *m* ridge pole, roof-tree.

maide poite *m* spirtle.

maids, maidse *m* match (*for striking*).

màidsear *m* (*rank*) major.

Màigh *f* (*with art*) **a' Mhàigh** May.

maighdeann *f* maiden; virgin; spinster; (*address*) **a Mhaighdeann X!** Miss X!

maighdeannas *m* maidenhood, virginity.

maighdeann-mhara *f* mermaid.

maigheach *m* hare.

maighistir, maighstir *m* master; (*address*) **a Mhaighstir X!** Mister X!

maighistir-sgoile, maighstir-sgoile *m* schoolmaster.

màileid *f* suitcase; briefcase; bag.

màilleid-droma *f* rucksack.

màilleid-làimh *f* handbag.

maille *f* slowness; delay.

maille ri *prep* with, along with.

maillich *v* delay; procrastinate.

mair *v* last, continue; **mair beò** live, survive.

maireann *adj* living; enduring; **X nach maireann** the late X.

maireannach *adj* eternal; durable; long-lived.

màirnealach *adj* dilatory; boring.

mairtfheoil *f* beef.

maise *f* beauty.

maiseach *adj* beautiful.

maisich *v* beautify; decorate; (*face*) make up.

màithrell *adj* same as **màthairell**.

màl *m* rent.

mala *f* brow; eyebrow.

malairt *f* trade, business; barter.

malairtich *v* trade; barter.

màlda *adj* coy, bashful.

mall *adj* slow, tardy.

mallachd *f* curse.

mallaich *v* curse.

mallaichte *adj* cursed, damned.

mamaidh *f* Mummy.

manach *m* monk.

manachainn *f* monastery.

manadh *m* omen.

manaidsear *m* manager.

Manainneach *m/adj* Manxman; Manx.

mang *f* fawn.

maodal *f* paunch.

maoidh *v* threaten.

maoil *f* forehead, brow.

Maoil *f* (*with art*) **a' Mhaoil** the Minch.

maolle *f* baldness.

maoin *f* wealth; goods, chattels.

maol *m* cape, promontory; rounded hill. • *adj* blunt; bald.

maorach *m* shellfish.

maor-eaglais *m* church officer.

maor-obrach *m* foreman, gaffer.

maoth *adj* soft; tender-hearted.

maothaich *v* soften.

mapa *m* map.

mar *prep* as; like. • *conj* **mar a** as, how; **mar gun** as if, as though.

mar a bheatha *adv* for dear life.

marag *f* pudding.

maraiche *m* sailor, seafarer.

mar an ceudna *adv* likewise, too.

marbh *v* kill. • *adj* dead.

marbhaiche *m* killer; murderer.

marbhan *m* corpse.

marbhrann *m* elegy.

marbhtach *adj* deadly, fatal.

mar bu chòir *adv* fittingly.

marcachadh *m* riding; horsemanship.

marcaich *v* ride.

marcaiche *m* rider, horseman.

marcaid *m/f* market.

mar eisimpleir (*abbrev* **m e**) *adv* for example.

margadh *m/f* market; **am Mar-**

gadh Coitcheann the Common Market.

margarain *m* margarine.

màrmor *m* marble.

mar ri *prep* with, along with.

màrsail *f* march; marching.

mar sin *adv* so.

mar sin leat/leibh! *excl* goodbye!

Màrt *m* Mars; (*with art*) **am Màrt** March.

mart *m* beef animal.

màs *m* buttock; (*fam*) arse, bum.

ma's e do thoil e *adv* please.

ma's fhìor *adv* kidding, pretending.

masg *m* mask.

maslach *adj* disgraceful, shameful.

masladh *m* disgrace, shame.

maslaich *v* disgrace, put to shame.

ma-tà *adv* then, in that case.

matamataig, matamataigs *m* mathematics.

math *m* good. • *adj* good.

ma-tha *adv* then, in that case.

mathachadh *m* manure; fertilizer.

mathaich *v* manure; enrich.

màthair *f* mother.

màthair-chèile *f* mother-in-law.

màthaireil, màithreil *adj* motherly, maternal.

màthair-uisge *m* fountainhead.

mathan *m* (brown) bear.

mathanas *m* forgiveness, pardon.

mathan bàn *m* polar bear.

mathas *m* goodness.

math dhà-rìreadh! *excl* excellent!

math do *v* forgive.

ma thogras tu if you like.

math thu-fhèin! *excl* well done! good for you!

meadhan *m* middle, centre; medium, mechanism; waist; average; *pl* **na meadhanan** (*press, etc*) the media.

meadhanach *adj* middling, so-so; average.

meadhan-aois *f* middle age.

meadhan-aoiseil *adj* medieval.

meadhan-chearcall *m* equator.

meadhan-là *m* midday, noon.

meadhan-oidhche *m* midnight.

Meadhan-thìreach *adj* Mediterranean.

meal *v* enjoy. • *excl* **meal do/ur naidheachd!** congratulations!

meal-bhucan *m* melon.

meall[1] *v* deceive; cheat; entice.

meall[2] *m* lump; lumpy hill.

meallach *adj* beguiling, bewitching.

mealladh *m* deceit, deception; enticement.

meall an sgòrnain *m* Adam's apple.

meallta *adj* deceived; cheated.

mealltach *adj* deceitful; cheating; deceptive.

mealltair *m* deceiver; cheat.

meall-uisge *m* heavy shower.

mean *adj* little, tiny; **mean air mhean** little by little.

mèanan *m* yawn.

mèananaich *f* yawning.

meanbh *adj* tiny, minute.

meanbh-chuileag *f* midge.

meang *f* fault, flaw; abnormality.

meangach *adj* abnormal.

meangan, meanglan *m* branch, bough.

meann *m* (*goat*) kid.

mearachadh *m* aberration.

mearachd *f* mistake, error.

mearachdach *adj* wrong, erroneous.

mèaran *m* yawn.

mèaranaich *f* yawning.

mèarrsaidh *m* march, marching.

meas[1] *m* valuation; respect, esteem; **is mise le meas** (*corres*) yours sincerely. • *v* estimate; evaluate; esteem; think.

meas[2] *m* fruit.

measach *adj* fruity.

measail *adj* respected; respectable; valued.

measail (air) *adj* fond (of).

measarra *adj* moderate; temperate.

measarrachd *f* moderation; abstinence.

meas-chraobh *f* fruit tree.

measgaich *v* mix, mingle.

measgaichear *m* mixer.

measgaich suas *v* confuse, mix up.

meata *adj* faint-hearted; feeble.

meatailt *f* metal.

meatair *m* metre.

meatrach *adj* metric.

meidh *f* scales; equilibrium.

meil *v* mill, grind.

meilleabhaid *f* velvet.

meilich *v* chill; numb.

mèilich *f* bleat, bleating; baa, baa-ing.

mèinn[1] *f* temperament; appearance.

mèinn[2], **mèinne** *f* mine; ore.

mèinneach *adj* mineral.

mèinneadair *m* miner.

mèinnear, mèinnearach *m* mineral.

mèinnearachd *f* mining; mineralogy.

mèinn-ghuail *see* **mèinn-ghuail**.

mèinneil *adj* mineral.

mèinn-eòlas *m* mineralogy.

mèinn-ghuail, mèinne-ghuail *f* coalmine.

meirg *v* rust. • *f* rust.

meirg-dhìonach *adj* rustproof.

meirgeach *adj* rusty.

meirgich *v* rust.

mèirle *f* theft.

mèirleach *m* thief.

meomhair *f* (*faculty*) memory.

meòmhraich *v* recollect; muse.

meud *m* size; amount; extent.

meudachd *f* magnitude.

meudaich *v* increase; enlarge.

m' eudail! *excl* love! darling!

meur *f* finger; branch; (*piano, etc*) key.

meuran *m* thimble.

meur-chlàr *m* keyboard.

meur-lorg *f* fingerprint.

mi *pron* I, me.

mì- *prefix* un-, dis-, in-, mis-, un-, -less.

mial *f* (*parasite*) tick.

mialaich *f* mewing, miauling.

mial-chaorach *f* sheep-tick.

miann *m/f* wish; longing; (*sexual*) desire.

miannaich *v* wish for; lust after.

mias *f* platter; basin.

mias-ionnlaid *f* wash-basin.

mì-bhlasta *adj* tasteless;.

mì-cheartas *m* injustice.

mì-dhìleas *adj* disloyal.

mì-earbsa *m* mistrust.

mì-fhoighidinn *f* impatience.

mì-fhoighidneach *adj* impatient.

mì-ghnàthach *adj* abnormal; unusual.

mil *f* honey.

mìle *m* thousand; mile.

milis *adj* sweet.

mill *v* damage; spoil; destroy.

millean *m* million.

millte *adj* damaged; spoilt; destroyed.

millteach *adj* destructive.

mìlseachd *f* sweetness.

mìlsean *m* dessert, pudding.

mì-mhodhail *adj* rude, ill-mannered.

mìn¹ *adj* smooth; soft.

mìn² *f* (*ground*) meal; **min-choirce** *f* oatmeal.

mì-nàdarra *adj* unnatural.

mìneachadh *m* explanation; interpretation.

mìneachail *adj* explanatory.

min-flùir *f* flour.

min-iarainn *f* iron filings.

mìnich *v* explain, illustrate; interpret; mean.

mìnich *v* smoothe.

minig *adj* frequent.

ministear *m* (*church, govt*) minister.

ministrealachd *f* (*church, govt*) ministry.

min-sàlbh *f* sawdust.

mìodal *m* flattery, fawning.

mìog *f* smirk.

mìogadaich *f* bleat, bleating.

mìolchu *m* greyhound.

mion *adj* small; minute; detailed; punctilious.

mionach *m* entrails, guts; (*fam*) belly.

mionaid *f* minute.

mionaideach *adj* thorough; detailed.

mion-aoiseach *adj* minor.

mion-bhraide *f* pilfering.

mion-chànan *m* minority language.

mìon-cheasnaich v question minutely, grill.

mìon-chuid f (*proportion*) minority.

mìon-chùiseach adj meticulous.

mìon-eòlas m detailed knowledge.

mìon-fhacal m (*gram*) particle.

mìon-gheàrr v cut up finely.

mìonnaich v curse, swear.

mìonnan m curse, swearword.

mìon-phuing f detail.

mìorbhail f marvel; miracle.

mìorbhaileach adj marvellous; miraculous.

mìos m/f month; **mìos nam pòg** honeymoon.

mìosach adj monthly.

mìosachan m calendar.

mìotag f glove; mitten.

mìr m bit, particle; scrap.

mìre f mirth; light-heartedness.

mì-rùn m malice, ill-will.

mìsde adj *same as* **mìste**.

mìse pron *emphatic form of* **mì**.

mìsg f drunkenness, intoxication.

mìsgear m drunkard, boozer.

mì-shealbhach adv unlucky, unfortunate.

mìsneachadh m encouragement.

mìsneachail adj courageous; spirited; in good heart; encouraging.

mìsneach, mìsneachd f courage.

mìsnich v encourage; inspire courage in.

mìste, mìsde adj the worse for; **cha bu mhìsde mi X** I'd be none the worse for X.

mìthich adj timely.

mo poss adj my.

moch adj early; **bho mhoch gu dubh** from morning til night.

mòd m (*with art*) **am Mòd (Nàiseanta)** the (National) Mod.

modh f manner, mode; manners; (*gram*) mood.

modhail adj polite, well-bred.

Mohamadanach m/adj Mohammedan, Muslim.

mòine f (*collective*) peat; **dèan/ buain mòine** v cut peat.

mòinteach f moor, moorland.

moit f pride.

moiteil adj proud.

mol[1] v praise; recommend.

mol[2] m shingle; shingly beach.

molach adj hairy; rough.

moladh m praise; recommendation.

moll m chaff.

molldair m (*jelly, etc*) mould.

molt, mult m wether.

mòmaid f moment, second.

monadail adj hilly, mountainous.

monadh m moor, moorland; common hill grazing.

mòr adj big; great; **mòr aig a chèile** great friends/pals.

mòrachd f greatness, grandeur.

morair m lord.

mòran m many, a lot of; much.

mòrchuis *f* pride, conceit.

mòr-chuid *f* (*with art*) a' mhòr-chuid the majority; most people.

morghan *m* gravel, shingle.

mòr-inbhe *f* eminence; high rank.

mòr longnadh *m* astonishment, stupefaction.

mòr-roinn *f* continent.

mòr-sluagh *m* multitude.

mort, murt *v* murder, assassinate. • *m* murder, assassination, manslaughter.

mortair, murtair *m* murderer, assassin.

mòr-uasal *m* nobleman, aristocrat.

mosach *adj* nasty; scruffy; niggardly.

mosg *m* mosque.

mosgail *v* (*from sleep*) wake, waken, rouse.

mo sgrios! *excl* woe is me!

motair *m* motor.

motair-rothar *m* motorbike.

motha *adj* bigger, greater.

mothachail *adj* aware; observant; sensitive; conscious.

mothaich *v* notice; feel; experience.

mo thruaighe! *excl* woe is me!

mo thruaighe ort! *excl* woe unto you!

mu *prep* around, about; concerning.

muc *f* pig; sow.

mu choinneimh *prep* opposite.

mucfheoil *f* pork.

mùch *v* extinguish, quench; smother; strangle; repress.

muc-mhara *f* whale.

mu dheas *adv* to/in the South.

mu dheidhinn *prep* about, concerning.

mu dheireadh *adj* last. • *adv* at last; mu dheireadh thall at long last.

muga *f* (*drinking*) mug.

mùgach *adj* morose, surly.

muidhe *m* churn.

mùlg *f* frown, scowl.

muilcheann, muinichill *m* sleeve.

Mulleach *m*/*adj* from Mull.

muilleann, muilinn *m*/*f* mill.

muilleann-gaoithe *m*/*f* windmill.

muile-mhàg *f* toad.

muilinn *m*/*f* same as **muilleann**.

muillean *m* million.

muillear *m* miller.

muilt-fheoil *f* mutton.

muime *f* stepmother.

muin *f* (*esp of animal*) back; top.

muineal *m* neck.

muing *f* mane.

muinichill *m* same as **muilcheann**.

muinntir *f* people; followers.

muir *m*/*f* sea.

muir-làn *m* high tide.

mulad *f* grief, sadness.

muladach *adj* sad.

m' ulaidh my darling, my love.
mullach *m* top; summit; roof.
mult *m* same as **molt**.
mun, mus *conj* before.
mùn *m* urine, piss.
muncaidh *m* monkey.
mun cuairt *adv* around, about.
mun cuairt air *prep* around, about.
mùr *m* bulwark, rampart.
mura *conj* if not.
murt *v/m* same as **mort**.

murtair *m* same as **mortair**.
mus *conj* same as **mun**.
mu seach *adv* in turn, one by one.
mùth *v* change, alter; mutate; deteriorate.
mùthadh *m* change, alteration; mutation; deterioration.
mu thimcheall *adv* around.
mu thràth *adv* already.
mu thuath *adv* to/in the North.

N

'n *art/poss pron/prep* **an** *after words ending with a vowel.*
na[1] *imper part* do not, don't.
na[2] *conj* than.
na[3] *rel pron* what, that which, those which.
na[4] *art* (*f sing*) of the; (*pl*) the.
nàbachas *m* neighbourliness.
nàbaidh *m* neighbour.
nàbaidheachd *f* neighbourhood.
nàbaidheil *adj* neighbourly.
nach *neg rel pron* that not.
nach math a rinn thu! *excl* well done!
'na chrùbagan *adv* crouched down.
'na chrùban *adv* crouching, squatting.
nàdar, nàdur *m* nature; temperament.

nàdarrach *adj* natural.
'na dhùisg *adv* awake.
'na dhùsgadh *adv* awake.
nàdur *m* same as **nàdar**.
na h-uile *pron* everybody, everyone.
naidheachd *f* piece of news; anecdote; (*pl TV, etc*) **na naidheachdan** the news.
naidheachdair *m* journalist.
nàidhlean *m* nylon.
nàire *f* shame, ignominy; bashfulness. • *excls* **mo nàire!** for shame! **mo nàire ort!** shame on you!
nàisean *m* nation.
nàiseanta *adj* national.
nàiseantach *m* nationalist.
nàiseantachd *f* nationalism; nationhood.

naisgear m (gram) conjunction.
nàimhdeas m enmity, hostility.
nàimhdeil adj inimical, hostile.
nàireach, nàrach adj shame-faced; bashful; diffident.
naisgear m (gram) conjunction.
nam see **nan**.
'nam aonar adv on my own.
'nam bheachd-sa in my opinion.
'nam chomain adj obliged to me.
nàmhaid m enemy.
nan¹ (**nam** before b, f, p) conj if.
nan² (**nam** before b, f, p) pl art of the.
naodh, naoi m/adj nine.
naoidhean m baby; infant.
naoinear m/f nine (people).
naomh m saint. • adj holy, sacred; saintly.
naomhachd f holiness; saintliness.
nàr adj shameful; disgraceful.
nàrach adj same as **nàireach**.
nàraich v put to shame; disgrace.
nas motha adv either, (with neg v) neither.
'na stad adj stationary; in abeyance.
'na shuidhe adv seated, sitting.
nathair f adder; serpent, snake.
'na thràill do addicted to.
'na trasg adv fasting.
neach m person; one, someone.
neach chungaidhean m chemist, pharmacist.
neach-teagaisg m teacher.

neach-treòrachaidh m guide.
neactair m nectar.
nead m nest.
nèamh m heaven(s).
nèamhaidh adj heavenly, celestial.
neapaigear m handkerchief.
neapaigin f napkin.
nearbhach adj nervous; nervy.
neart m strength, might; vigour; **an trèine a neirt** in his prime.
neartaich v strengthen; invigorate.
neartmhor adj strong; mighty.
neas m/f weasel; ferret; **neas mhòr** stoat.
neasgaid f boil; ulcer, abscess.
nèibhi, nèibhidh m/f navy.
neimh, nimh m poison; malice.
Neiptiùn m Neptune.
neo conj same as **no**.
neo- prefix un-, in-, non-.
neo-chrìochnach adj infinite.
neo-eisimeileach adj independent.
neo-eisimeileachd f independence.
neòinean m daisy.
neòinean-grèine m sunflower.
neò-làthaireachd f absence.
neònach adj strange, curious.
neo-sheachanta adj unavoidable, inevitable.
neul m cloud; complexion; faint.
neulach adj cloudy.
neulaich v cloud over; obscure.

nì¹ *m* thing; matter; circumstance; **an Nì Math** God.

nì² *future tense of v* **dèan**.

Nic (*in surnames*) daughter of.

nigh *v* wash.

nigheadair *m* washer, washing machine.

nigheadaireachd *f* washing.

nigheadair-shoithichean *m* dishwasher.

nighean *f* girl; young woman; daughter; **nighean bràthar/ peathar** niece.

nimh *m same as* **neimh**.

nimheil *adj* poisonous; malicious.

Nirribhidh *f* Norway.

nitheigin *pron* something.

nitheil *adj* concrete, actual.

no, neo *conj* or.

nobhail *f* novel.

nochd *v* show; appear; **nochd an clò** be printed/published.

Nollaig *f* Christmas.

norrag *f* nap, snooze; **norrag cadail** a wink of sleep.

nòs *m* way; custom; style.

nota *f* note; (*money*) pound.

nuadh *adj* new.

nuadhaich *v* renovate.

nuallaich *v* howl; roar; bellow.

nurs *f* nurse.

O

o *prep* from; since.

òb *m* bay.

obair *f* work; job, employment.

obair-ghrèise *f* (*the product of*) embroidery, needlework.

obair-làimhe *f* handiwork.

obair-taighe *f* housework.

obann *adj* sudden.

obh! obh! *excl* dear oh dear! good heavens!

obraich, oibrich *v* work, function; operate.

och (nan och)! *excl* alas! woe is me!

ochd *m/adj* eight.

ochdad *m* eighty.

ochdamh *adj* eighth.

ochd-deug *m/adj* eighteen.

ochdnar *m/f* eight (people).

o chionn *prep* ago; since; **o chionn ghoirid** recently; **o chionn fhada** long ago.

ocsaidean *m* oxygen.

odhar *adj* dun(-coloured); sallow.

òg *adj* young.

ògan *m* shoot, tendril.

òganach *m* young man; adolescent.

ogha *m* grandchild.

Og-mhìos *m* (*with art*) **an t-Og-mhìos** June.

oibrich *v same as* **obraich**.

oibriche *m* worker, workman.

oide *m* stepfather.

oideachas *m* education; learning.

oidhche *f* night; oidhche mhath leat/leibh! goodnight! Oidhche Challainn Hogmanay, New Year's Eve; Oidhche Shamhna Halloween.

oidhirp *f* attempt, try; effort.

oifig *f* same as oifis.

oifigeach, oifigear *m* officer; official.

oifigeil *adj* official.

oifis, oifig *f* office; position; oifis a' phuist post office; Oifis na h-Alba the Scottish Office.

òige *f* youth.

òigear *m* youngster, adolescent.

òigh *f* virgin; young woman.

òigheil *adj* virginal.

òighre *m* heir, inheritor.

òighreachd *f* (*land*) estate; inheritance.

òigridh *f* (*collective*) young people.

oilbheum *m* offence.

oilbheumach *adj* offensive.

oileanach *m* student.

oileanaich *v* train; instruct.

oillt *f* terror; horror.

oillteil *adj* frightful, dreadful; horrible.

oilltich *v* terrify.

oilthigh *m* university.

òinseach *f* fool, idiot.

oir *f* edge, margin; rim; oir an rathaid verge; oir a' chabhsair kerb.

oir *conj* for.

oirbh *prep pron* on you (*pl*).

òirdheirc *adj* magnificent; illustrious.

òirleach *m/f* inch.

oirnn *prep pron* on us.

oirre *prep pron* on her, on it (*f*).

oirthir *f* coast, seaboard.

oisean, oisinn *m* corner.

oiteag *f* breeze; breath of wind.

òl *v* drink.

ola *f* oil.

olann *f* wool.

olc *m* evil, wickedness. • *adj* evil, wicked.

ollamh *m* learned man; (*academic*) doctor.

òmar *m* amber.

on a *conj* since, as.

onair *f* honour; honesty; esteem. • *excl* air m'onair! honestly!

onorach *adj* honourable; honest; honorary.

onoraich *v* honour.

on taigh *adv* out; away from home.

opairèisean *m* (*med*) operation.

òr *m* gold.

òraid *f* speech, address; lecture.

òraidiche *m* speaker.

orainds, orains *adj* orange.

oraindsear, orainsear *m* orange.

òran *m* song; òrain luadhaidh waulking songs; na h-òrain

mhòra the classic(al) songs.
òr-chèard *m* goldsmith.
òrd *m* hammer.
òrdag *f* thumb.
òrdag-coise *f* toe.
òrdaich *v* order, command; organise, tidy.
òrdaighean *mpl* (*with art*) **na h-òrdaighean** (*relig*) communion.
òrdail *adj* orderly; ordinal.
òrdugh *m* order, sequence; command.
òrgan *m* organ.
orm *prep pron* on me.
orra *prep pron* on them.
òrraiseach *adj* squeamish.
ort *prep pron* on you (*sing*).
ortha *f* spell, charm.
osan *m* stocking, hose.

osann *m same as* **osna**.
os cionn *prep* above, over.
òsdair, òstair *m* hotelier, landlord, licensee.
o shean *adv* of old, long ago.
os ìosal *adv* quietly; secretly.
osna, osnadh *m/f*, **osann** *m* sigh; breeze.
osnaich *v* sigh.
ospadal *m* hospital.
ospag *f* sigh; breath of wind.
òstair *m same as* **òsdair**.
Ostair *f* (*with art*) **an Ostair** Austria.
Ostaireach *m/adj* Austrian.
othail *f* hubbub, uproar.
othaisg *f* hogg, ewe-lamb.
o thùs *adv* originally.
òtrach *m* dunghill, midden.

P

paca *m* pack.
pacaid *f* packet.
pàganach *m/adj* pagan, heathen.
paidh *m* pie.
paidhir *m/f* pair.
paidir *f* Lord's Prayer.
paidirean *m* rosary.
pàigh *v* pay (for); atone (for).
pàigh, paigheadh *m* pay, remuneration.
pàileis *f* palace.

pàillean *m* pavilion; large tent.
pailt *adj* plentiful.
pailteas *m* plenty.
pàipear *m* paper.
pàipear-balla *m* wallpaper.
pàipear-gainmhich *m* sandpaper.
pàipear-naidheachd *m* newspaper.
pàirc *f* field; park.
paireafain *m* paraffin.

pàirt *m* part.

pàirt-càraidh *m* spare, spare part.

pàirtich *v* share out; divide up.

pàisde, pàiste *m* baby; infant; small child.

paisg *v* wrap (up); fold (up).

pàiste *m same as* pàisde.

pàiteach *adj* thirsty.

pana *m* pan.

pannal *m* panel.

Pàpa *m* Pope.

pàpanach *m/adj* (*derog*) papist, popish.

pàrant *m* parent.

pàrlamaid *f* parliament.

pàrlamaideach *adj* parliamentary.

parsail *m* parcel, package.

pàrtaidh *m* party.

partan *m* (*edible*) crab.

pasgadh *m* packing.

pasgan *m* bundle; package.

pastra *f* pastry.

pathadh *m* thirst.

pàtran *m* pattern.

peacach *m* sinner. • *adj* sinful.

peacadh *m* sin.

peacadh-bàis *m* mortal sin.

peacadh-gine *m* original sin.

peacaich *v* sin.

peanas *m* punishment; penalty.

peanasaich *v* punish.

peann *m* pen.

peansail *m* pencil.

peant *v* paint.

peanta *m* paint.

peantair *m* painter.

pearraid *f* parrot.

pearsa *m* person; (*play, etc*) character.

pearsanta *adj* personal.

pearsantachd *f* personality.

pears-eaglais *m* clergyman.

peasair *f* pea.

peata *m* pet.

peatroil, peatrol *m* petrol.

peighinn *f* penny.

peile *m* pail.

pèilleag *f* porpoise.

peilear *m* bullet; pellet.

peile-frasaidh *m* watering can.

peinnsean *m* pension.

peirceall *m* jaw, jawbone.

pèist *f* reptile.

peitean *m* vest; waistcoat.

pèitseag *f* peach.

peur *f* pear.

pian *v* pain, distress; torture. • *f* pain.

piàna *m* piano.

pianail *adj* painful.

pic *m* (*tool*) pick.

picil *f* pickle.

pile *f* pill.

pìleat, plodhlead *m* pilot.

pillean *m* cushion; pillion.

pinc *adj* pink.

pinnt *m* pint.

pìob *f* pipe; tube.

pìobaire *m* piper.

pìobaireachd *f* (bag-)piping; pibroch.

plobar *m* pepper.

plòb mhòr *f* Highland bagpipes.

plobraich *v* add pepper to; pep up.

plòb-thombaca *f* (tobacco) pipe.

plòb-uilne *f* uileann pipes.

ploc *v* peck; nibble.

plodhlead *m same as* **pìleat**.

plòs *m* piece, bit; packed lunch.

plseach *m* progress, improvement.

plseag *f* kitten.

plt *f* vulva.

pluthar *f* sister.

pluthar-chèile *f* sister-in-law.

plaide *f* blanket.

plàigh *f* plague; infestation; nuisance.

plàighell *adj* pestilential.

plana *m* plan.

planaid *f* planet.

planaig *v* plan.

plangaid *f* blanket.

plap *v* flutter. • *m* fluttering.

plaoisg *v* shell; peel; skin.

plaosg *m* shell; peel; skin; husk.

plàsd *m* sticking plaster.

plastalg *f*/*adj* plastic.

plathadh *m* glance; glimpse; instant.

pleadhag *f* (*canoe, etc*) paddle.

pleadhagaich *v* paddle.

plèana *f* (aero)plane.

ploc *m* clod; turf; block; lump.

ploc-prìne *m* pinhead.

plosg *v* gasp, pant; palpitate, throb. • *m* gasp; palpitation; throb.

plub, plubraich *m* splash, plop. • *v* splash, plop, slosh.

plucan *m* pimple; (*sink, etc*) plug.

pluic *f* (plump) cheek.

plumair *m* plumber.

Pluta *m* Pluto.

poball *m* people.

poballach, poblach *adj* public.

poballachd, poblachd *f* republic.

poca *m* bag; sack.

pòca *m*, **pòcaid** *f* pocket.

poca-cadail *m* sleeping-bag.

pòcaid *see* **pòca**.

pòg *v* kiss. • *f* kiss.

poidsear *m* poacher.

poileas *m same as* **polas**.

poileasman *m same as* **polasman**.

poileataiceach *adj* political.

poileataics *f* politics.

polt *f* pot.

polt-dhubh *f* (whisky) still.

pòltear *m* drinker, boozer.

pòltearachd *f* boozing, tippling.

polt-fhlùran *f* flowerpot.

polt-mhùln *f* chamberpot.

polt-teatha *f* teapot.

pòla *m* pole; **am Pòla a Tuath/a Deas** the North/South Pole.

Pòlach *m*/*adj* Pole; Polish.

Pòlainn *f* (*with art*) **a' Phòlainn** Poland.

polas, poileas *m* police; policeman.

polasman, polleasman *m* policeman.

poll *m* mud; bog.

poll-mòna, poll-mònach *m* peat bog.

pònaidh *m* pony.

pònair *f* bean(s); **pònair leathann** broad bean(s); **pònair Fhrangach** French bean(s).

pong *m* (*mus*) note.

pongail *adj* concise; punctual; punctilious.

pòr *m* seed; crops; growth.

port[1] *m* port, harbour; **port-adhair** airport.

port[2] *m* tune; **port a-beul** mouth music.

Portagail *f* (*with art*) **a' Phortagail** Portugal.

Portagalleach *m/adj* Portuguese.

portair *m* porter; doorman.

pòs *v* marry.

pòsadh *m* marriage.

pòsda, pòsta *adj* married; **pòsda aig** married to; **nuadh-phòsda** newly married.

post *m* post, stake; post, mail; postman; **post-adhair** air mail.

posta *m* postman.

pòsta *adj same as* **pòsda**.

post dealain *m* electronic mail.

prabar *m* rabble, mob.

prab-shùilleach *adj* bleary-eyed.

prais *f* cooking pot.

pràis *f* brass.

pràiseach *adj* brass.

preantas *m* apprentice.

preas[1] *v* crease; corrugate; crush.

preas[2] *m* bush, shrub.

preas[3], **preasa** *m* cupboard.

preasach *adj* wrinkly, wrinkled.

preasadh *m* wrinkle.

preasag *f* wrinkle, crease.

preas-aodaich *m* wardrobe.

preas-leabhraichean *m* bookcase.

prìne *m* pin.

prìne-banaltraim *m* safety pin.

prìob *v* wink; blink.

prìobadh *m* wink; blink; instant.

prìobhaideach *adj* private.

prìomh *adj* main, head.

prìomhaire *m* prime minister.

prionnsa *m* prince.

prionnsabal *m* principle.

prìosan *m* prison.

prìosanach *m* prisoner.

prìs *f* price, cost.

prìseil *adj* precious; valuable.

prògram *m* programme; (*comput*) program.

proifeasair *m* professor.

proifeiseanta *adj* professional.

pròis *f* pride.

pròiseict *f* project.

pròiseil *adj* proud.

pronn *v* mash, pulverise; (*fam*) bash, beat up. • *adj* mashed, pulverised.

pronnasg *m* sulphur; brimstone.

prosbaig *f* binoculars; telescope.

Pròstanach *m/adj* Protestant.

prothaid f (*fin*) profit; gain, benefit.

puball m marquee.

pùdar m powder.

pùdaraich v powder.

pulng f point (in scale, etc); (*orthog*) stop, mark; **stad-phulng** full stop; **clisg-phulng** exclamation mark; **dà-phulng** colon.

pulnnsean m poison.

pulnnseanach adj poisonous.

pulnnseanaich v poison.

pumpa m pump.

punnd m (*weight and money*) pound; **punnd Eireannach** punt; **punnd Sasannach** pound sterling.

purpaidh adj purple.

purpar, purpur m purple.

put[1] v push, jostle.

put[2] m buoy.

putan m button.

R

rabald f rabbit.

rabhadh m warning; alarm.

rabhd, ràbhart m idle talk; obscene talk.

ràc[1] v rake.

ràc[2] m drake.

racald f (*sports*) racket.

ràcan m rake.

rach v go.

rach à blth v cease to be.

rach a cadal v go to bed.

rach à culmhne v be forgotten.

rach a dhìth v go short.

rach alr dìochulmhne v be forgotten.

rach alr lomrall v wander; go astray, err.

rach alr lteig v fly.

rach alr muln v have sex with; (*animals*) serve.

rach alr seachran v wander; go astray.

rach am fad v get/grow longer.

rach am feabhas v improve, get better.

rach am meud v get bigger.

rach an geall gu v bet that.

rach an laigse v faint.

rach an neul v faint, pass out.

rach an sàs an v get involved in.

rach an urras (alr) v guarantee, vouch (for).

rach an urras gu v guarantee that.

rach à sealladh v disappear, go out of sight.

rach às mo chulmhne v be forgetten.

rach às mo leth v side with me.

rach bhualthe v deteriorate.

rach car mu char v roll over and over.

rach fodha v sink; (firm, etc) fail.

rach 'na laighe v lie down; go to bed.

rach 'na lasair v go up in flames.

rach 'na shaighdear v become a soldier.

rach ri taobh X v take after X.

rach seachad (air) v pass by, go past.

rach thar a chèlle v fall out, quarrel.

radan m rat.

ràdh m saying, proverb.

radharc m eyesight; sight, view.

rag adj stiff; stubborn.

ragaich v stiffen.

rag-mhuinealach adj pig-headed.

raidhfil f rifle.

raineach f bracken, fern(s).

ràinig past tense of v ruig.

ràith f season; quarter (of year); while.

ràitheachan m (magazine) quarterly, periodical.

ràmh m oar.

ràn v roar, yell; weep. • m roar, yell; weeping.

rann f poetry; a verse.

rannsaich v search; rummage; research; ransack.

raon m field.

raon-adhair m airfield.

raon-cluiche m playing field.

rapach adj slovenly, scruffy.

rathad m road; way, route.

rathad mòr m main road.

Ratharsach m/adj from Raasay.

Ratharsair Raasay.

rè f time, period.

rè prep during, throughout.

reachd m rule; command; law.

reamhar adj fat.

reamhraich v fatten.

reic v sell. • m sale; selling.

reiceadair m vendor; salesman; auctioneer.

rèidh adj level; smooth; cleared; **rèidh ri** on good terms with.

rèidhlean m green.

rèidio m radio.

rèile f rail, railing.

rèilig f kirkyard.

rèis f (sport, etc) race.

rèiseamaid f regiment.

rèite f agreement; reconciliation; betrothal; atonement.

rèiteach, rèiteachadh m betrothal.

rèitear m referee.

reithe m tup, ram.

rèitich v reconcile; appease; arbitrate; settle; adjust.

reòdh v freeze.

reòiteag f ice cream.

reòta adj frozen.

reòth v same as **reòdh**.

reothadair m freezer, deep freeze.

reothadh m frost.

reothairt f spring-tide.

reub v tear; lacerate; mangle.

reubadh m rip, rent.

reubalach m rebel.

reudan m wood-louse.

reul f star.

reuladair m astronomer.

reul-bhad m constellation.

reul-eòlas m astronomy.

reul-iùil f pole star.

reusan m reason; sanity.

reusanta adj reasonable; sensible; fair.

ri prep to; against; during.

riabhach adj brindled; grizzled; drab; dun.

riadh (fin) interest.

riaghail v rule (over), govern; regulate; manage.

riaghailt f rule, regulation; system, order.

riaghailteach adj regular; systematical.

riaghailteachd f orderliness; regularity.

riaghailtich v regularise; regulate.

riaghaltas m government.

riaghladair m ruler, governor.

riaghladh m governing; administration; management.

rian m orderliness; system; reason; (mus) arrangement.

rianadair m (mus) arranger; computer.

rianail adj methodical.

riaraich v please; satisfy; distribute; (cards) deal.

riatanach adj essential.

rib v trap, ensnare.

ribe f trap, snare.

ribean-tomhais m tape measure.

ribh prep pron to you (pl).

ribheid f (mus) reed.

rìbhinn f (songs) maiden, girl.

ridhil m (dance) reel; **ridhil-ochdnar** eightsome reel.

ridire m knight.

rìgh m king.

Rìgh nan Dùl m Lord of the Universe, God.

righinn adj (material, etc) tough.

rim bheò adv all my life; in my lifetime.

rinn¹ past tense of v dèan.

rinn² m point, promontory.

rinn³ prep pron to us.

rioban m ribbon.

riochd m likeness, form; appearance.

riochdaich v represent; portray; impersonate.

riochdair m (gram) pronoun.

riochdaire m representative.

rìoghachadh m reign; reigning.

rìoghachd f kingdom.

rìoghaich v reign.

rìoghail adj royal; kingly, regal.

rìomhach adj beautiful; splendid.

rionnach m mackerel.

rionnag f star.

ris¹ prep pron to him, to it (m).

rls² *adv* showing, exposed.

rls a' bhruthalch *adv* against the slope.

rls a' ghaolth *adv* against the wind.

rls an t-sruth *adv* against the current.

rl taobh *prep* beside, alongside.

rl taobh a chèlle *adv* abreast.

rl teachd *adv* future, to come.

rlthe *prep pron* to her, to it (*f*).

rl tìde *adv* in time, eventually.

rl uchd bàls *adv* at the point of death.

rlum *prep pron* to me.

rlut *prep pron* to you (*sing*).

rlutha *prep pron* to them.

ro *prep* (*time and space*) before; in front of.

ro *adv* too; very, extremely.

ro- *prefix* fore-, pre-.

robach *adj* hairy, shaggy; slovenly.

robh *past tense, neg and interrog, of v* **blth**.

roc *f* wrinkle.

rocald *f* rocket.

ròcall *f* croak(ing), caw(ing).

ròcals *f* rook.

ro-chralceann *m* foreskin.

roghalnn *m* choice; preference.

roghnalch *v* choose.

rollig *v* roll.

rolmhe *prep pron* before him, before it (*m*).

rolmhe *adv* before.

rolmhear *m* preposition.

rolmh-lnnleachd *f* strategy.

rolmhpe *prep pron* before her, before it (*f*).

ròlneag *f* (*single*) hair.

rolnn *v* divide (up); distribute; (*cards*) deal; (*arith*) divide.

rolnn *f* division; share; department; (*govt*) region; continent.

ròlsd *v* roast; fry.

ro làlmh *adv* beforehand.

ròlalst *m* romance, romantic novel.

ro-leasachan *m* (*gram*) prefix.

ròmach *adj* woolly, hairy, shaggy; bearded.

Romàlnla *f* Romania.

Romàlnlanach *m/adj* Romanian.

romhad *prep pron* before you (*sing*).

romhalbh *prep pron* before you (*pl*).

romhalnn *prep pron* before us.

romham *prep pron* before me.

romhpa *prep pron* before them.

ròn *m* (*animal*) seal.

rong¹ *f* rung; spar; hoop.

rong² *m* vital spark.

ron mhlthlch *adv* premature(ly).

ronn *m* mucus, phlegm.

ro-nochd *v* overexpose.

ro-òrdachadh *m* predestination.

ro-òrdalch *v* predestine, predetermine.

ròpa *m* rope.

ròp-aodalch *m* clothes-line.

ro-ràdh *m* foreword, preamble.

ròs *m* rose.

ròsda *adj* roast(ed); fried.

rosg[1] *m* eyelash.

rosg[2] *m* prose.

rosg-rann *f* sentence.

ròst *v same as* **ròisd**.

ròsta *adj same as* **ròsda**.

roth *m/f* wheel.

rothach *adj* wheeled.

rothar *m* bicycle.

ro-throm *adj* overweight.

ruadh *adj* red; red-haired, ginger.

rualg *v* chase; put to flight, (*milit*) rout. • *f* chase, pursuit; flight; rout; hunt.

ruamhair *v* dig; rummage.

rubair *m* rubber.

rubha *m* point, promontory.

rùchd *v* grunt; belch; retch. • *m* grunt; belch; retching.

rud *m* thing; fact.

rùda *m* ram, tup.

rudail *adj* concrete, actual, real.

rùdan *m* knuckle, finger-joint.

rudbeag *adv* a bit, somewhat.

rudeigin *pron* something, anything. • *adv* somewhat.

rudhadh *m* blush(ing), flush(ing).

rud sam bith *m* anything at all.

rug *past tense of v* **beir**.

rugadh mi *v* I was born.

ruidhle *m same as* **ridhil**.

ruig *v* arrive (at), reach.

ruig air *v* reach for; take, seize;.

ruighe *m/f* forearm; hillslope.

rùllear *m* (*measuring*) rule, ruler.

Ruis *f* (*with art*) **an Ruis** Russia.

ruisean *m* (*with art*) **an ruisean** the midday meal.

Ruiseanach *m/adj* Russian.

rùisg *v* bare, strip; shear, fleece; peel; chafe.

rùisgte *adj* stripped; shorn; peeled.

Ruisia *f* Russia'.

ruiteach *adj* ruddy; blushing, flushed.

ruith *v* run; flow; chase. • *f* run, running; pursuit; rout; rate, pace.

rùm *m* room; space.

Rumach *m/adj* from Rum.

rùm-bidhe *m* dining-room.

rùm ionnlaid *m* bathroom.

rùn *m* secret; love, affection; wish, purpose; ambition.

rùnaich *v* wish, desire; resolve.

rùnaire *m* secretary; **Rùnaire na Stàite** the Secretary of State.

rùraich *v* rummage, grope; explore.

rus *m* rice.

rùsg *m* fleece; peel, skin, husk; (*tree*) bark.

S

's (*for* **agus, is**) *conj* and.

-sa *suffix* this.

sabaid *v* fight, scrap, brawl. • *f* fight(ing), scrap(ping), brawl-(ing).

sàbaid *f* sabbath.

sàbh *v* saw. • *m* saw.

sàbhail *v* save, rescue; econo-mise.

sàbhailte *adj* safe.

sabhal *m* barn.

sàbhaladh *m* rescuing; (*relig*) salvation; savings.

sabhs *m* sauce.

sac *m* sack.

sad *v* throw, toss, chuck.

sagart *m* priest.

saibhear *m* culvert; sewer.

saideal *m* satellite.

saidhbhir *adj* wealthy, affluent.

saidhbhreas *m* wealth, afflu-ence.

saighdear *m* soldier.

saighead *f* arrow.

saidheans *m* science.

sail *f* beam, joist.

sàil *f* heel.

sailead *m* salad.

saill[1] *v* salt; season (*with salt*).

saill[2] *f* fat, grease.

saillear *f* salt-cellar.

saillte *adj* salt, salted; salty.

saimeant *m* concrete, cement.

sal *m* filth; dross; stain.

sàl *m* salt water, brine; (*with art*) **an sàl** (*songs, etc*) the sea, the briny.

salach *adj* dirty, filthy; foul.

salaich *v* dirty, soil; defile, sully.

salann *m* salt.

salchar *m* dirt, filth.

salm *m/f* psalm.

saltair *v* tread, trample.

sàmhach *adj* quiet, peaceful, tranquil; silent.

samhail *m* likeness; match; the like(s) of.

Samhain *f* Hallowtide; All Saints'/Souls' Day; **Oidhche Shamhna** *f* Halloween; (*with art*) **an t-Samhainn** November.

sàmhchair *f* quiet(ness), tran-quility; silence.

samhla, samhladh *m* resem-blance; sign; (*lit*) symbol, simile, comparison, allegory; parable.

samhlaich (ri) *v* resemble; com-pare, liken (to).

samhradh *m* summer.

sanas *m* announcement; notice; hint.

sanas-reic *m* advertisement.

san fharsaingeachd *adv* gener-ally, broadly speaking.

san fhradharc *adv* in sight.

sannt *m* avarice, covetousness.

sanntach *adj* greedy, avaricious.

sanntaich *v* covet.

saobh *adj* foolish, wrong-headed.

saobhaidh *f* den, lair.

saobh-chràbhadh *m* superstition.

saobh-shruth *m* eddy, counter-current.

saobh-smuain *m* whim.

saoghal *m* world; life; lifetime.

saoghalta *adj* wordly; materialistic.

saoil *v* think, believe; suppose.

saor¹ *v* free; (*relig*) save, redeem.
• *adj* free (of charge); cheap; free, at liberty.

saor² *m* joiner, carpenter.

saoradh *m* liberation; absolution; salvation.

saor-àirneis *m* cabinet maker.

saor-làithean *mpl* holiday(s).

saor o *adv* free from, untroubled by.

saorsa *f* freedom; (*relig*) redemption.

saor 's an asgaidh *adv* free of charge.

saor-tholleach *adj* voluntary.

saothair *f* labour, toil.

saothraich *v* labour, toil.

sàr *adv* very, extremely; through and through.

sàraich *v* oppress; distress; vex; weary.

sàr-mhath *adj* excellent.

sàr obair *f* masterpiece.

sàsaich *v* content, satisfy; satiate.

sàsaichte *adj* contented, satisfied; sated.

Sasainn *f* England.

Sasannach *m/adj* Englishman; English.

sàsar *m* saucer.

sàth *v* stab; push, shove.

seabhag *f* hawk, falcon.

seacald *f* jacket.

seac àraidh *adv* especially, particularly.

seach¹ *prep* instead of; rather than; in comparison to.

seach² *adv/prep* past, by.

seachad¹ *adj* over, finished; (*space and time*) past.

seachad² *adv* past, by.

seachad air *prep* past, by.

seachain, seachainn *v* avoid; shun, abstain from.

seachanta *adj* avoidable.

seachd *n/adj* seven.

seachdad *m* seventy.

seachdain *f* week.

seachdamh *adj* seventh.

seachdnar *m/f* (*people*) seven.

seachran *m* wandering; going astray.

seac searbh sgìth (de) sick and tired (of).

seada *m/f* shed.

seadag *f* grapefruit.

seadh *adv* (*non-affirmative*) yes, uh-uh.

seagal *m* rye.

seagh *m* sense, meaning.

seàla *f* shawl.

sealbh *m* luck; fortune, providence; heaven. • *excl* **sealbh ort!** good luck! **alg Sealbh tha brath** Heaven knows.

sealbh *f* property; possession.

sealbhach *adj* lucky; possessive.

sealbhadair *m* owner, proprietor.

sealbhaich *v* own, possess.

sealg *v* hunt.

sealg *f* hunt, hunting.

sealgair *m* hunter, huntsman; **an Sealgair Mòr** Orion.

seall *v* see; look; show; watch over.

seall air *v* look at.

sealladh *m* sight; view, prospect; eyesight; look; **an dà shealladh** second sight.

sealladh-taoibh *m* sideways look/glance.

Sealtainn *m* Shetland.

Sealtainneach *m/adj* Shetlander; from Shetland.

seamrag *f* shamrock; clover.

sean *adj* old; former.

seana-ghille *m* old batchelor.

seanair *m* grandfather; ancestor, forebear.

seanalair *m* general.

seana-mhaighdeann *f* old maid.

seanchaidh *m* shenachie, tradition-bearer; story-teller.

seanchas *m* traditional lore; chat, gossip; news.

seanfhacal *m* proverb, saying, adage.

sean-fhasanta *adj* old-fashioned.

sean-fhleasgach *m* old bachelor.

seang *adj* thin; slim; lank, skinny.

seangan *m* ant.

seanmhair *m* grandmother.

seann *adj same as* **sean**.

seann-phàrant *m* grandparent.

sean-seanair *m* great grandfather.

sean-sheanmhair *f* great grandmother.

seantans *m* (*gram*) sentence.

Seapan *f* (*with art*) **an t-Seapan** Japan.

Seapanach *m/adj* Japanese.

sear *adj/adv* east, eastern.

sear air *adv* east of.

searbh *adj* bitter; sour, acrid; pungent; harsh; disagreeable; sharp, sarcastic.

searbhadair *m* towel.

searbhanta *m/f* servant, maid.

searg *v* wither, shrivel, dry up; fade away; pine away; blight.

seargach *adj* (*tree*) deciduous.

searmon *f* sermon.

searmonaich *v* preach.

searrach *m* colt, foal.

searrag *f* flask; bottle.

seas *v* stand (up); stand by; support; last.

seasamh *m* standing position; **'na sheasamh** standing (up).

seasamh-chas *m* footing.

seasg *adj* barren, sterile; (*cattle, etc*) dry.

seasgad *m* sixty.

seasgair *adj* cosy, snug; comfortably off.

seasmhach *adj* firm, stable; reliable; enduring; durable.

seathar *m* chair.

seathar-tulgaidh *m* rocking-chair.

seatlair *m* settler.

seic *f* cheque.

Seic *f* (with art) **an t-Seic** the Czech Republic.

Seiceach *m/adj* Czech.

seiche *f* skin, pelt, hide.

seic-leabhar *m* chequebook.

sèid *v* blow; swell, puff up.

seilbh, seilbheach, seilbh-eadair, seilbhich *same as* **sealbh, sealbhach, sealbh-adair, sealbhaich.**

seilcheag *f* snail; slug.

seile *m* saliva, spittle.

seileach *m* willow.

seillean *m* bee.

seillean mòr *m* bumble-bee.

sèimh *adj* calm, mild, gentle.

sèimhe *f* calm(ness), mildness, gentleness.

seinn *v* sing; (*instrument, etc*) play, sound.

seinn *m* singing; sounding.

seinneadair *m* singer.

seirbheis *f* service; favour.

seirbheiseach *m* servant.

seirc *f* love, affection; (Christian) charity.

seirm *v* ring (out), sound.

sèisd *m/f* siege.

seis, seise *m* like(s) of; equal, match.

seisean *m* (*meeting, etc*) session; kirk session.

sèist *m/f* refrain, chorus.

seo *adj/pron* this.

seòbhrach *f* primrose.

seòclaid *f* chocolate.

seòd *m* hero.

seòl *v* sail; steer; navigate; guide, direct; manage; govern. • *m* sail; course; method; means.

seòladair *m* sailor, seaman.

seòladh *m* sailing; (*house, etc*) address.

seòl-beatha *m* way of life.

seòl-mara *m* (high) tide.

seòlta *adj* cunning; resourceful; shrewd.

seòmar *m* room.

seòmar-cadail *m* bedroom.

seòmar-ionnlaid *m* bathroom.

seòmar-leapa *m* bedroom.

seòmar-mullaich *m* attic.

seòrsa *m* sort, kind; genus, species; class.

seòrsaich *v* classify; sort.

seud *m* jewel, gem.

seumarlan *m* factor, land-agent; chamberlain.

seun *m* spell; charm, amulet.

seunta *adj* enchanted, spellbound.

's e ur beatha! *excl* you're welcome!

sgadan *m* herring.

sgàll *v* shade, darken, eclipse; veil, mask. • *f* shade, shadow; covering; (*occas*) ghost, spectre.

sgailc *v* slap, smack. • *f* slap, sharp blow; sharp sound; (*liquid*) swig; baldness.

sgàilc *n* same as **sgàil**.

sgàillean-grèine *m* parasol.

sgàillean-uisge *m* umbrella.

sgàil-lampa *f* lampshade.

sgàil-sùla *f* eyelid.

sgàin *v* burst, crack, split.

sgàineadh *m* split, crack.

sgàird *f* (*with art*) **an sgàird** diarrhoea.

sgairt¹ *f* diaphragm.

sgairt² *f* yell; gusto; vigour, activity.

sgairteil *adj* brisk; active, bustling; enthusiastic; (*weather*) blustery.

sgait *f* (*fish*) skate.

sgal *v* yell, squeal. • *m* yell; outburst; squall.

sgàl *m* tray.

sgàla *f* (*mus*) scale.

sgalag *f* farm servant; skivvy.

sgalanta *adj* shrill.

sgall *m* baldness; bald patch.

sgallach *adj* bald-headed.

Sgalpach *m/adj* from Scalpay.

Sgalpaigh *n* Scalpay.

sgamhan *m* lung.

sgaoil *v* spread (out); stretch out; disperse; release.

sgaoth *m* mass, multitude, swarm.

sgaothaich *v* (*crowds, etc*) flock, mass, swarm.

sgap *v* scatter.

sgar *v* separate; sever.

sgaradh *m* separation.

sgaradh-pòsaidh *m* divorce, separation.

sgarbh *m* cormorant.

sgarbh an sgumain *m* (*bird*) shag.

sgarfa *m* scarf.

sgàrlaid *f/adj* scarlet.

sgath *v* cut off; prune.

sgàth *m* shadow; protection; fear.

sgàthan *m* mirror.

sgeadaich *v* adorn, embellish; dress up; (*lamp, fire, etc*) attend to, trim.

sgealb *v* split; shatter; chip; carve. • *f* chip; splinter, fragment.

sgealbag *f* index finger.

sgealp *f* slap, smack; sharp sound.

sgeap *f* beehive.

sgeilb *f* chisel.

sgeileid *f* skillet.

sgeilp *f* shelf.

sgeir *f* rock, skerry.

sgeith *v* vomit, throw up.

sgeul *m* story; (*of person*) news, sign.

sgeulach adj like a story; fond of stories.

sgeulachd f story.

sgeulachd ghoirid f short story.

sgeulaiche m storyteller.

sgeumhach adj beautiful.

sgeumhaich v beautify; adorn, ornament.

sgeunach adj timid, shy; skittish, mettlesome.

sgi, sgith f ski.

sgiamh v squeal, shriek. • m squeal, shriek.

sgian f knife.

sgiath f wing; shield; shelter.

sgiathaich v fly.

Sgiathanach, Sgitheanach m/adj from Skye. • m an t-Eilean Sgitheanach (the Isle of) Skye.

sgil m skill.

sgileil adj skilled; skilful.

sgillin f penny.

sgillinn ruadh f brass farthing.

sgioba m/f crew; team.

sgiobair m skipper, captain.

sgiobalta adj neat, tidy; quick, active; handy.

sgiobalaich v tidy; put right/straight.

sgiorradh m accident; stumble, slip.

sgiort f skirt.

sgios f tiredness; weariness.

sgire f (local govt) district; area, locality; parish.

sgireachd f parish.

sgith f same as **sgi**.

sgith adj tired; weary.

sgitheach m whitethorn, hawthorn.

Sgitheanach m/adj same as Sgiathanach.

sgithell adj tiring; wearisome.

sgithich v tire; weary.

sgithich v ski.

sgiths adj same as **sgios**.

sgiurs v whip, scourge.

sgiursair m whip, scourge.

sglaib f (building, etc) plaster.

sglaibeadair m plasterer.

sgleat m slate.

sgleatair m slater.

sgleog f slap.

sgob v snatch; sting; peck; sprain.

sgoil f school; schooling.

sgoil-àraich f nursery school.

sgoilear m pupil; scholar.

sgoilearachd f scholarship; bursary.

sgoilt, sgolt v split, cleave; slit.

sgoinneil adj (fam) great, smashing.

sgol v rinse.

sgolt see **sgoilt**.

sgoltadh m split, cleft; chink; slit.

sgona f scone.

sgonn m lump, hunk.

sgòr m (games, etc) score.

sgòrnan m throat; gullet, windpipe.

sgoth f skiff, sailing boat.

sgòth *f* cloud.

sgòthach *adj* cloudy.

sgoth long *f* yacht.

sgraing *f* frown, scowl.

sgreab *f* scab.

sgread *v* scream, shriek. • *m* scream, shriek.

sgreadhail *f* trowel.

sgreamh *m* loathing, disgust.

sgreamhail *adj* loathsome, disgusting.

sgreataidh *adj* loathsome, nauseating.

sgreuch *v* scream, screech. • *m* scream, screech.

sgrìob *v* scratch, scrape; furrow. • *f* scratch, scrape; furrow; trip, jaunt.

sgrìobach *adj* abrasive.

sgrìoban *m* hoe.

sgrìobh *v* write.

sgrìobhadair *m* writer.

sgrìobhadh *m* writing; handwriting.

sgrìobhaiche *m* writer.

sgriobtar *m* scripture.

sgrios *v* destroy; ruin. • *m* destruction; ruin.

sgriosail *adj* destructive; pernicious; (*fam*) terrible, dreadful.

sgriubha *f* screw.

sgriubhaire *m* screwdriver.

sgròb *v* scratch; cross out.

sgrùd *v* scrutinize; investigate; research; audit.

sgrùdadh *m* scrutiny; investigation; research; audit.

sguab¹ *v* sweep, brush. • *f* brush, broom.

sguab² *f* sheaf of corn.

sguabadair *m* hoover, vacuum-cleaner.

sguab fhliuch *f* mop.

sgud *v* chop.

sgudal *m* rubbish, refuse; nonsense.

sguir *v* stop, cease; desist.

sguir de *v* give up, stop.

sgur *m* stopping, ceasing.

sgùrr *m* peak, pinnacle.

shìos *adv* down; below.

shìos bhuam *adv* below me, down from me.

shuas *adv* up; above.

shuas bhuam *adv* above me, up from me.

sia *n/adj* six.

siab *v* wipe, rub; (*snow*) drift.

siabann *m* soap.

siach *v* sprain, strain.

sia-deug *m/adj* sixteen.

sian¹ *f* storm; (*wind*) blast; *pl* (*with art*) **na siantan** the elements.

sian² *m* thing; anything, (*with neg v*) nothing.

sianar *m/f* (*people*) six.

siar *adj/adv* west, western. • **na h-Eileanan Siar** *mpl* the Western Isles; **an Cuan Siar** *m* the Atlantic Ocean; **an taobh siar** *m* the west.

siar air *prep* west of.

sibh *pers pron pl* you.

sìde *f* weather; **sìde nan seachd sìan** appalling weather.

sil *v* (*liquids*) drip, drop, flow, rain.

silidh *m* jam; jelly.

silteach *adj* (*liquids*) dripping, dropping, flowing.

similear *m* chimney.

simplidh *adj* simple, uncomplicated; simple-minded.

sin *adj* that; those. • *pron* that.

sìn *v* stretch, extend; pass, hand.

sinc *m* zinc.

since *f* (*kitchen*) sink.

sine *f* nipple, teat.

sineach *adj* mammal.

sìneadh *m* stretching; recumbent position. • **'na shìneadh** *adv* stretched out, lying down.

singilte *adj* single; (*gram*) singular.

sinn *pron* we.

sinn-seanair *m* great-grandfather.

sinn-seanmhair *f* great-grandmother.

sinnsear *m* ancestor, forefather.

sinn-sinn-seanair *m* great-great-grandfather.

sinn-sinn-seanmhair *f* great-great-grandmother.

sinteag *f* hop; stride.

sin thu!, sin thu-fhèin! *excl* well done! good for you!

slobhag *f* wick.

sìobhalta *adj* civil, polite.

sìobhaltair *m* civilian.

sìochail *adj* peaceful.

sìoda *m* silk.

sìol *m* seed; race; progeny.

sìolachan *m* strainer, filter.

sìolaidh *v* subside, settle; filter, strain.

sìol-cuir *m* seed corn.

sìol-ghinidh *m* semen.

sìoman *m* straw rope.

sìon *m* same as **sìan²**.

Sìona *f* China.

Sìonach *m/adj* Chinaman; Chinese.

sionnach *m* fox.

sionnsar *m* (*bagpipe*) chanter.

sìor- *prefix* ever-.

sìor-mhaireannach *adj* everlasting; immortal.

sìorrachd *f* sheriffdom; county, shire.

sìorraidh *m* sheriff.

sìorraidh *adj* everlasting, eternal.

sìorraidheachd *f* eternity.

sìorram *m* same as **sìorraidh**.

sìorramachd *f* same as **sìorrachd**.

sìor-uaine *adj* evergreen.

sìos *adv* down.

siosar *f* scissors.

siosarnaich *f* hissing; whispering; rustling.

sìos 'na inntinn *adv* depressed.

sir *v* seek, search for; require.

siris, sirist *f* cherry.

siteag f dunghill, midden.

sìth[1] f peace; tranquility.

sìth[2] adj fairy.

sìthean m fairy hill.

sìtheann f venison; game.

sìtheil adj peaceable; tranquil.

sìthich v pacify.

sìthiche m fairy.

sitir f braying, neighing, whinnying.

slubhail v travel; seek; die.

slubhal f travel.

slùbhlach adj speedy; fluent; fluid.

slùcar m sugar; pl **slùcairean** sweets.

slud pron that, yonder.

sluga f jug.

sluthad (sing), **sluthadaibh** (pl) imper on you go! get on with it!

slabhraidh f chain.

slac v thrash, beat, thump; bruise, maul.

slàinte f health. • excls **slàinte!** cheers! good health! **slàinte mhath/mhòr!** good health! **air do dheagh shlàinte!** your very good health!

slaman m curds, crowdie.

slàn adj well, healthy; complete. • excl **slàn leat!** goodbye! farewell!

slànaich v heal, cure; get better.

slànaighear m (with art) **an Slànaighear** the Saviour.

slàn is fallain safe and sound.

slaod v drag, haul. • m sledge.

slaodach adj slow; long-drawn-out, boring.

slaodair m trailer.

slaod-uisge m raft.

slaoightear m rascal, rogue.

slapag f slipper.

slat f (length) yard; twig; rod; (vulg) penis, cock; spear, javelin.

slat-iasgaich m fishing rod.

slat-rìoghail f sceptre.

slat-thomhais f yardstick.

sleamhainn adj slippy, slippery.

sleamhnag f (children's) slide.

sleamhnaich v slip, slide.

sleuchd v bow down; prostate oneself.

sliabh m moor, moorland; hill.

sliasaid f thigh.

slige f (mollusc, military) shell.

slighe f path, road, track; way, route.

slinnean m shoulder.

sliob v stroke.

sliochd m descendants, lineage.

slios m side, flank.

slis f slice.

sliseag-èisg f fish slice.

slisnich v slice.

sloc, slochd m hollow; pit.

sloinneadh m surname, family name.

sluagh m people, populace, crowd; army.

sluagh-ghairm m war-cry; slogan.

sluaghmhor adj populous.

sluasaid f shovel.

slugadh m swallow, gulp; swallowing.

sluig v swallow; devour.

smachd m authority, discipline; control; rule.

smachdail adj commanding, authoritative.

smàil, smàl v (fire) put out; quench.

smal m spot, stain.

smàl v same as **smàil**.

smàladair m candle snuffers.

smàladh m extinguishing.

smalan m gloom, melancholy.

smalanach adj gloomy, melancholy.

smaoin f thought, notion, idea.

smaoinich, smaointich v think, reflect; consider.

smàrag f emerald.

's mar sin air adhart and so on.

smèid (air) v beckon (to); wave (to).

smeòrach f thrush.

smeur[1] v smear, daub; grease.

smeur[2] f blackberry, bramble.

smid f (with neg v) word, syllable.

smig, smiogaid m chin.

smior m marrow; courage, spirit, guts; manliness, strength, vigour; best/pick of.

smiorail adj strong; spirited; plucky; manly, vigorous.

smlùr v same as **smeur**[1].

smoc v (tobacco) smoke.

smocadh m smoking; **chan fhaodar smocadh** no smoking.

smuain f same as **smaoin**.

smuainich, smuaintich v same as **smaoinich**.

smuais v smash, splinter.

smugaid f spit.

smùid v smoke; smash. • f smoke, steam, vapour, fumes; drunkenness.

smùr m dust; dross.

snagan-daraich m woodpecker.

snaidhm m knot.

snàig v crawl, creep; grovel.

snaigh v hew; carve.

snàmh v swim; float. • m swimming, floating.

snasail, snasmhor adj neat, trim; elegant.

snàth m (coll) thread.

snàthad m needle.

snàthainn m (single) thread.

sneachd m snow.

snèap f turnip, swede.

snigh v drip, seep.

snìomh v spin; twist; wring.

snìomhaire m (tool) drill.

snodha-gàire m smile.

snog adj pretty; nice.

snuadh m appearance; complexion.

so- prefix -able, -ible.

sòbair adj sober.

sòbhrach f same as **seòbhrach**.

socair adj mild; tranquil, relaxed;

at peace. • *f* comfort; ease, leisure. • *excl* **socair!** take it easy!

socais *f* sock.

sochar *f* bashfulness; weakness, compliance; indulgence.

socharach *adj* bashful; weak; soft, over-indulgent.

socrach *adj* at ease; sedate, leisurely.

socraich *v* abate; assuage; settle; set, fix.

sodal *m* adulation; fawning, flattery.

so-dhèanta *adj* possible, feasible.

sòfa *f* sofa.

soilire *m* celery.

soilleir *adj* bright, clear; obvious.

soilleirich *v* brighten (up); clarify, explain.

soillse *m* light.

soillsich *v* shine; gleam.

soirbh *adj* easy.

soirbheachail *adj* successful; prosperous.

soirbhich le *v* turn out well for.

sòisealach *adj* socialist.

sòisealta *adj* social. • *fpl* **seirbhisean shòisealta** social services.

soisgeul *m* gospel.

soisgeulach *adj* evangelical.

soisgeulaiche *m* evangelist.

soitheach *m* (*sailing*) vessel; dish, container.

soitheamh *adj* gentle, good-natured.

sòlaimte *adj* solemn; ceremonious.

solair *v* supply, purvey.

solas *m* light.

sòlas *m* solace, consolation; joy.

sòlasach *adj* comforting, consoling; joyful.

solta *adj* meek, gentle.

so-lùbadh *adj* flexible, pliable.

sona *adj* happy, content.

sònraich *v* distinguish; specify, single out.

sònraichte *adj* special, particular; specific.

sop *m* wisp.

soraidh *f* farewell; greeting. • *excl* **soraidh leat!** farewell!

so-ruighinn *adj* attainable; accessible.

so-thuigsinn *adj* intelligible, comprehensible.

spàid *f* spade.

spaideil *adj* (*esp dress*) smart.

spaidirich *v* strut.

spàin *f* spoon.

spàin-mhilsein *f* dessert spoon.

Spainn *f* (*with art*) **an Spàinn** Spain.

Spàinneach, Spàinnteach *m/adj* Spaniard; Spanish.

Spàinnis *f* (*language*) Spanish.

spàirn *f* exertion, effort; struggle.

spanair *m* spanner.

spàrr[1] *v* drive, thrust.

spàrr[2] *m* joist, beam; roost.

speach *f* wasp.

speal f scythe.

spealg v smash, splinter. • f splinter, fragment.

spèll v skate. • f ice-skate.

spèis f love; affection; regard.

speuclairean mpl spectacles, glasses.

speuclairean-grèine mpl sunglasses.

speur m sky; space; pl na **speuran** the heavens.

speur-sheòladh m space travel.

speuradair m astrologer.

speuradaireachd f astrology.

speurair m spaceman, astronaut.

spìc f spike.

spìdeag f nightingale.

spìocach adj miserly, mean.

spìocaire m miser.

spìon v snatch, grab; pluck.

spionnadh m strength; energy.

spiorad m spirit, ghost; **an Spiorad Naomh** the Holy Spirit/ Ghost.

spioradail adj spiritual.

spìosradh m spice.

spìosraich v spice; embalm.

spiris f perch, roost.

spleuchd v stare, gape; squint. • m stare; squint.

spliuchan m pouch.

spòg f paw; (of clock or watch) hand; spoke.

spong m sponge.

sporan m purse; sporran.

spòrs f sport; fun.

spot m spot, stain.

spoth v castrate.

spreadh v burst; explode.

spreadhadh m explosion.

sprèidh f livestock.

sprèig v incite, urge.

sprùilleach m crumbs.

sprùilleag f crumb.

spùill v plunder, despoil.

spùinneadair m plunderer, brigand.

spùinneadair-mara m pirate, buccaneer.

spuir, spur m claw, talon.

spùt v spurt; squirt. • m spout; spurt, gush; waterfall.

sràbh m drinking straw.

srac v rip, tear.

sradag f spark.

sràid f street.

sràidearaich v stroll, saunter.

srainnsear m stranger.

srann v snore.

srann f snore; snoring.

srannartaich f snoring.

sreang f string.

sreath m row, line, rank; layer; series.

sreothart m sneeze.

sreothartaich f sneezing.

srian f bridle, rein(s); streak, stripe.

sròn f nose; ridge; point, promontory.

sròn-adharcach m rhinoceros.

srùb v spout; spurt; slurp. • m (pot, etc) spout.

srùbag f sip; snack, stroupach.

srùban m cockle.

sruth v flow, stream, run. • m stream, burn; flow; current.

stàball m stable.

stad v stop, cease; halt, pause. • m stop, end; halt, pause.

stad-phuing f (orthog) full stop.

stald f state, condition.

staldhre f stair, staircase.

stailc f (industry, etc) strike.

stàillinn f steel.

staing f difficulty, tight corner, fix.

stàirn f crashing, clattering, rumbling.

stairseach, stairsneach f threshold.

stàlt f (nation) state; (pl) **na Stàitean Aonaichte** the United States. • m **Rùnaire na' Stàite** the Secretary of State.

stàiteil adj stately.

stalc m starch.

stalcaire m fool, blockhead.

stalcaireachd f stupidity; stupid action.

stamag f stomach.

stamh m (seaweed) tangle.

stamp v stamp. • f (postage) stamp.

staoig f steak.

staoin f (the metal) tin.

steall v spout, squirt, spurt, gush. • f outpouring. spout, spurt; (fam) swig, slug.

steallair, steallaire m syringe.

stèidh f base, foundation, basis.

stèidhich v found, establish.

stèidhichte adj founded, established. • f **an Eaglais Stèidhichte** the Established Church.

stèisean m station.

stiall v stripe, streak.

stiall f stripe; tape; (of clothing) stitch, scrap.

stìopall m steeple.

stiùbhard m steward.

stiùir v steer, direct; run, manage. • f rudder, helm.

stiùireadair m steersman, helmsman.

stiùireadh m steering, directing; managing.

stob m fence post; stake; (tree) stump.

stòbha f stove.

stoc m (tree) trunk, stump; livestock; scarf, cravat.

stocainn f stocking.

stoidhle f style.

stòir, stòr v store.

stòiridh m story; humorous anecdote.

stoirm f storm.

stòl m stool.

stòlda adj sedate, staid, serious; sober.

stòr[1] m store; riches, wealth.

stòr[2] v same as **stòir**.

stòras m riches, wealth.

stòr-dàta m database.

stràc m stroke, blow; (orthog) accent.

stràic m (school, formerly) belt, tawse.

streap v climb.

streap-monaidhean f hillwalking, mountain climbing.

strì v struggle; compete. • f struggle, strife; contest.

strìoch f hyphen.

strìochag f (marking, etc) tick.

strìochd v surrender, yield; cringe.

strìopach f prostitute.

structair m structure.

struidheil adj extravagant, prodigal. • m am mac struidheil the prodigal son.

struth m/f ostrich.

stuadh f (sea) wave; (house) gable.

stuaim f abstemiousness, moderation, temperance; sobriety.

stuama adj abstemious, moderate, temperate; sober.

stuamachd f abstinence, sobriety.

stùlceach adj surly, morose.

stulg v incite, urge.

stùr m dust.

stuth m material, stuff.

sualcheantas m badge, emblem.

sualmhneach adj calm, quiet.

suain[1] v wrap, entwine.

suain[2] f sleep, slumber.

Suain f (with art) **an t-Suain** Sweden.

Suaineach m/adj Swede; Swedish.

suairc, suairce adj kind; courteous; affable.

suarach adj insignificant; petty; despicable.

suarachas m insignificance; pettiness.

suas adv up.

suath v rub, wipe.

suath ri v brush against.

sùbailte adj supple, flexible.

subh m berry.

subh-làir m strawberry.

sugan m straw rope.

sùgh v absorb; suck (up).

sùgh m juice; sap.

sùghach adj absorbent.

sùgh-measa m fruit juice.

sùghmhor adj juicy; sappy.

sùgradh m mirth, merrymaking; lovemaking.

suidh v sit (down); **suidh sìos** sit down.

suidhe m seat; sitting position. • adv 'na shuidhe adv sitting.

suidheachadh m setting, site; situation.

suidheachan m seat; stool; pew.

suidhich v seat; place; decide/agree upon;.

suidhichte adj settled, arranged; resolute; sedate, grave.

suidse f switch.

sulgeart m cheerfulness.

sùil f eye; look, glance.

sùilbhir *adj* cheerful.

sùll-chrItheach *f* quagmire.

sùlleach *adj* forward-looking, far-sighted.

sùllich *v* expect.

sulm[1] *f* regard; attention.

sulm[2] *f* (*money*) amount, sum; (*arith*) sum.

sulpear *f* supper.

suirghe, suIrIdhe *f* courting, courtship.

suIteas *m* sweet.

sùith *m* soot.

sùlaire *m* solan goose.

sult *m* fat, fatness;.

Sultain, SuItuIne *f* (*with art*) an

t-Sultain, an t-SuItuIne September.

sultmhor *adj* fat, plump; lusty, in rude health.

sumaInn *f* (*sea*) surge, swell.

sùnnd *m* cheerfulness; mood.

sùnndach *adj* cheerful, in good spirits.

Suòmach *m/adj* Finn; Finnish.

Suòmaldh *f* Finland.

sùrd *m* cheerfulness; alacrity.

sùrdag *f* jump, skip; bounce; caper.

sùrdagaIch *v* jump, skip; bounce; caper.

suth *m* embryo.

sutha *f* zoo.

T

tàbhachdach *adj* sound, substantial.

tabhaIrteach, tabhaIrtaIche *m* donor, benefactor.

tabhannaIch *v* bark. • *f* barking.

tabhartach *adj* generous, liberal; (*gram*) dative.

tabhartas *m* donation; presentation; grant.

taca *f* proximity.

tacaId *f* tack, tacket.

tacan *m* little while.

tachaIr *v* happen.

tachaIr rI *v* meet.

tachaIs *v* scratch; itch, tickle.

tachartas *m* happening; incident.

tachas *m* scratching; itching; tickling.

tachd *v* smother, choke, throttle.

tacsaIdh *m* taxi.

tadhall (aIr) *v* visit, call (on).

tadhal *m* visit; (*sport*) goal.

tagaIr *v* claim; (*legal*) plead, argue.

tagh *v* choose; elect, vote in.

taghadh *m* choosing, choice; election.

taghta *adj* chosen; elected; (*fam*) great! perfect!

tagradh *m* claim; (*legal*) plea.

taibhse *m/f* ghost.

taibhsearachd *f* second sight.

taic, taice *f* contact; proximity; prop; (*moral and phys*) support; patronage

taic airgid *f* (*fin*) support, backing.

taicell *adj* supporting, supportive.

taidhir *f* tyre.

taifeld *m* bowstring.

taigeis *f* haggis.

taigh *m* house. • *adv* **aig an taigh** at home. • *m/f* **fear/bean an taighe** the landlord/lady.

taigh beag *m* toilet.

taigh-bìdh *m* café, restaurant.

taigh-cluiche *m* theatre.

taigh comhairle *m* council house.

taigh-dhealbh *m* cinema.

taigh-eiridinn *m* hospital.

taigh-grùide *m* brewery.

taigh na galla do X! *excl* damn X! sod X!

taigh-nighe *m* wash-house, laundry.

taigh-òsda *m* hotel; inn, pub.

taigh-tasgaidh *m* museum.

tailceas *m* contempt, disdain.

tailceasach *adj* reproachful; contemptuous.

tàilleasg *m* chess; backgammon.

tàillear *m* tailor.

taing *f* thanks, gratitude. • *excl* **taing dhut/dhuibh** thank you.

taingeil *adj* thankful, grateful.

tàir¹ *v* escape, make off.

tàir² *f* contempt, disparagement.

tairbhe *f* advantage, benefit; profit.

tairbheach *adj* advantageous, beneficial; profitable.

tairbhich *v* benefit, profit, gain.

tàirell *adj* contemptible.

tairg *v* propose, offer; bid.

tairgse *f* offer, bid.

tàirneanach *m* thunder.

tairsgeir *f* peat iron.

tais *adj* damp, moist, humid.

taisbean *v* show, reveal; display, exhibit; demonstrate.

taisbeanach *adj* clear, distinct; (*gram*) indicative.

taisbeanadh *m* display, exhibition; demonstration.

taisbean-lann *f* art gallery; exhibition hall.

taise, taiseachd *f* moisture, damp, dampness, humidity.

taisg *v* store; hoard.

taisich *v* dampen, moisten.

taitinn (ri) *v* please.

taitneach *adj* agreeable, pleasant.

taitneas *m* pleasantness; pleasure.

tàladh *m* attraction; allurement; soothing, calming; lullaby.

talaich *v* complain, grumble.

tàlaidh *v* attract; allure; tempt; calm; sing/rock to sleep.

tàlaidheach *adj* attractive.

talamh *m* earth, soil; land; (*with art*) **an Talamh** the Earth.

tàlann *m* talent, gift.

tàlantach *adj* talented, gifted.

talla *m* hall; **talla a' bhaile** the village/town hall.

talmhaidh *adj* earthly.

tàmailt *f* disgrace, shame; insult.

tàmailteach *adj* scandalous, shameful; insulting.

tàmailtich *v* insult.

tamall *m* while, time.

tàmh[1] *v* dwell, live.

tàmh[2] *m* rest, peace; inactivity, idleness; leisure.

tana *adj* thin, runny; shallow; sparse.

tanaich *v* thin.

tancair *m* tanker.

tannasg *m* ghost.

taobh *m* side; way, direction.

taobh an teine *m* fireside.

taobh-duilleige *m* page; **taobh-duilleige a dhà** page two.

taobh ri taobh *adv* side by side.

taois *f* dough.

taom *v* pour (out), flow (out); empty; bale.

tap *f* (*water*) tap.

tapadh *m* handiness, smartness; willingness.

tapadh leat/leibh! *excl* thank you!

tapag *f* slip of the tongue.

tapaidh *adj* clever, quick; sturdy, manly; active.

tarbh *m* bull.

tarbh-nathrach *m* dragonfly.

tarcais *m* contempt, disdain.

tarcaiseach *adj* reproachful; contemptuous.

targaid *f* target; shield.

tàrmaich *v* beget; breed; propagate; produce.

tàrr *v* escape, make off.

tarrag *f* (*joinery*) nail.

tarraing *v* draw; drag, pull; attract.

tarraing à *v* tease, kid.

tarraingeach *adj* attractive.

tarraing gu *v* approach.

tarrang *f* same as **tarrag**.

tarsainn *adv* across, over.

tarsainn air *prep* across, over.

tart *m* thirst.

tartmhor *adj* thirsty, dry.

tasgadh *m* storehouse; museum; investment.

tasgaidh *m* store, hoard.

tastan *m* shilling.

tàth *v* join together; glue; cement; weld; solder.

tathaich *v* frequent, haunt; visit.

tathaich air *v* call on.

tàthan *m* hyphen.

tè *f* one (*f*); woman.

teachd *defective v* come; fit, be contained. • *m* arrival, coming.

teachdaire *m* messenger; missionary.

teachdaireachd *f* message; mission, commission.

teachd-an-tir *m* living, livelihood.

teachd-a-steach *m* entry, entrance; income.

teadhair *f* tether.

teagaisg *v* teach, instruct.

teagamh *m* doubt, uncertainty.

teagamhach *adj* doubtful, doubting; sceptical.

teagasg *m* teaching.

teaghlach *m* family.

teallach *m* hearth, fireside; fireplace.

teallach ceàrdaich *m* forge.

teampall *m* temple.

teanchair *m* clamp, vice; pincers; tongs.

teanga *f* tongue; (*occas*) language.

teann[1] *v* move, go, proceed.

teann[2] *adj* tight, tense; firm, secure; strict, severe.

teannachair *m same as* **teanchair**.

teannaich *v* tighten, tense; constrict, squeeze.

teann air[1] *v* approach; begin.

teann air[2] *prep* close to.

teann ri *v* begin (to), set about.

teanta *f* tent.

tèarainte *adj* safe, secure.

tèarainteachd *f* safety, security.

tearc *adj* scant, scarce, few.

tèarmann *m* protection; refuge, sanctuary.

teàrr *f* tar, pitch.

teas *m* heat.

teasach *f* fever.

teasaich *v* heat (up).

teasairg *v* save, rescue.

teas-meadhan *m* dead centre.

teas-mheidh *f* thermometer.

teasraig *v same as* **teasairg**.

teatha *f* (*drink*) tea.

tè bheag *f* nip, dram.

teich *v* flee, abscond; desert.

teicheadh *m* running away; desertion.

teicneolach *adj* technical, technological.

teicneolaiche *m* technician; technologist.

teicneolas *m* technology.

teicneolas fiosrachaidh *m* information technolology, IT.

teignigeach *adj* technical.

teine *m* fire.

teinntean *m* hearth, fireplace.

teip *f* tape; cassette.

teip clàraidh *f* recording tape.

teip-tomhais *f* measuring tape.

teirinn *v* come down; go down; climb down; dismount; alight, descend.

teisteanas *m* testimony, evidence; certificate, diploma; testimonial.

teisteanas breith *m* birth certificate.

telebhisean *m* television.

teòclaid *f/adj* chocolate.

teodhachd *f* temperature.

teòthaich *v* warm (up); warm to, take to.

teòma *adj* expert, skilful; ingenious.

teòth ri *v* take to.

teth *adj* hot.

teud *m* (harp, etc) string.

tha *present tense of v* **bith**.

tha amharas agam *v* I suspect.

tha an t-eagal orm I'm frightened.

tha dùil agam air X *v* I expect X.

tha eagal orm I'm afraid, I'm sorry to say.

tha fallas orm *v* I'm sweating.

tha feum agam air X *v* I need X.

tha fios *adv* of course, naturally.

tha fios agam *v* I know.

tha gràin agam air *v* I hate him/it.

thàinig *past tense of v* **thig**.

thairis *prep pron* over him, over it (m). • *adv* across, over; beyond.

thairis air *prep* across, over; beyond.

thairte *prep pron* over her, over it (f).

thall *adv* over there, over yonder.

thalla (sing), **thallaibh** (pl) *imper* go, off you go.

thall 's a bhos *adv* here and there; hither and thither.

tha mi an dòchas *v* I hope.

tha mi an dùil *v* I hope, I expect.

tha mi duilich! I'm sorry!

tha mi gu dòigheil! I'm fine!

thar *prep* across, over; beyond; more than.

thar a chèile *adv* in confusion; at loggerheads.

tharad *prep pron* over you (sing).

tharaibh *prep pron* over you (pl).

tharainn *prep pron* over us.

tharam *prep pron* over me.

thar mo chomais *adv* beyond my ability.

tharta *prep pron* over them.

tha smùid orm I'm drunk.

tha ùidh agam ann *v* I'm interested in it.

theab *defective v* nearly; **theab mi tuiteam** I nearly fell.

theagamh *conj* perhaps, maybe.

thèid *future tense of v* **rach**.

thig *v* come; approach; arrive.

thig air adhart *v* make progress.

thig am bàrr *v* surface.

thig am follais *v* come to light.

thig an uachdar *v* surface; manifest itself.

thig a-steach air *v* occur to.

thig còmhla *v* congregate, unite.

thig do *v* (clothes, etc) suit; please, suit.

thig gu inbhe *v* grow up.

thig ri *v* suit.

thoir *v* give; bring; take.

thoir adhradh *v* worship.

thoir air *v* make, force.

thoir air èiginn *v* rape.

thoir air falbh *v* abduct.

thoir air gabhail *v* lease.

thoir am bith *v* bring into being/existence.

thoir am follais *v* bring to light.

thoir an aire *v* pay attention; take care.

thoir an car à *v* cheat.

thoir an t-siteag ort! *v* get out! outside!

thoir bàrr airr *v* beat, cap, top.

thoir breith *v* pass judgement.

thoir bualdh air *v* defeat; influence, affect.

thoir creideas do *v* trust; believe.

thoir culreadh do *v* invite.

thoir do chasan leat! get the hell out of here!

thoir dùbhlan do *v* challenge; defy.

thoir facal air *v* swear to.

thoir flanals *v* give evidence, testify.

thoir flos air *v* send for.

thoir gealladh *v* promise; vow.

thoir gu bull *v* achieve; see through.

thoir gu stad *v* bring to an end/a stop.

thoir guth air *v* mention.

thoir lonnsalgh air *v* attack, assault; have a shot/an attempt at.

thoir na bulnn asam *v* take to my heels.

thoir oldhirp (air) *v* make an attempt (at).

thoir rabhadh do *v* warn; alert.

thoir seachad *v* give, give away.

thoir seachad òrald *v* give/deliver a speech.

thoir sùll air *v* have a look at.

thoir tairgse (air) *v* make an offer/a bid (for).

thoir tarralng air *v* mention, refer to.

thoir tualream air *v* guess at.

thoir urram do *v* respect.

thoir uspag *v* (*horse, etc*) start, shy.

thoir X orm *v* take myself off to X.

thu *pers pron sing* you.

thuca *prep pron* to them.

thug *past tense of v* **thoir**.

thugad *prep pron* to you (*sing*).

thugalbh *prep pron* to you (*pl*).

thugalnn *prep pron* to us.

thugam *prep pron* to me.

thulce *prep pron* to her, to it (*f*).

thulge *prep pron* to him, to it (*m*).

thun *prep* to, towards, up to.

thulrt *past tense of v* **abair**.

tì *f* (*drink*) tea.

tlamhaidh *adj* melancholy; plaintive.

tibhre *m* dimple.

tlcead *f* ticket.

tìde *m/f* time; weather; (*with art*) **an tìde, an tìde-mhara** the tide. • *excl* **bha a thìde algel** he took his time!

tldsear *m* teacher.

tlgh *m* house.

tighearna *m* lord; laird, landowner; (*with art*) **an Tlghearna** the Lord, God. • *excl* **a Thlghearnal** (Oh) Lord!

Tìleach *m/adj* Icelander; Icelandic.

tilg *v* throw; throw up; (*weapon*) fire.

tilg air *v* accuse of, reproach with.

tilg smugaid *v* spit.

till *v* return, come/go back.

tilleadh *m* return; returning.

tìm *f* time.

timcheall[1] *adv* round.

timcheall[2] *adv/prep* round, around, about.

timcheall air *prep* round, around, about.

timcheallan *m* roundabout.

tinn *adj* ill, sick.

tinneas *m* illness, disease.

tinneas cridhe *m* heart disease.

tinneas mara *m* seasickness.

tinneas na dighe *m* alcoholism.

tiodhlac *m* gift, present.

tiodhlacadh *m* burial, funeral.

tiodhlaic *v* give, donate; bury.

tiomnadh *m* will, testament; bequest; **an Seann Tiomnadh** the Old Testament; **an Tiomnadh Nuadh** the New Testament.

tiomnaich *v* bequeathe, leave.

tiompan *m* cymbal.

tional *v* assemble, congregate; (*stock*) gather.

tionndaidh *v* turn.

tionnsgail *v* devise, invent.

tionnsgal *m* inventiveness; invention.

tionnsgalach *adj* inventive.

tionnsgalair *m* inventor.

tioraidh! *excl* cheerio!

tioram *adj* dry; thirsty.

tiormachd *f* dryness; drought.

tiormadair *m* dryer.

tiormaich *v* dry; dry up.

tiota *m* second, instant.

tiotag *f* instant, tick.

tiotal *m* title.

tiotan *m* second, instant.

tìr *m/f* land; country; area, region; ground, landscape.

tìr-eòlas *m* geography.

tìr mòr *m* mainland; continent.

tiugainn! *imper* come along! let us go!

tiugh *adj* thick, dense; slow-witted.

tighead *m* thickness; density.

tlachd *f* pleasure, enjoyment; affection, liking.

tlachdmhor *adj* pleasant; likeable.

tnù *m* envy; malice.

tobar *m/f* spring, well.

tobhta *m/f* ruin(s).

tocasaid *f* barrel, hogshead.

tòchd *m* stink.

tochradh *m* dowry.

todha *m* hoe.

todhaig *v* hoe.

todhair *v* manure; bleach.

todhar *m* manure, dung.

tog *v* raise, lift; pick up; build; (*family, etc*) bring up.

togair *v* wish for; covet; **ma thogras tu** if you like.

togalach *m* building.

tog dealbhan *v* take photos.

tog ort *excl* stir your stumps! get a move on!

togradh *m* wish, desire.

toibheum *m* blasphemy.

toigh *adj* pleasing; **is toigh leam X** I like X.

toil *f* will.

toileach *adj* willing; content; glad.

toileachas *m* contentment; gladness.

toilich *v* please, content.

toilichte *adj* happy; pleased, satisfied.

toil-inntinn *f* (*mental*) pleasure; peace of mind.

toill *v* deserve.

toillteanach (air) *adj* worthy (of).

tòimhseachan *m* puzzle; riddle.

tòimhseachan-tarsainn *m* crossword puzzle.

toinisg *f* common sense.

toinisgeil *adj* sensible; intelligent.

toinn *v* twist, wind, twine.

tòir *f* pursuit.

toirm *f* noise, din.

toirmeasg *m* forbidding; prohibition.

toirmeasgach *adj* prohibitive.

toirmisg *v* forbid, prohibit.

toiseach *m* start, beginning; vanguard; (*vehicle, etc*) front.

tòiseachadh *m* beginning.

tòiseachadh ùr *m* fresh start.

tòisich (air/ri) *v* start (to).

tòisich as ùr *v* start afresh.

tolt *f* steam; smoke.

toitean *m* cigarette.

toll *v* bore, pierce, perforate; dig a hole. • *m* hole, pit, hollow; (*vulg*) arsehole.

tolladh-chluasan *m* ear-piercing.

tolltach *adj* full of holes.

toll-tòine *m* anus.

tolman *m* knowe, knoll.

tom *m* hillock; thicket.

tomaltach *adj* sizeable, bulky; burly.

tombaca *m* tobacco.

tomhais *v* measure; calculate; guess; survey.

tomhas *m* measuring; dimension; calculation; guess, guessing; surveying.

tomhas-teas *m* thermometer.

tòn *f* anus, rectum; (*fam*) arse, bum, backside; (*building, etc*) back.

tonn *m/f* wave.

tonna *m* ton, tonne.

tonn teasa *m* heat wave.

torach *adj* fruitful, productive; fertile, fecund; pregnant; (*egg, etc*) fertilised.

torachadh *m* fertilisation.

torachas *m* fertility.

toradh *m* produce, fruit(s); result, effect.

toraich v fertilise.

torc m boar.

torman m murmur, drone, hum; rumble.

tòrr m heap, mound, hill; (fam) lots, loads.

tòrradh m burial, funeral.

tosd m silence.

tosdach adj silent, quiet.

tosgaire m ambassador; envoy.

tosgaireachd f embassy.

tractar m tractor.

trafaig f traffic.

tràghadh m draining; subsiding; (car) exhaust.

tràigh¹ v drain, empty; subside, settle; ebb.

tràigh² f shore, beach; tide.

tràill m/f slave; drudge; addict.

tràilleachd f slavery; addiction.

tràillich v enslave.

traisg v fast.

tràlair m trawler.

trang adj busy.

trannsa f corridor, passage.

trasg f fast, fasting.

tràth¹ adv early.

tràth² m time, season; while, period; (gram) tense.

tràth bìdh m mealtime.

tràthach m hay.

treabh v plough.

trealaich f jumble; odds and ends, stuff, paraphernalia; trash, rubbish; (pl) **trealaichean** luggage, baggage.

trèan v train.

trèana f train.

treas adj third.

treas deug adj thirteenth.

trèig v leave; abandon; relinquish.

trèigte adj abandoned, deserted.

treis f while, time.

treiseag f short while.

treòrachadh m guiding, leading; guidance.

treòraich v guide, lead.

treubh f tribe.

treud m flock, herd; group; (derog) crowd, gang.

treun adj strong, stout. • f **treun a neirt** his prime.

trì n/adj three.

triall (do) v travel, journey (to).

trian m third.

triath m lord.

tric adj/adv frequent(ly).

trì-cheàrnag f triangle.

trìd-shoilleir adj transparent.

trioblaid f trouble.

trìthead m thirty.

triubhas m trews, trousers.

triùir m/f (people) three, threesome.

triuthach f (with art) **an triuthach** whooping cough.

tro prep through.

trobhad (sing), **trobhadaibh** (pl) imper come here, come to me; come along.

tròcair f mercy.

tròcaireach adj merciful.

trod *m* quarrel, row; quarreling.

trolch *m/f* dwarf.

troid *v* quarrel, squabble, fight.

troigh *f* (*measure*) foot.

troighean *m* pedal.

troimh *prep* same as **tro**.

troimh chèile *adv* at loggerheads; in confusion; untidy.

troimhe *prep pron* through him, through it (*m*).

troimhpe *prep pron* through her, through it (*f*).

trom *adj* heavy; serious; important; depressed; pregnant.

tromalach *f* preponderance, majority.

trombaid *f* trumpet.

tromhad *prep pron* through you (*sing*).

tromhaibh *prep pron* through you (*pl*).

tromhainn *prep pron* through us.

tromham *prep pron* through me.

tromhpa *prep pron* through them.

trom-laighe *m/f* nightmare.

trosg *m* cod.

trotan *m* trot; trotting.

truacanta *adj* compassionate, humane.

truacantas *m* compassion, pity.

truagh *adj* sad; poor, pitiable, abject.

truaghan *m* wretch. • *excl* **a thruaghain!** poor man/creature!

truaill *v* pollute; corrupt, pervert; defile, profane.

truas *m* pity, compassion.

truileis *f* rubbish, junk.

truimead *m* heaviness.

truinnsear *m* plate.

truis, trus *v* bundle, roll up; (*skirt, etc*) tuck up; (*stock*) gather.

trusgan *m* clothes, clothing.

tuagh *f* axe.

tuagh-chatha *f* battleaxe, Lochaber axe.

tuainealach *adj* dizzy, giddy.

tuainealaich *f* dizziness, vertigo.

tuaiream *f* guess, conjecture.

tuaireamach *adj* random, arbitrary.

tuairisgeul *m* description.

tuar *m* complexion, hue; appearance.

tuarasdal *f* salary, wage(s); stipend; fee.

tuasaid *f* quarrel; scrap, tussle.

tuath[1] *adj/f* northern, north.

tuath[2] *f* peasantry; tenantry.

tuath air *prep* north of.

tuathal *adj* widdershins; anticlockwise; awry, wrong.

tuathanach *m* farmer.

tuathanachas *m* farming.

tuathanas *m* farm.

tubaist *f* accident; mishap.

tubhailte *f* towel.

tubhailte-sholthichean *f* tea-towel.

tùch *v* make hoarse; smother; extinguish.

tùchadh *m* hoarseness.

tùchanach *adj* hoarse.

tudan *m* stack; turd.

tugh *v* thatch.

tughadh *m* thatch.

tulg *v* understand.

tulgse *f* comprehension; intelligence; sense, judgement.

tulgseach *adj* understanding; intelligent; sensible.

tull *f* flood, deluge.

tuilleadh *m* more, additional; tuilleadh 's a chòir more than enough.

tuinich *v* settle; dwell.

Tuirc *m* (*with art*) an Tuirc Turkey.

tuireadh *m* mourning; lament.

tùirse *f* sorrow.

tuiseal *m* (*gram*) case.

tuislich *v* stumble, slip, trip.

tuit *v* fall.

tuit do *v* happen to, befall.

tuiteamach *adj* accidental, chance.

tuiteamas *m* occurence, event; incident; accident.

tulach *m* hillock.

tulg *v* rock, lurch, swing, toss.

tulgach *adj* rocking, lurching, swinging, tossing; rocky, unsteady.

tulgadh *m* rocking, lurching, swinging, tossing.

tum *v* dip, immerse; steep.

tunnag *f* duck.

tur *adj* whole, complete. • *adv* gu tur completely, altogether.

tùr[1] *m* understanding; sense.

tùr[2] *m* tower.

turadh *m* dry weather/spell.

turald *f* tower; turret.

tùrail *adj* sensible.

turas *m* journey; trip; tour, touring; time.

turasachd *f* tourism.

turas-mara *m* voyage.

turas-tillidh *m* return journey.

Turcach *m/adj* Turk; Turkish.

tursa *m* standing stone.

tùrsach *adj* sorrowful.

tùs *m* beginning, origin.

tùsanach *adj* aborigene.

tùthag *f* patch.

U

uabhar *m* pride, haughtiness, arrogance.

uachdar *m* surface; top; cream; upland.

uachdarach *adj* upper; superior; superficial.

uachdaran *m* superior; landowner, laird.

uachdar-fhiaclan *m* toothpaste.

uaibh *prep pron* from you (*pl*).

uaibhreach *adj* proud; haughty, arrogant.

uaibhreas *m* pride; haughtiness, arrogance.

uaigh *f* grave.

uaigneach *adj* lonely, solitary; secluded; private, secret.

uaimh *f* cave.

uaine *adj* green.

uainn *prep pron* from us.

uaipe *prep pron* from her, from it (*f*).

uaipear *m* botcher, bungler.

uair *f* hour; (*clock*) time; time, occasion. • *adv* once.

uaireadair *m* timepiece, clock; watch.

uaireadair-gloinne *m* hourglass.

uaireadair-grèine *m* sundial.

uaireannan *adv* sometimes.

uairiginn *adv* some time.

uair is uair *adv* time and time again.

uair no uaireiginn *adv* some time or other.

uair sam bith *adv* any time.

uaisle *f* nobility, gentility.

uaithe *prep pron* from him, from it (*m*).

uallach *m* load, burden; onus, responsibility; stress, worry.

uam *prep pron* from me.

uamhann *m* dread, horror.

uamhas *m* dread, horror, terror; atrocity.

uamhasach *adj/adv* dreadful(ly), awful(ly), terrible, terribly.

uamhasach fhèin math *adv* (*fam*) wonderful, brilliant.

uan *m* lamb.

uapa *prep pron* from them.

uasal *adj* noble, aristocratic; genteel. • *m* gentleman; (*pl with art*) **na h-uaislean** the nobility, the aristocracy.

uat *prep pron* from you (*sing*).

ubhal *m* apple.

ubhalghort *m* orchard.

uchd *m* breast, bosom; lap.

uchd-leanabh *m* adopted child.

uchd-mhacaich *v* adopt.

ud *adj* that, yonder.

ud ud! *excl* tut tut! now now!

uèir *f* wire.

ugan *m* chest area.

ugh *m* egg.

ughach *m* oval. • *adj* oval.

ughagan *m* custard.

ùghdar *m* author.

ùghdarras *m* authority; (*govt*) **ùghdarras ionadail** local authority.

ughlann *f* ovary.

uibhir *f* number; amount, quantity; **na h-uibhir de** a certain amount of; such a lot of; **uibhir eile** as much again.

uibhir ri *prep* as much as.

Uibhist *m* Uist.

Uibhisteach *m/adj* from Uist.

ùidh *f* hope; fondness; interest.

uidh *f* step; gradation; journey; **uidh air n-uidh** step by step, gradually.

uidheam *f* equipment, tackle, gear; furnishings, trappings; harness; rigging.

uidheamaich *v* equip, fit out; get ready.

uile *adj/adv* all, every; fully, completely; **a h-uile** every. • *npl* **na h-uile** everybody.

uilleann *f* angle; corner; elbow.

uilebheist *m* monster.

uile-chumhachdach *adj* all-powerful, omnipotent.

uile fhiosrach *adj* all-knowing.

uile gu lèir *adv* altogether, completely.

ùilleach *adj* oily.

uilleagan *m* spoilt brat.

uillinich *v* jostle, elbow.

uime *prep pron* about him, about it (*m*).

uimpe *prep pron* about her, about it (*f*).

ùine *f* time; while; (*pl fam*) **ùineachan** (**is ùineachan**) ages (and ages).

uinneag *f* window.

uinnean *m* onion.

uinnsean *m* (*tree*) ash.

ùir *f* soil, earth.

uircean *m* piglet.

uiread *f* a certain amount/quantity; **na h-uiread** such a lot; **uiread eile** as much again; **uiread ri** as much as. • *adv* (*sums*) times, multiplied by.

uireasbhach *adj* needy; lacking. • *m* needy person.

uireasbhaidh *f* indigence; lack, need; shortage.

uirsgeul *m* fable, legend, myth; fiction.

uirsgeulach *adj* legendary; fictional.

uiseag *f* skylark.

uisge *m* water; rain; **tha an t-uisge ann** it's raining.

uisge-beatha *m* whisky.

uisge-dìonach *adj* waterproof, watertight.

uisge na stiùireach *m* (*of boat, etc*) wake.

uisgich *v* water.

ulaidh *f* treasure; precious object.

ulbhag *f* large stone, boulder.

ulfhart *m* howl, howling.

ullaich *v* prepare; provide.

ullamh *adj* ready; handy; finished.

ultach *m* load; armful; bundle.

umad *prep pron* about you (*sing*).

umaibh *prep pron* about you (*pl*).

ùmaidh *m* blockhead, dolt, fool.

umainn *prep pron* about us.

umam *prep pron* about me.

umha *m* bronze.

umhail, umhal *adj* humble; lowly; obedient; obsequious.

ùmhlachd *f* humbleness; lowliness; obedience; obsequiousness; bow.

ùmhlaich *v* humble; humiliate.

umpa *prep pron* about them.

Ungair *f* (*with art*) **an Ungair** Hungary.

Ungaireach *m*/*adj* Hungarian.

ùnnlagh *m* fine.

ùnnsa *m* ounce.

ùpag *f* jostle, jab.

ùpraid *f* uproar; confusion; dispute.

ùpraideach *adj* rowdy, unruly.

ùr *adj* new; recent; fresh.

ur *poss adj* your.

ùrachadh *m* renewal; renovation; change.

ùraich *v* renew; renovate; refresh.

urchair *f* shot.

urchair gunna *f* gun-shot.

urchasg *m* antidote.

ùrlar *m* floor.

ùrnaigh *f* prayer; praying; **Urnaigh an Tighearna** the Lord's Prayer.

ùr-nodha *adj* brand new; up-to-date.

urra *f* person; authority; responsibility.

urrainn *f* power, ability.

urram *m* respect; honour.

urramach *adj* honourable; honorary; (*with art*) (*minister*) **an t-Urramach X** the Reverend X.

urras *m* guarantee, surety; bond; bail; insurance; (*fund, etc*) trust.

ursainn *f* prop, support; jamb.

ursainn chatha *f* (*warrior*) champion.

usgar *m* jewel.

uspag *f* (*horse, etc*) start, shy.

ùth *m* udder.

English-Gaelic Dictionary

A

abandon *v* tréig.
abate *v* lùghdaich.
abbey *n* abaid *f*.
abbot *n* aba *m*.
abbreviate *v* giorraich.
abdicate *v* leig dhe.
abdication *n* leigeil dhe *m*.
abdomen *n* balg *m*.
abduct *v* thoir air falbh.
abet *v* cuidich.
abhor *v* is lugha air.
abhorrence *n* gràin.
abide *v* fuirich.
abject *adj* truagh; dìblidh.
ability *n* comas *m*.
able *adj* comasach.
able-bodied *adj* fallain; corp-làidir.
abnormal *adj* mì-ghnàthach.
abnormality *n* mì-ghnàthas *m*.
aboard *adv* air bòrd.
abode *n* àite còmnaidh *m*.
abolish *v* cuir às do.
abolition *n* cur às *m*
abominable *adj* gràineil.
aborigine *n* prìomh neach-àiteach-aidh *m*.
abortion *n* breith an-abaich *f*.
abound *v* bi lìonmhor.
about *adv* timcheall; mun cuairt. • *prep* mu; mu dheidhinn; mu thimcheall; mun cuairt air; tim-cheall air. • *pron* **about her** uimpe; **about him, it** uime; **about me** umam; **about them** umpa; **about us** umainn; **about you** (*sing*) umad; **about you** (*pl*) umaibh;
above *adv* shuas; gu h-àrd. • *prep* os cionn.
abrade *v* sgrìobaich.
abridge *v* giorraich.
abridged *adj* giorraichte.
abroad *adv* thall thairis.
abrupt *adj* cas; aithghearr.
abruptness *n* caise *f*.
abscess *n* niosgaid *f*.
abscond *v* teich, teich air falbh.
absence *n* neo-làthaireachd *f*.
absent *adj* nach eil an làthair.
absent-minded *adj* cian-aireach-al.
absent oneself *v* dìochuimh-neach cùm air falbh.
absolve *v* saor; sgaoil.
absolute *adj* iomlan; làn.
absolutely *adv* gu h-iomlan.
absolution *n* saoradh, fuasgladh *m*.
absorb *v* sùgh, deoghail.
absorbent *adj* sùghach.
abstain *v* na buin (ri).
abstemious *adj* stuama.
abstinence *n* stuamachd *f*.

abstracted *adj* beachdail.

abstract *n* às-tharraing *f*.

abstract *v* às-tharraing, tarraing à.

absurd *adj* gòrach.

absurdity *n* gòraiche *f*.

abundance *n* pailteas *m*.

abundant *adj* pailt.

abuse[1] *n* mì-ghnàthachadh *m*; (*verbal*) càin-eadh *f*.

abuse[2] *v* mì-ghnàthaich; (*verbally*) càin.

abysmal *adj* uabhasach.

abyss *n* àibheis *m*.

academic *adj* sgoileireach. • *n* oilthigheach *m*.

academy *n* àrd-sgoil *f*.

accelerate *v* luathaich, greas.

acceleration *n* luathachadh, greasad *m*.

accelerator *n* inneal-luathach-aidh *m*.

accent *n* blas *m*.

accept *v* gabh.

acceptable *adj* furasda ghabhail.

access *n* inntrigeadh *m*.

accessible *adj* fosgailte.

accident *n* tubaist *f*.

accidental *adj* tubaisteach.

accommodate *v* gabh.

accommodation *n* rùm *m*.

accompaniment *n* compàirt *f*.

accompanist *n* compàirtiche *m*.

accomplice *n* fear-cuideachaidh *m*.

accomplish *v* coimhlion, thoir gu buil.

accomplished *adj* coimhlionta, deas.

accord *n* aonta, co-chòrdadh *m*.

accordion *n* bocsa-ciùil *m*.

according to *adv* a-rèir.

accordingly *adv* mar sin.

account *n* cùnntas, tuairisgeul *m*. • *v* thoir cùnntas air.

accountancy *n* cùnntasachd *f*.

accountant *n* cùnntasair *m*.

accounts book *n* leabhar-cùnntais *m*.

accumulate *v* cruinnich.

accumulation *n* co-chruinneach-adh *m*.

accuracy *n* cruinneas *m*.

accurate *adj* cruinn, grinn.

accusation *n* casaid *f*.

accuse *v* dèan casaid.

accustom *v* gnàthaich.

accustomed *adj* gnàthach; àbh-aist.

ace *n* an t-aon *m*.

acerbic *adj* geur.

acerbity *n* goirte *f*.

ache *n* goirteas, cràdh *m*.

achieve *v* coimhlion.

achievement *n* euchd *m*.

acid *adj* searbh; geur.

acidity *n* searbhachd *f*.

acknowledge *v* aidich.

acknowledgement *n* aideachadh *m*.

acoustic *adj* fuaimneach.

acoustics *n* fuaimearrachd *f*.

acquaintance *n* fear-eòlais *m*.

acquainted adj eòlach.

acquiesce v aontaich.

acquire v faigh, buannaich.

acquit v fuasgail.

acre n acaire m.

across adv tarsainn, thairis.
• prep tarsainn air, thairis air, thar.

act n gnìomh m; (play) earran f; achd. • v obraich, dèan gnìomh; cluich.

action n gnìomh m.

active adj deas, èasgaidh; spreigeach.

activity n gnìomhachd f.

actor n cleasaiche, actair m.

actress n bana-chleasaiche, bana-actair f.

actual adj dearbh, fìor.

acute adj dian, geur.

adapt v fàs suas ri, dèan freagar-rach.

adaptable adj freagarrach.

add v cuir ri, meudaich, leasaich.

adder n nathair f.

addict n tràill m/f.

addicted adj fo bhuaidh.

addiction n tràilleachd f.

addition n meudachadh, leasach-adh m.

additional adj a bharrachd, a thu-illeadh.

address n seòladh m; (oration) òraid f. • v cuir seòladh air; dèan òraid ri.

adequate adj iomchaidh.

adhere v lean.

adherent n fear leanmhainn m.

adhesive n stuth leanmhainn m.

adjacent adj dlùth.

adjective n buadhair m.

adjudication n breitheamhnas m.

adjust v ceartaich, rèitich.

adjustable adj so-rèitichte.

administer v riaghlaich.

administration n riaghladh m.

administrative adj riaghlach.

administrator n fear-riaghlaidh m.

admirable adj ionmholta.

admiration n meas m.

admire v tha meas air.

admissible adj ceadaichte.

admission n cead m; (confes-sion) aideachadh m.

admit v leig a steach; (confess) aidich.

ado n othail f.

adolescence n òigeachd f.

adolescent n òigear m.

adopt v uchd-mhacaich.

adoption n uchd-mhacachd f.

adore v trom-ghràdhaich.

adorn v sgeadaich.

adrift adj leis an t-sruth.

adult adj inbheach. • n inbheach m.

adulterate v truaill.

adulteration n truailleadh m.

adulterer n adhaltraiche m.

adultery n adhaltranas m.

advance n dol air adhart m; (fi-

nancial) eàrlas *m*. • *v* rach air thoiseach; (*financial*) thoir eàrlas.

advanced *adj* adhartach.

advancement *n* àrdachadh *m*.

advantage *n* tairbhe, buannachd *f*.

advantageous *adj* tairbheach.

adventure *n* tachartas *m*.

adventurous *adj* dàna.

adverb *n* co-ghnìomhair *m*.

adverse *adj* an aghaidh.

adversity *n* cruaidh-chas *f*.

advertise *v* thoir sanas.

advertisement *n* sanas, sanas-reic *m*.

advice *n* comhairle *f*.

advise *v* comhairlich.

adviser *n* comhairleach *m*.

advocacy *n* tagradh *m*.

advocate *n* fear-tagraidh *m*.

advocate *v* tagair.

aerial *n* aer-ghath *m*.

aeronaut *n* speur-sheòladair *m*.

aeroplane *n* pleuna *f*, itealan *m*.

affable *adj* suairce.

affair *n* gnothach *m*.

affect *v* drùidh air; (*let on*) leig air.

affection *n* gaol *m*.

affectionate *adj* gaolach.

affinity *n* dàimh *m/f*.

affirm *v* dearbh, daingnich.

affirmative *adj* aontach.

aflict *v* goirtich, sàraich.

affliction *n* doilgheas *m*.

affluence *n* beairteas *m*.

affluent *adj* beairteach.

afford *v* ruig air.

affront *v* maslaich.

afloat *adj* air fleòdradh.

afoot *adj* air chois; air bhonn.

aforementioned *adj* roimh-ainmichte.

afraid *adj* fo eagal, eagalach.

afresh *adv* às ùr, a-rithist.

Africa˙*n* Afraga *f*.

African *adj* Afraganach.

after *adv* an dèidh làimhe. • *prep* an dèidh.

afternoon *n* feasgar, tràth-nòin *m*.

afterthought *n* ath-smuain *f*..

again *adv* a-rithist.

against *prep* an aghaidh.

age *n* aois *f*. • *v* fàs aosda.

aged *adj* sean, aosda.

agency *n* ionadachd *f*.

agent *n* fear-ionaid *m*; dòigh *m*.

aggravate *v* antromaich.

aggression *n* (*phys*) ionnsaigh *m*; (*mental*) miann *m*.

aggressive *adj* ionnsaigheach.

agile *adj* lùthmhor.

agitate *v* gluais.

agitation *n* gluasad *m*.

ago *adv* air ais.

agog *adv* air bhiod.

agonise *v* bi an ioma-chomhairle.

agony *n* dòrainn *f*.

agree *v* aontaich; còrd.

agreeable *adj* taitneach.

agreement *n* còrdadh *m*, rèite *f*.

agricultural *adj* àiteachail.
agriculture *n* àiteachd *f*, tuathan achas *m*.
aground *adv* an sàs.
ahead *adv* air thoiseach.
aid *n* cuideachadh *m*. • *v* cuidich.
ailment *n* tinneas, galar *m*.
ailing *adj* tinn.
aim *n* (*missile*) cuimse *f*, (*intent*) amas *f*. • *v* cuimsich; amais.
air *n* àile; (*mus*) fonn; (*look*) aogas. • *v* leig an àile gu.
airborne *adj* air sgèith.
airmail *n* post-adhair *m*.
airport *n* port-adhair *m*.
airwave *n* tonn-adhair *m*.
aisle *n* trannsa *f*.
ajar *adv* leth-fhosgailte.
akin *adj* (*related*) càirdeach.
alacrity *n* sùrd *m*.
alarm *v* cuir eagal air.
alarming *adj* eagalach.
album *n* leabhar-chuimhneachan *m*.
alcohol *n* alcol *m*.
alcoholic *n* alcolach *m*.
alcoholism *n* alcolachd *f*.
alder *n* feàrna *f*.
ale *n* leann *m*.
alert *adj* furachail.
algebra *n* ailgeabra *f*.
alias *adv* fo ainm eile.
alien *adj* coigreach. • *n* coigreach *m*; Gall *m*.
alienate *v* fuadaich.
alight *v* teirinn.

alike *adj* co-ionnan.
alimony *n* airgead sgaraidh *m*.
alive *adj* beò.
all *adj* uile, na h-uile, iomlan.
allay *v* caisg.
allegation *n* cur às leth *m*.
allegiance *n* ùmhlachd *f*.
allegory *n* samhla *m*.
alleviate *v* aotromaich, lùgh-daich.
alleviation *n* aotromachadh *m*.
alliance *n* càirdeas *m*.
alliteration *n* uaim *f*.
allow *v* leig le, ceadaich.
allowance *n* cuibhreann *f*.
allusion *n* iomradh *m*.
ally *n* caraid *m*; co-chòmragh-aiche *m*.
almighty *adj* uile-chumhachdach.
Almighty *n* An t-Uile-chumhach-dach *m*.
almost *adv* gu ìre bhig.
alms *npl* dèircean.
aloft *adv* gu h-àrd, shuas.
alone *adj* aonarach.
along *adv* air fad; **along with** còmhla ri.
alongside *adv* ri taobh.
aloud *adv* gu h-àrd ghuthach.
alphabet *n* aibidil *f*.
alphabetical *adj* aibidileach.
already *adv* mar thà.
also *adv* cuideachd.
altar *n* altair *f*.
alter *v* atharraich.
alteration *n* atharrachadh *m*.

alternative *adj* eile. • *n* roghainn eile *m*.

although *conj* ged a.

altitude *n* àirde *f*.

altogether *adv* gu lèir, uile gu lèir.

aluminium *n* almain *m*.

always *adv* an còmhnaidh, daonnan.

amalgamate *v* cuir le chèile.

amateur *adj* neo-dhreuchdail.

amaze *v* cuir iongnadh air.

amazement *n* iongantas *m*.

amazing *adj* iongantach.

ambassador *n* tosgaire *m*.

ambidextrous *adj* co-dheaslamhach.

ambiguity *n* dà-sheaghachas *m*.

ambiguous *adj* dà-sheaghach.

ambit *n* cuairt *f*.

ambition *n* glòir-mhiann *m*.

ambitious *adj* glòir-mhiannach.

ambulance *n* carbad-eiridinn *m*.

ambush *n* feallfhalach *m*.

ameliorate *v* dèan nas fheàrr.

amen *int* amen.

amenable *adj* fosgailte.

amend *v* leasaich.

amendment *n* leasachadh *m*.

amenity *n* goireas *m*.

America *n* Ameireagaidh *f*.

American *adj* Ameireaganach.

amiable *adj* càirdeil.

amid, amidst *prep* a-measg.

amiss *adv* gu h-olc.

ammunition *n* connadh làmhaich *m*.

amnesty *n* mathanas na coitcheann *m*.

among, amongst *prep* a-measg, air feadh.

amorous *adj* gaolach.

amount *n* suim, uimhir *f*, meud *m*.

amphibian *n* muir-thìreach *m*.

amphibious *adj* dà-bhitheach.

ample *adj* mòr, tomadach.

amplification *n* meudachadh *m*.

amplify *v* meudaich.

amputate *v* geàrr air falbh.

amputation *n* gearradh air falbh *m*.

amuse *v* toilich.

amusement *n* greannmhorachd *f*.

amusing *adj* greannmhor.

anachronism *n* às-aimsireachd *f*.

anaemic *adj* clon-falach.

anaesthetic *n* an-fhaireachdair *m*.

analogy *n* co-fhreagarrachd *f*.

analyse *v* mion-sgrùdaich.

analysis *n* mion-sgrùdadh *m*.

analyst *n* mion-sgrùdaire *m*.

anarchist *n* ceannairceach *m*.

anatomical *adj* bodhaigeach.

anatomy *n* eòlas bodhaig *m*.

ancestor *n* sinnsear *m*.

ancestry *n* sinnsearachd *f*.

anchor *n* acair *f*.

ancient *adj* àrsaidh.

and *conj* agus, is, 's.

anecdote *n* naidheachd *f*.

anew *adv* às-ùr.

angel *n* aingeal *m*.

angelic *adj* mar aingeal.

anger *n* fearg *f*.

angina *n* grèim chridhe *m*.

angle *n* uilinn *f*.

angler *n* iasgair *f*.

angling *n* iasgachd *m*.

angry *adj* feargach.

anguish *n* dòrainn *f*.

animal *n* ainmhidh *m*.

animate *v* beothaich.

animated *adj* beothail.

animation *n* beothachadh *m*.

ankle *n* adhbrann *f*.

annex *n* ath-thaigh *m*.

annihilate *v* dìthich.

annihilation *n* lèirsgrios *m*.

anniversary *n* cuimhneachan, bliadhnail *m*.

annotate *v* notaich.

annotation *n* notachadh *m*.

announce *v* cuir an cèill.

annoy *v* cuir dragh air.

annoyance *n* dragh; buaireas *m*.

annoyed *adj* diombach.

annoying *adj* buaireil.

annual *adj* bliadhnail.

annually *adv* gach bhliadhna.

annul *v* cuir às.

anoint *v* ung.

anon *adv* a dh'aithghearr.

anonymous *adj* neo-ainmichte.

another *pron* fear eile. • *adj* eile.

answer *n* freagairt *f*.

answer *v* freagair.

ant *n* seangan *m*.

antagonist *n* nàmhaid *m*.

antediluvian *adj* roimh 'n Tuil.

anthem *n* laoidh *m*.

anthology *n* duanaire, cruin-neachadh *m*.

anthropology *n* daonn-eòlas *m*.

anticipate *v* sùilich.

anticipation *n* sùileachadh *m*.

antidote *n* urchasg *m*.

antipathy *n* fuath *m*.

antiquary *n* àrsair *m*.

antique *adj* seann-saoghlach. • *n* seann-rud *m*.

antiseptic *n* loit-leigheas *m*.

antler *n* cabar fèidh *m*.

anvil *n* innean *m*.

anxiety *n* iomagain *m*.

anxious *adj* iomagaineach.

any *adj* sam bith, air bith, idir. • *pron* aon sam bith; aon; gin.

anyone *pron* neach sam bith.

anything *n* càil, dad *m*.

apartheid *n* sgaradh cinnidh *m*.

apartment *n* seòmar *m*; taigh *m*.

apathy *n* cion ùidhe *m*.

ape *n* apa *f*.

aperture *n* toll, fosgladh *m*.

apex *n* binnean *m*; bàrr *m*.

apiece *adv* an-t-aon.

apologise *v* dèan leisgeul.

apology *n* leisgeul *m*.

apostle *n* abstol *m*.

apostrophe *n* ascair *m*.

appal *v* cuir uabhas air.

apparatus *n* uidheam *m*.

apparent *adj* soilleir, faicsin-neach.

apparition n taibhse f.

appeal n tarraing f, (legal) ath-agairt m. • v tarraing; ath-agair.

appear v nochd.

appearance n taisbeanadh m; teachd an làthair m.

appease v rèitich.

append v cuir ri.

appendage n sgòdan m.

appendix n (anat) aipeandaig f; (book) ath-sgrìobadh m.

appetite n càil f.

applaud v bas-bhuail.

apple n ubhal m.

apple-tree n craobh-ubhal f.

appliance n goireas m.

applicable adj freagarrach.

applicant n tagraiche m.

application n cur an sàs m; (for a job) tagradh m.

applications npl (comput) cleach-daidhean mpl.

apply v cuir a-steach.

appoint v suidhich.

appointment n suidheachadh m.

apportion v dèan rionn air.

appraise v meas.

appreciate v cuir luach air, lu-achaich; (grow) àrdaich.

appreciation n luachachadh m.

apprehend v (infer) thoir fa-near; (arrest) glac.

approach n modh-gabhail f. • v dlùthaich.

appropriate adj cubhaidh. • v gabh seilbh air.

approval n deagh bharail f.

approve v gabh beachd math air.

approximate adj dlùthach.

apricot n apracot m.

April n An Giblean m.

apron n aparan m.

apropos adv a thaobh.

apt adj deas; freagarrach.

aptitude n sgil m; buailteachd f.

Arab n Arabach m.

Arabic adj Arabach.

arable adj àitich.

arbitrate v rèitich.

arbitrator n neach-rèiteachaidh.

arch n stuagh m.

archaeologist n àrsair m.

archbishop n àrd-easbaig m.

archetype n prìomh-shamhla m.

architect n ailtire m.

architecture n ailtireachd f.

archive n tasg-lann f.

ardent adj dian, bras.

arduous adj deacair.

area n farsaingeachd, lann f.

argue v connsaich; dearbh.

argument n connsachadh m; arga-maid f.

argumentative adj connsachail.

arid adj loisgte.

arise v èirich suas.

arithmetic n cùnntas m.

ark n àirc f.

arm n gàirdean m. • v armaich.

armchair n cathair-ghàirdeanach f.

armistice n fosadh m.

armour *n* armachd *f*.

armpit *n* achlais *f*.

army *n* arm, armailt *m*.

around *adv* mun cuairt. • *prep* timcheall, mu chuairt.

arouse *v* dùisg.

arrange *v* rèitich, còirich.

arrangement *n* rèiteachadh *m*; (*mus*) rian *m*.

array *v* cuir an ordugh.

arrears *n* fiachan gun dìoladh *m*.

arrest *v* cuir an làimh.

arrival *n* teachd *m*.

arrive *v* ruig, thig.

arrogance *n* dànadas *m*.

arrogant *adj* dàna.

arrow *n* saighead *f*.

arsenal *n* arm-lann *f*.

art *n* ealdhain, ealain *f*; dòigh *f*; alt *m*; (*artifice*) seoltachd *f*.

artery *n* cuisle *f*.

artful *adj* innleachdach; seòlta.

arthritis *n* tinneas nan alt *m*.

article *n* alt *m*; (*clause*) bonn *m*.

articulate *adj* pongail.

artifice *n* seòltachd *f*.

artificial *adj* brèige.

artist *n* fear-ealain *m*.

as *adv* cho . . . ri, cho . . . is. • *conj* mar, ceart mar.

ascend *v* dìrich, streap.

ascent *n* dìreadh *m*.

ascertain *v* lorg; faigh fios.

ascribe *v* cuir às leth.

ash *n* uinnseann *m*.

ashamed *adj* nàraichte.

ashes *n* luaithre *f*.

ashore *adv* air tìr.

ashtray *n* soitheach-luaithre *f*.

Asia *n* An Aisia *f*.

Asiatic, Asian *adj* Aisianach.

aside *adv* a thaobh.

ask *v* (*request*) iarr; (*inquire after*) faighnich, feòraich.

askew *adv* cam; claon.

asleep *adj* an cadal.

asparagus *n* creamh na muice fiadhaich *m*.

aspect *n* snuadh *m*.

aspen *n* critheann *m*.

asperity *n* gairbhe *f*.

aspiration *n* dèidh *m*.

aspire *v* iarr, bi an dèidh air.

ass *n* asal *f*.

assail *v* thoir ionnsaigh air.

assailant *n* fear-ionnsaigh *m*.

assassin *n* mortair *m*.

assassinate *v* moirt, dèan mort.

assault *n* ionnsaigh *f*.

assemble *v* cruinnich.

assembly *n* mòrdhail *m*.

assent *n* aonta *m*.

assert *v* tagair.

assertion *n* tagradh *m*.

assertive *adj* tagrach.

assess *v* meas; (*for taxation*) meas a thaobh cis.

assessment *n* meas *m*; meas a thaobh cis *m*.

assessor *n* measadair *m*.

asset *n* taic *f*.

assiduity *n* dùrachd *f*.

assiduous *adj* leanmhainneach.
assign *v* cuir air leth.
assignation *n* cur air leth *m*; (*tryst*) coinneamh-leannan *f*.
assignment *n* obair shònraichte *f*.
assimilate *v* gabh a-steach.
assist *v* cuidich.
assistance *n* cuideachadh *m*.
assistant *n* fear-cuideachaidh.
associate *v* theirig am pàirt; cuir as leth.
association *n* comann *m*; ceangal *m*.
assonance *n* fuaimreagadh *m*.
assortment *n* measgachadh *m*.
assuage *v* caisg.
assume *v* gabh air.
assumption *n* gabhail *m*; (*supposition*) barail *f*.
assurance *n* dearbhachd *f*.
assure *v* dearbh.
assuredly *adv* gun teagamh.
asterisk *n* reul *f*.
astern *adv* an deireadh na luinge.
asthma *n* a' chuing *f*.
astonish *v* cuir iongnadh air.
astonishment *n* iongnadh *m*.
astray *adv* air seachran.
astride *adv* casa-gobhlach.
astringent *adj* ceangailteach; geur is tioram.
astronaut *n* speur-sheòladair *m*.
astrologer *n* speuradair *m*.
astrology *n* speuradaireachd *f*.
astronomer *n* reuladair *m*.

astronomical *adj* reul-eòlasach.
astronomy *n* reul-eòlas *m*.
asunder *adv* air leth.
asylum *n* àite-dìon *m*.
at *prep* aig.
atheism *n* neo-dhiadhachd *f*.
atheist *n* neo-dhiadhaire *m*.
athletic *adj* lùthmhor.
athletics *n* lùth-chleasachd *f*.
athwart *adv* trasd.
Atlantic Ocean *n* An Cuan Siar *m*.
atlas *n* atlas *m*.
atmosphere *n* àile *m*.
atom *n* dadam *m*.
atomic *adj* dadamach.
atone *v* dèan èirig.
atonement *n* rèite *f*.
atrocious *adj* uabhasach.
atrocity *n* buirbe *f*.
attach *v* ceangail.
attached *adj* ceangailte.
attachment *n* dàimh, gràdh *m*.
attack *n* ionnsaigh *m*. • *v* thoir ionnsaigh.
attain *v* ruig.
attainable *adj* so-ruigsinn.
attainment *n* ruigsinn *m*; (*ability*) sgil *m*.
attempt *n* oidhirp *f*. • *v* dèan oidhirp.
attend *v* fritheil; **attend to** thoir aire.
attendance *n* frithealadh *m*.
attendant *n* fear-frithealaidh *m*.
attentive *adj* furachail.

attenuate v tanaich.
attest v thoir fianais.
attestation n teisteas m.
attire n aodach, trusgan m. • v sgeadaich.
attitude n seasamh m.
attract v tarraing.
attraction n sùgadh m.
attractive adj tarraingeach.
attribute v cuir às leth.
attrition n bleith f.
attune v gleus.
attuned adj air ghleus.
auburn adj buidhe-ruadh.
auction n reic-tairgse f.
audible adj àrd-ghuthach.
audience n luchd-èisdeachd m.
audiovisual adj claistinn-léirsinneach.
audit n sgrùdadh m. • v sgrùd.
auditor n sgrùdaire m.
augment v meudaich.
augur n fiosaiche m.
augury n tuar m.
August n Lùnasdal m.
aunt n antaidh f.
aurora borealis n Na Fir Chlis.
auspicious adj fàbharach.
austere adj teann.
austerity n teanntachd f.
Australasia n Astrailàisia f.
Australia n Astràilia f.

Austria n An Ostair f.
authentic adj cinnteach.
author n ùghdar m.
authorise v thoir ùghdarras.
authority n ùghdarras, smachd m.
autobiography n fèin-eachdraich f.
automatic adj fèin-ghluasadach.
autumn n Am Foghar m.
auxiliary adj taiceil.
avail v foghainn.
available adj ri fhaotainn.
avarice n sannt m.
avaricious adj sanntach.
avenge v dìol.
average adj gnàthach. • n meadhan m.
aversion n fuath m.
avid adj gionach.
avoid v seachainn.
await v fuirich ri.
awake v dùisg.
award n duais f. • v thoir duais.
aware adj fiosrach.
away adv air falbh.
awesome adj fuathasach.
awful adj eagalach, uabhasach.
awhile adv tacan.
awkward adj cearbach.
awry adj cam.
ax, axe n tuagh f.
axle n aiseil f.

B

babble *n* glagais *f*.

baby *n* leanabh *m*.

bachelor *n* fleasgach *m*.

back *adv* air ais. • *n* cùl *m*; (*person*) druim *m*. • *v* theirig air ais; (*support*) seas.

backbone *n* cnàmh-droma *m*.

backgammon *n* tàileasg *m*.

backside *n* tòn *f*.

backsliding *n* cùl-sleamhnachadh *m*.

backwards *adv* an coinneamh a chùil.

bacon *n* muicfheòil *f*.

bacterial *adj* bacteridheach.

bad *adj* dona, olc.

bad-tempered *adj* greannach.

badge *n* suaicheantas *m*.

badger *n* broc *m*.

badness *n* donas *m*.

baffle *v* dèan a chuis air.

bag *n* poca *m*.

baggage *n* treallaichean *f*.

bagpipe *n* pìob, a' phìob mhor *f*.

bail *n* fuasgladh air urras *m*. • *v* thoir urras air.

bailiff *n* bàillidh *m*.

bait *n* maghar *m*. • *v* biadh.

bake *v* fuin; bruich ann an àmhainn.

baker *n* fuineadair, bèicear *m*.

bakery *n* taigh-fuine *m*.

balance *n* meidh *f*; (*mental*) co-throm *m*; (*fin*) còrr *m*. • *v* cuir air meidh; cothromaich.

balcony *n* for-uinneag *f*.

bald *adj* maol.

baldness *n* maoile *f*.

baleful *adj* millteach.

ball *n* ball *m*; (*dance*) bàl.

ballad *n* bailead *m*.

ballast *n* balaiste *f*.

balloon *n* bailiùn *m*.

ballot *n* bhòtadh *m*.

balm *n* ìocshlaint *f*.

bamboo *n* cuilc Innseanach *f*.

bamboozle *v* cuir an imcheist.

ban *n* toirmeasg *f*. • *v* toirmisg.

banana *n* banàna *m*.

band *n* bann *m*; còmhlan *m*; (*mus*) còmhlan ciùil *m*.

bandage *n* stìom-cheangail *f*.

bandy-legged *adj* camachasach.

baneful *adj* nimheil.

bang *n* cnag *f*; bualadh *m*. • *v* cnag; buail.

banish *v* fògair.

banishment *n* fògradh *m*.

basking shark *n* cearban *m*.

battery *n* bataraidh *m*.

bawdy *adj* drabasda.

bead *n* grìogag *m*.

beak *n* gob *m*.

beans *npl* pònair *m*.

beard *n* feusag *f*.

beast *n* beathach *m*, biast *m*.

beat v thoir buille.

beautiful adj bòidheach.

beauty maise, bòidhchead m.

beckon v smèid air.

bed n leabaidh m.

bedroom n seòmar leapa m.

bee n seillean, beach m.

beef n mairtheoil.

beer n leann m.

beetle n daolag m.

beg v iarr; dèan faoighe.

beggar n dèirceach m.

behave v giùlain.

behaviour n giùlan m; modh m.

bell n clag m.

bellow v beucaich.

bellows n balg-sèididh m.

belly n brù, broinn f.

belong v buin.

beloved adj gràdhach.

below adv shìos.

belt n crios m.

bench n being f.

bend n lùb m. • v lùb.

beneath prep fo.

benediction n beannachadh m.

benefaction n tabhartas m.

benefactor n taibheartach m.

beneficent adj deagh-ghnìomh-ach.

beneficial adj tairbheach.

benefit n sochair m.

benevolence n deagh-ghean m.

benevolent adj coibhneil.

benign adj suairc.

bent adj lùbte.

benumb v meilich.

bequeath v tiomnaich.

bequest n dìleab m.

bereaved adj rùisgte.

berry n dearc f, subh m.

beseech v dèan guidhe.

beside prep ri taobh.

besides adv a bhàrr air.

besiege v dèan sèisd air.

best adj as fheàrr. • n rogha m. • v fairtlich air.

bestial adj brùideil.

bestow v builich.

bet v cuir geall.

betray v brath.

betrayer n brathadair m.

betrayal n brathadh m.

betroth v rèitich.

better adj nas fheàrr.

between adv eadar. • prep eadar.

bewail v caoidh.

beware v thoir an aire.

bewitch v cuir fo gheasaibh.

beyond prep air taobh thall; seachad air.

bias n claonadh m.

bible n bìoball m.

biblical adj sgriobturail.

bicycle n bàidhseagal m.

bid n tairgse f. • v thoir tairgse.

bidding n (invitation) cuireadh m.

bide v fuirich.

biennial adj dà-bhliannach.

bier n carbad-adhlacaidh, giùlan m.

big adj mòr.

bigamy n dà-chèileachas m.
bigot n dalm-bheachdaiche m.
bigotry n dalm-bheachd m.
bilateral adj dà-thaobhach.
bile n domblas m.
bilingual adj dà-chànanach.
bill n gob m; (account) bileag.
billion n billean m.
bin n biona f.
binary adj càraideach.
bind v ceangail.
binding n ceangal m.
biochemist n bith-cheimicear m.
biochemistry n bith-cheim-iceachd f.
biography n beath-eachdraidh f.
biological adj bith-eòlasach.
biology n bith-eòlas m.
biped n dà-chasach m.
birch n beithe f.
bird n eun m.
bird-song n ceilear m/f.
birth n breith f.
birth certificate n teisteanas-breith m.
birthday n ceann-bliadhna m.
birthright n còir-bhreith f.
biscuit n briosgaid f.
bisect v geàrr sa' mheadhan.
bishop n easbaig m.
bit n mìr, bìdeag m; (horse) cab-stair m.
bitch n galla f.
bite v bìd, thoir grèim à.
biting adj bìdeach.
bitter adj geur.

black adj dubh, dorch.
blackbird n lon-dubh m.
blackboard n bòrd-dubh m.
blacken v dubh, dèan dubh.
black-humoured adj gruamach.
blackness n duibhead m.
blacksmith n gobha m.
bladder n aotroman m.
blade n (of grass) bilean; (of weapon) lann.
blame n coire f. • v coirich.
blameless adj neo-choireach.
blanch v gealaich.
bland adj mìn.
blank adj bàn.
blanket n plaide, plangaid f.
blasphemy n toibheum m.
blast n sgal m. • v sgrios.
blaze n teine lasrach m. • v las.
bleach v todhair.
bleak adj lom, fuar.
bleat v dèan mèilich.
bleed v leig fuil.
blemish n gaoid f.
blend n coimeasgadh m. • v coimeasgaich.
bless v beannaich.
blessed adj beannaichte.
blessing n beannachd f.
blight n fuar-dhealt.
blind adj dall. • n sgàil m.
blind man n dallaran m.
blindness n doille f.
blink v caog.
bliss n aoibhneas m.
blissful adj aoibhneach.

blister n leus m. • v thoir leus air; thig leus air.

blithe adj aoibhinn.

block n ploc m. • v caisg.

blockhead n bumailear m.

blonde n te bhàn f.

blood n fuil f.

blood feud n folachd f.

blood group n seòrsa fala m.

blood pressure n bruthadh fala m.

bloodshed n dòrtadh-fala m.

blood transfusion n leasachadh-fala m.

bloody adj fuileach.

bloom n blàth m.

blot n dubhadh m.

blotting paper n pàipear-sùghaidh m.

blouse n blobhsa f.

blow v sèid.

blubber n saill (muice-mara) f.

blue adj gorm.

blueness n guirme f.

bluff v meall.

blunder n iomrall m.

blunt adj maol. • v maolaich.

blur v dèan doilleir.

blush n rudhadh m.

bluster v bagair.

boar n torc m.

board n bòrd m, dèile f. • v rach air bòrd.

boarding house n taigh-aoigheachd m.

boarding pass n cead dol air bòrd m.

boast n bòsd. • v dèan bòsd.

boaster n bòsdair m.

boastful adj bòsdail.

boat n bàta m.

body n corp m; (person) neach, creutair m; (band) buidheann m.

bog n boglach, fèithe f.

bog-cotton n canach m.

boggle v bi an teagamh.

boil v goil; bruich.

boiled adj bruich.

boiler n goileadair m.

boisterous adj stoirmeil; iorgh-aileach.

bold adj dàna.

boldness n dànadas m.

bolster v misnich.

bolt n crann m. • v cuir crann air.

bomb n bom, boma m. • v leag bom air.

bond n ceangal m.

bondage n daorsa m.

bone n cnàmh m.

boneless adj gun chnàimh.

bonfire n tein-aighear m.

bonnet n bonaid f.

bonny adj maiseach.

bonus n còrr m.

bony adj cnàmhach.

book n leabhar m.

bookcase n lann leabhraichean f.

bookish adj dèidheil air leughadh.

book-keeper n fear chumail leabhraichean m.

book-keeping n leabhar-chùn-
ntas m.

bookseller n leabhar-reiceadair m.

bookshop n bùth-leabhraichean
m.

boor n amhasg m.

boorish n amhasgail m.

boot n bròg m.

booty n cobhartach m/f.

booze n stuth òil m. • v òl.

border n crìoch f.

borderer n fear àiteach nan
crìoch m.

bore n duine ràsanach m.

bore v cladaich.

boring adj fadalach.

borrow v faigh, gabh iasad.

borrower n fear gabhail iasaid m.

bosom n uchd m.

boss n ceann m.

botanise v cruinnich luibhean.

botanist n luibh-eòlaiche m.

botany n luibh-eòlas m.

both adj araon, le chèile, an dà;
(people) an dithis.

bother n sàrachadh m. • v sàraich.

bottle n botal m.

bottom n lochdar m; grùnnd m;
màs m.

bottomless adj gun ghrùnnd.

bough n geug f.

bound n sìnteag f. • v thoir leum.

bountiful adj fialaidh.

bourgeois adj bùirdeasach.

bow n bogha m; (ship) toiseach m;
(head) ùmhlachd m.

bowels n innidh f.

bowl n cuach f, bòbhla m.

bowsprit n crann-spreòid m.

bowstring n taifeid m.

box n bocsa, bocas m. • v (sport)
dèan sabaid.

boxer n fear-sabaid, bocsair m.

boxer shorts npl pantaichean
bocsair.

boy n balach, gille m.

brace n (pair) dithis m.

braces npl galars.

bracken n raineach f.

bracket n camag f.

brae n bruthach f.

brag v dèan bòsd.

bragging n bòsd, spaglainn m.

brain n eanchainn f.

bramble n smeur f.

bramble-bush n dris f.

branch n meangan m, geug f. • v
sgaoil.

brandish v beartaich.

brandy n branndaidh f.

brass n pràis f.

brat n isean m.

brave adj gaisgeil.

bravery n misneachd f.

brawl n stairirich m. • v dèan
stairirich.

bray v dèan sitir.

breach n briseadh m. • v dèan briseadh.

bread n aran m.

breadcrumb n criomag arain f.

breadth n leud m.

break *v* bris; sgar.

breakfast *n* biadh-maidne *m*.

breast *n* clòch *f*.

breath *n* anail *f*.

breathe *v* (*out*) leig anail; (*in*) tarraing anail.

breathless *adj* plosgartach.

breed *n* seòrsa *m*. • *v* tarmaich.

breeding *n* oilean *m*.

breeze *n* tlàth-ghaoth *f*.

brevity *n* giorrad *m*.

brew *v* dèan grùdaireachd; tarraing.

brewer *n* grùdaire *m*.

bribe *n* brìb *f*. • *v* brìb.

bribery *n* brìbeireachd *f*.

brick *n* breice *f*.

bricklayer *n* breicire *m*.

bridal *adj* pòsda.

bride *n* bean-bainnse *f*.

bridegroom *n* fear-bainnse *m*.

bridesmaid *n* maighdean-phòsaidh *f*.

bridge *n* drochaid *f*.

brief *adj* geàrr.

brigand *n* spùinneadair *m*.

bright *adj* soilleir; (*mind*) tuigseach.

brighten *v* soillsich.

brightness *n* soilleireachd *f*.

brilliant *adj* boillsgeach; (*mind*) air leth geur.

brim *n* oir *m*.

brine *n* sàl *m*.

bring *v* thoir.

brink *n* oir *m*.

brisk *adj* beothail.

briskness *n* beothalachd *f*.

bristle *n* calg *m*. • *v* cuir calg air.

Britain *n* Breatainn *f*.

British *adj* Breatannach.

brittle *adj* brisg.

broach *v* (*open*) toll; (*introduce*) tog.

broad *adj* leathann.

broadcast *v* craobh-sgaoil.

broadcaster *n* craobh-sgaoileadair *m*.

brochure *n* leabhran *m*.

brogue *n* bròg èille *f*; (*language*) dual-chainnt *f*.

broken *adj* briste.

broker *n* fear-gnothaich *m*.

brokerage *n* duais fir-gnothaich *f*.

bronchial *adj* sgòrnanach.

bronchitis *n* at sgòrnain *m*.

bronze *n* umha *m*.

bronzed *adj* (*tanned*) donn, grianloisgte.

brooch *n* bràiste *f*.

brood *n* àl *m*. • *v* àlaich.

brook *n* alltan *m*.

broom *n* bealaidh *m*; sguab *m*.

broth *n* eanraich *f*, brot *m*.

brothel *n* taigh-siùrsachd *m*.

brother *n* bràthair *m*.

brotherhood *n* bràithreachas *m*.

brotherly *adj* bràithreil.

brow *n* mala *f*; (*of hill*) maoilean *m*.

brown *adj* donn.

brownness n duinne f.
browse v criom; (book) thoir ruith air.
bruise n pronnadh m. • v pronn.
brunette n tè dhonn f.
brush n sguab f. • v sguab.
Brussels n A' Bhruiseal f.
brutal adj brùideil.
brutality n brùidealachd f.
brute n brùid m.
bubble n builgean m.
buck n boc m.
bucket n cuinneag f.
buckle n bucall m.
bud n gucag f.
budge v caraich.
budget n càin-aisneis f.
buffet n beum m; (food table) clàr bìdh m.
bug n (infection) galar m.
bugle n dùdach f.
build v tog.
builder n fear-togail m.
building n togalach m.
building society n comann thogalach m.
bulb n bolgan m.
bulk n meudachd f.
bulky adj tomadach.
bull n tarbh m.
bulldog n tarbh-chù m.
bulldozer n tarbh-chrann m.
bullet n peilear m.
bulletin n cùirt-iomradh m.
bullock n tarbh òg m.
bully n pulaidh m.

bum n màs m.
bump n meall; bualadh m.
bumper n bumpair m.
bun n buna m.
bunch n bagaid f.
bundle n pasgan m.
bung n tùc m.
bungle v dèan gu cearbach.
bungler n cearbaire m.
buoy n put m.
buoyancy n fleodradh m.
buoyant adj aotrom.
burden n eallach m. • v uallaich.
bureau n biùro m.
burgh n borgh m.
burglar n gadaiche-taighe m.
burglary n gadachd-taighe f.
burial n adhlacadh m.
burlesque n sgeigeireachd f.
burly adj tapaidh.
burn[1] n losgadh m. • v loisg.
burn[2] n (stream) alltan m.
burning n losgadh m.
burnish v lìomh.
burst v spreadh.
bury v adhlaic.
bus n bus, baos m.
bush n preas m.
bushy adj preasach.
business n gnothach m, malairt f.
businessman n fear-gnothaich m.
bust n ceann is guaillean m.
bustle n othail f.
busy adj trang.
busybody n gobaire m.

but *conj, adv, prep* ach.
butcher *n* feòladair *m*. • *v* casgair.
Bute *n* Bòid.
butler *n* buidealair *m*.
butt[1] *n* cùis-bhùirt *m*; (*cask*) baraill *m*; (*target*) targaid *f*.
butt[2] *v* sàth.
butter *n* ìm *m*.
buttercup *n* buidheag-an-t-samraidh *f*.
butterfly *n* dealan-dè *m*.
buttery *adj* ìmeach.
buttock *n* màs *m*.
button *n* putan *m*. • *v* putanaich.

buxom *adj* tiugh.
buy *v* ceannaich.
buyer *n* ceannaiche *m*.
buzz *n* srann *f*. • *v* srann.
buzzard *n* clamhan *m*.
by *adv* seachad; (*aside*) an dara taobh. • *prep* fasg air; le; **by and by** *adv* a dh' aithghearr, dh' aithgearr.
by-election *n* frith-thaghadh *m*.
bypass *n* seach-rathad *m*.
byre *n* bàthach *f*.
bystander *n* fear-amhairc *m*.

C

cab *n* tagsaidh *m*.
cabbage *n* càl *m*.
caber *n* cabar *m*.
cabin *n* seòmar luinge, cèaban *m*.
cadaverous *adj* cairbheach.
cadence *n* dùnadh *m*.
cadger *n* fear-faoighe *m*.
café *n* cafaidh *m*.
cage *n* cèidse *f*.
cairn *n* càrn *m*.
cajole *v* breug.
cake *n* breacag *f*.
calamitous *adj* dosgainneach.
calamity *n* dosgainn *f*.
calculate *v* tomhais.
calculation *n* tomhas *m*.
calculator *n* àireamhair *m*.

calculus *n* riaghailt-àireamh *f*.
Caledonia *n* Albann *f*.
calendar *n* mìosachan *m*.
calf *n* laogh *m*; (*leg*) calpa *m*.
calibre *n* meudachd *f*.
call *v* glaodh.
call-box *n* bocsa-fòn *m*.
calligraphy *n* làmh-sgrìobhaidh *f*.
calling *n* eigheachd *f*; (*vocation*) dreuchd *f*.
calliper *n* cailpear *m*.
callous *adj* cruaidh-chridheach.
calm *adj* ciùin; fèathach.
calm *v* ciùinich.
calumniate *v* cùl-chàin.
calve *v* beir laogh.

camel *n* càmhal *m*.

camera *n* camara *m*.

camouflage *n* breug-riochd *m*.

camp *n* càmpa *m*.

camp *v* càmpaich.

campaign *n* còmhrag *f*.

can[1] *n* canastair *m*.

can[2] *v* (*may*) faod; (*be able*) is ur-rainn do.

Canadian *adj* Canèideanach.

canal *n* clais-uisge *f*.

cancel *v* dubh a-mach.

cancellation *n* dubhadh a-mach *m*.

cancer *n* aillse *f*.

cancerous *adj* aillseach.

candid *adj* neo-chealgach.

candidate *n* fear-iarraidh *m*.

candle *n* coinneal *f*.

candlestick *n* coinnlear *m*.

candour *n* fosgarrachd *f*.

canine *adj* conail.

cannibal *n* canabail *m*.

canny *adj* cùramach.

canonise *v* cuir an àireamh nan naomh.

canter *n* trotan *m*.

canvas *n* canabhas *m*.

canvass *v* beachd-rannsaich.

canvasser *n* sireadair *m*.

cap *n* bonaid *m/f*, ceap *m*.

cap *v* còmhdaich; (*fig*) thoir bàrr air.

capability *n* cumhachd *m*.

capable *adj* comasach.

capacious *adj* farsaing.

capacity *n* comas *m*.

cape *n* rubha *m*; cleòc *m*.

caper *v* leum.

capital *n* ceanna-bhaile *m*.

capital letter *n* corr-litir *f*.

capitalism *n* calpachas *m*.

capitalist *n* calpaire *m*.

capitulate *v* strìochd.

capitulation *n* strìochdadh *m*.

caprice *n* neònachas *m*.

capricious *adj* neònach.

capsule *n* capsal *m*.

captain *n* caiptean *m*.

caption *n* tiotal *m*; fo-thiotal *m*.

captive *n* ciomach *m*.

captivity *n* ciomachas *m*.

capture *n* glacadh *m*.

capture *v* glac.

car *n* càr, carbad *m*.

carbohydrate *n* gualaisg *m*.

carbon *n* gualan *m*.

carcass *n* cairbh *m*.

card *n* cairt *f*.

card *v* càrd.

cardboard *n* cairt-bhòrd *m*.

cardiac *adj* cridhe.

cardiac disease *n* tinneas cridhe *m*.

cardinal *adj* prìomh. • *n* càirdineal.

card index *n* clàr-amais cairt *m*.

care *n* cùram *m*. • *v* gabh cùram.

career *n* (*rush*) rèis *f*; (*work*) dreachd *f*.

careful *adj* cùramach.

careless *adj* mì-chùramach.

carelessness *n* mì-chùram *m*.

caress *v* cnèadaich.

caretaker *n* fear-aire *m*.

cargo *n* luchd *m*.

caricature *n* dealbh-magaidh *m*.

carnage *n* àr *m*.

carnal *adj* feòlmhor.

carnival *n* fèill *f*.

carnivorous *adj* feòil-itheach.

carousal *n* fleadh *m*.

carpark *n* pàirc-chàraichean *f*.

carpenter *n* saor *m*

carpet *n* brat-ùrlair *m*.

carriage *n* carbad *m*; (*gait*) giùlan *m*.

carrier *n* fear-ghiùlain *m*.

carrion *n* ablach *m*.

carrot *n* curran *m*.

carry *v* giùlain, iomchair, thoir.

cart *n* cairt *f*. • *v* giùlain le cairt.

cartilage *n* maoth-chnàimh *m*.

cartoon *n* dealbh-èibhinn *m/f*.

cartridge *n* catraisde *f*.

carve *v* geàrr; snaigh.

carving *n* snaigheadh *m*.

cascade *n* eas *m*.

case *n* còmhdach *m*; ceus *m*; staid *m*; cùis *m*; tuiseal *m*.

cash *n* airgead ullamh *m*.

cash-book *n* leabhar-airgid *m*.

cashier *n* gleidheadair airgid *m*.

cash machine *n* inneal-airgid *m*.

cash register *n* inneal-cùnntaidh airgid *m*.

cask *n* buideal *m*.

cassock *n* casag *f*.

cast *v* tilg, cuir; cast loose *v* sgaoil.

caste *n* dual-fhine *f*.

castigate *v* cronaich.

castle *n* caisteal *m*.

castrate *v* spoth.

casual *adj* tuiteamach.

casualty *n* leòinteach *m*.

cat *n* cat *m*.

catalogue *n* ainm-chlàr *m*.

catalyse *v* cruth-atharraich.

catapult *n* tailm *m*.

cataract *see* cascade; (*eye*) *n* meam-ran sùla *m*.

catarrh *n* an galar smugaideach *m*.

catastrophe *n* droch thubaist *f*.

catch *n* glacadh *m*. • *v* glac, greimich.

catching *adj* gabhaltach.

catechism *n* leabhar-cheist *m*.

categorical *adj* làn-chinnteach.

category *n* gnè *f*.

cater *v* solair.

caterpillar *n* burras *m*.

caterpillar-tracked *adj* burrasach.

cathedral *n* cathair-eaglais *f*.

Catholic *adj* Caitligeach.

catholic *adj* coitcheann.

cattle *n* spreidh *f*.

cattle show *n* fèill a' chruidh *f*.

cauldron *n* coire mòr *m*.

cauliflower *n* colag *f*.

causal *adj* adhbharach.

causation *n* adhbharachadh *m*.

cause n adhbhar m; cùis m. • v dèan, thoir gu buil.

causeway n cabhsair m.

caustic adj loisgeach.

caution n cùram m. • v cuir air fhaicill.

cautious adj cùramach.

cavalry n marc-shluagh m.

cave n uamh f.

cavity n lag m/f, sloc f.

cease v stad.

cease-fire n stad-losgaidh m.

ceaseless adj gun stad.

cedar n seudar m.

cede v gèill.

ceilidh n cèilidh m/f.

ceiling n mullach m.

celebrate v glèidh; bi subhach.

celebrity n neach iomraiteach m.

celestial adj nèamhaidh.

celibacy n aontamhachd f.

celibate adj aontamhach.

cell n cealla; prìosan f.

cellar n seilear m.

cello n beus-fhidheall f.

cellular adj ceallach.

celluloid n ceallaloid m.

Celt n Ceilteach m.

Celtic adj Ceilteach.

cement n saimeant m. • v tàth.

cemetery n cladh m.

censor n caisgire m. • v caisg.

censorious adj cronachail.

censure n coire f. • v coirich.

census n cùnntas-sluaigh m.

centenary n ceud blianna m.

centennial adj ceud-bhliannach.

centimetre n ciadameatair m.

central adj anns a' mheadan.

central heating n teasachadh meadhanach m.

central processing unit n prìomh ghnìomh-inneal m.

centre n meadhan m.

centrifugal adj meadhan-sheachnach.

centripetal adj meadhan-aomachail.

century n ceud blianna, linn m.

cereal n gràn m.

ceremony n deas-ghnàth m.

certain adj cinnteach.

certainly adv gu cinnteach.

certainty n cinnt f.

certificate n teisteanas m.

certify v teistich.

cesspool n poll-caca m.

chagrin n mìghean m.

chain n slabhraidh f. • v cuibhrich.

chain store n bùth-sreatha f.

chair n cathair f.

chairman n fear-cathrach m.

chalk n cailc f.

challenge n dùbhshlan m.

chamber n seòmar m.

chambered adj seòmrach.

champ v cagainn.

champion n gaisgeach m.

championship n urram gaisgeachd m.

chance n tuiteamas m.

change n caochladh m; (money) iomlaid f. • v mùth.
changeable adj caochlaideach.
channel n amar, caolas m.
chant v sianns.
chanter n feadan m.
chaos n eucruth m.
chapel n caibeal m.
chapter n caibideil m/f.
character n beus, mèinn f; (story) pearsa m.
characteristic adj coltach.
charcoal n gual-fiodha m.
charge n earbsa f; ionnsaigh f; prìs f. • v earb; thoir ionnsaigh; cuir.
charity n gràdh, coibhneas m.
charm n mealladh m; (spell) ortha f. • v meall; cuir fo dhraoidheachd.
chart n cairt-iùil f.
charter v fasdaidh.
chase n sealg. • v ruith.
chaste adj geanmnaidh.
chastity n geanmnachd f.
chat v dèan còmhradh.
chatter v dèan cabaireachd.
cheap adj saor; air bheag prìs.
cheapness n saoiread m.
cheat n mealltair m. • v dèan foill air.
check n casg m. • v caisg.
checkmate n tul-chasg m.
cheek n gruaidh f.
cheer v brosnaich.
cheese n càise m, càbag f.

chemical adj ceimiceach.
chemist n ceimicear m; fear-chungaidhean.
cheque n seic f.
cherry n sirist f.
chess n fidhcheall m.
chest n ciste f; cliabh f.
chew v cagainn.
chicken n isean m.
chief n ceann-feadhna m.
chilblain n cusp f.
child n leanabh m.
childhood n leanabas m.
childless adj gun sliochd.
children n clann f.
chill v fuaraich.
chilly adj fuar.
chimney n similear m.
chin n smig m.
China n Sìna.
chocolate n teòclaid f.
choice n roghainn m.
choir n còisir-chiùil f.
choke v tachd.
choose v roghnaich.
chop n staoig. • v sgud.
chord n còrda f.
chorus n sèist f; co-sheirm f.
Christ n Crìosd m.
christen v baist.
Christmas n Nollaig f.
chronic adj leantalach.
chronicle n eachdhraidh f.
church n eaglais f.
churchyard n cladh m.
churlish adj mùgach.

cigarette n toitean m.

cinema n taigh-dhealbh m.

circle n cearcall; còmhlan m. • v cuairtich.

circuit n cuairt f.

circular adj cruinn.

circulate v cuir mun cuairt.

circumnavigate v seòl mun cuairt.

circumstance n cùis f.

circus n soircas m.

citizen n fear-àiteachaidh m.

city n cathair f.

civil adj sìobhalta.

civilian n sìobhaltair m.

civilisation n sìobhaltachd f.

civilise v sìobhail.

claim n tagairt f. • v tagair.

claimant n fear-tagraidh m.

clan n fine f, cinneadh m.

clanship n cinneadas m.

clap n buille f. • v buail ri chèile.

claret n clàireat f.

clarify v soilleirich.

clash v dèan glagadaich.

clasp n dubhan m.

class n buidheann f, clas m. • v seòrsaich.

classical adj clasaiceach.

classify v seòrsaich.

claw n iongna f.

clay n crèadh f.

claymore n claidheamh-mòr m.

clean adj glan. • v glan.

cleanness n gloinead m.

clear adj soilleir. • v soilleirich.

cleft n sgoltadh m.

cleg n crèithleag f.

clench v dùin.

clergy n clèir f.

clergyman n pears-eaglais m.

clever adj tapaidh.

click v cnag.

clientèle n luchd-dèilig m.

cliff n creag f, sgùrr m.

climate n clìomaid f.

climb v dìrich, streap.

climber n streapaiche m.

climbing n dìreadh m.

cling v slaod.

clinic n clionaic f.

clink v thoir gliong.

clip v geàrr.

clipper n gearradair m.

clock n uaireadair, cleoc m.

clod n ploc m.

clog v tromaich.

cloister n clabhstair m.

clone n lethbhreac ginteil m. • v mac-samhlaich.

close¹ adj (near) faisg; (stuffy) dùmhail. • n (entry) clobhsa m.

close² v dùin. • n dùnadh m.

clot n meall m.

cloth n aodach m.

clothe v còmhdaich.

clothes npl aodach, trusgan m.

cloud n neul m.

cloudy adj neulach.

clout, n (cloth) clùd m.

clover n clòbhar m.

clown n amadan m.

cloy v sàsaich.

club n (*stick*) cuaille, caman m.

cluck v dèan gogail.

clump n tom m.

clumsy adj cearbach.

cluster n bagaid f.

clutch n grèim m; (*car*) put. • v greimich.

coagulate v binndich.

coal n gual m.

coalesce v aonaich.

coarse adj garbh.

coast n oirthir f.

coastguard n freiceadan-oirthire m.

coastline n iomall-fairge m.

coat n còta m. • v cuir brat air.

coax v tàlaidh.

cobweb n eige f.

cockle n coilleag f.

cocksure adj coccanta, spairisteach.

cock n coileach m.

cod n trosg m.

code n riaghailt f.

co-education n co-fhoglam m.

coerce v ceannsaich.

coeval adj co-aimsireach.

co-exist v bi beò le.

coffee n cofaidh m.

coffin n ciste-laighe f.

cog n fiacaill f.

cogent adj làidir.

cohabitation n co-fhuireachd f.

cohere v lean.

coherent adj so-leantainn.

coll n cuibhleachadh m. • v cuibhlich.

coin n bonn airgid m.

coinage n cùinneadh m.

coincide v co-thirit.

coincidence n co-thuiteamas m.

cold adj fuar. • n fuachd m; cnatan m.

coldness n fuairead m.

collaborate v co-oibrich.

collapse v tuit am broinn a chèile.

collapsible adj so-sheacaich.

collar n coilear m.

collarbone n ugan m.

colleague n co-oibriche m.

collect v cruinnich.

collective adj co-choitcheann.

college n colaisde f.

collision n co-bhualadh m.

collusion n co-rùn m.

colonel n còirneal m.

colony n tìr-imrich f.

colour n dath m. • v dath.

column n colbh m.

coma n trom-neul m.

comb n cìr f. • v cìr.

combination n co-aontachadh m.

combine v co-aontaich.

come v thig; (*imper*) trobhad!

comedian n cleasaiche m.

comedy n cleas-chluich f.

comet n reul-chearbach f.

comfort n cofhurtachd f.

comfortable adj cofhurtail.

comic adj àbhachdach.

coming *n* teachd *m*.
comma *n* cromag *f*.
command *n* òrdugh *m*.
commemorate *v* cuimhnich.
commend *v* mol.
commendable *adj* ri a mholadh.
comment *n* facal *m*. • *v* thoir tarraing.
commerce *n* malairt *f*.
commercial *adj* malairteach.
commiserate *v* co-bhàidhich.
commission *n* ùghdarras *m*.
commit *v* earb; (*crime, etc*) ciontaich.
committee *n* comataidh *f*.
commodious *adj* luchdmhor.
commodity *n* badhar *m*.
common *adj* coitcheann.
Commonwealth *n* Co-fhlaitheas *m*.
communicate *v* com-pàirtich.
communication *n* com-pàirteachadh *m*; **communications** *npl* eadar-cheangal *m*.
community *n* pobal *m*.
commute *v* malairtich; triall.
compact *adj* teann.
compact disc *n* meanbh-chlàr *m*.
companion *n* companach *m*.
company *n* cuideachd *f*; companaidh *f*.
compare *v* coimeas.
compass *n* combaist *f*; meud *m*.
compassion *n* truas *m*.
compatible *adj* co-fhulangach.
compatriot *n* co-fhear-dùthcha *m*.

compel *v* co-èignich.
compensate *v* diol.
compete *v* strì.
competition *n* co-fharpais *f*.
competitor *n* farpaiseach *m*.
complacent *adj* somalta.
complain *v* gearain.
complaint *n* gearan *m*; (*illness*) galar.
computer *n* coimpiutair *m*.
conjugate *v* co-naisg.
conjunction *n* naisgear *m*.
conjure *v* cuir impidh air.
connection *n* ceangal *m*.
connoisseur *n* fear-eòlach *m*.
conquer *v* ceannsaich.
conquest *n* buaidh *f*.
conscience *n* cogais *f*.
conscientious *adj* cogaisach.
conscious *adj* mothachail.
consciously *adv* le mothachadh.
consecrate *v* coisrig.
consecutive *adj* leanmhainneach.
consent *n* aonta *m*.
consent *v* aontaich.
consequence *n* toradh *m*.
consequently *adv* uime sin.
conservancy *n* glèidhteachas *m*.
conservation *n* gleidheadh *m*.
conserve *v* taisg.
consider *v* smaoinich.
considerable *adj* math, cudromach.
consideration *n* tuigse *f*.
consignment *n* lìbhrigeadh *m*.
consistency *n* seasmhachd *f*.

consolation n sòlas m.

console v furtaich.

consonant n co-fhoghar m.

consort n cèile m.

conspicuous adj faicsinneach.

conspire v dèan co-fheall.

constancy n neo-chaochlaideachd f.

constant adj daingeann.

constellation n reul-bhad m.

constipation n teannachadh-innidh m.

constituency n roinn-taghaidh f.

constitution n dèanamh, nàdar m; (political) bonn-stèidh.

constriction n teannachadh m.

construct v tog.

construction n togail f.

consult v gabh comhairle.

consume v caith.

consumer n fear-caitheamh m.

consummate v crìochnaich.

contact v (physical) suath ann; (message) cuir fios gu.

contain v cùm; caisg.

container n bocsa-stòraidh m.

contemplate v beachd-smuainich.

contemporary adj co-aoiseach.

contempt n tàir f.

contemptuous adj tarcaiseach.

content adj toilichte.

context n co-theacs m.

continent n mòr-thìr f.

contingent adj tuiteamach.

continual adj sìor.

continually adv gun sgur.

continue v lean air.

continuous adj leanailteach.

contour n (map) loidhne àirde f.

contraception n casg-gineamhainn m.

contract n cùnnnradh. • v teannaich; rèitich.

contraction n teannachadh m.

contradict v cuir an aghaidh.

contradiction n breugnachadh m.

contrary adj an aghaidh.

contrast v eadar-dhealaich.

contravene v bris.

contribute v cuir ri.

contribution n cuideachadh m.

contrivance n innleachd f.

control n smachd m.

control v ceannsaich; stiùir.

controversial adj connsachail.

controversy n connspaid f.

convalescence n iar-shlànachadh m.

convalescent adj iar-shlànach.

convener n fear-gairm m.

convenient adj goireasach.

convent n clochar m.

converge v co-aom.

conversation n còmhradh m.

converse v dèan còmhradh.

conversion n iompachadh m.

convert v iompaich.

convex adj os-chearclach.

conveyance n còir-sgrìobhte f.

conveyancer n sgrìobhadair-chòirichean m.

convict *n* ciomach *m*. • *v* dearbh.
conviction *n* dìteadh *m*.
convivial *adj* cuideachdail.
convulsion *n* criothnachadh *m*.
cook *n* còcaire *m*. • *v* deasaich, bruich.
cooker *n* cucair *m*.
cookery *n* còcaireachd *f*.
cool *v* fuaraich.
cooperate *v* co-oibrich.
cope *v* dèan an gnothach.
copious *adj* pailt.
copper *n* copar *m*.
copulate *v* cuplaich.
copy *n* lethbhreac *m*. • *v* ath-sgrìobh.
copyright *n* dlighe-sgrìobhaidh.
coral *n* corail *m*.
cord *n* còrd *m*.
cordial *adj* càirdeil.
core *n* cridhe *m*.
cork *n* àrc *f*. • *v* cuir àrc ann.
corkscrew *n* sgriubha àrc *m*.
corn *n* coirce *m*.
corner *n* oisean *f*.
cornice *n* bàrr-mhaise *m*.
coronary *adj* coronach.
coronation *n* crùnadh *m*.
corpse *n* corp *m*.
corpuscle *n* corpag *f*.
correct *adj* ceart. • *v* ceartaich.
correspond *v* co-fhreagair.
correspondence *n* (*mail*) co-sgrìobhadh *m*.
corridor *n* trannsa *f*.
corrie *n* coire *m*.

corrode *v* meirgnich.
corrosion *n* meirg *f*.
corrugated *adj* preasach.
corrupt *adj* grod.
cosmetic *n* cungaidh maise *f*.
cosmopolitan *n* os-nàiseanta *m*.
cost *n* cosgais *f*. • *v* cosg.
costly *adj* cosgail.
costume *n* culaidh *f*.
cosy *adj* seasgair.
cottage *n* bothan *m*.
cotton *n* cotan *m*.
couch *n* uirigh *f*.
cough *n* casd *m*. • *v* dèan casd.
council *n* comhairle *f*.
councillor *n* comhairliche *m*.
count *v* cùnnt.
countenance *n* gnùis *f*.
counter *n* cuntair *m*.
counteract *v* cuir bacadh air.
counter-clockwise *adv* tuathal.
counterfeit *v* feall-chùinneach.
countersign *v* cuir ainm ri.
counting *n* cùnntas *m*.
countless *adj* do-àireamh.
country *n* dùthaich, tìr *m*.
countryman *n* fear-dùthcha *m*.
county *n* siorrachd *f*.
couple *n* càraid *f*.
couplet *n* rann dà-shreathach *f*.
coupon *n* cùpon *m*.
courage *n* misneach *f*.
courageous *adj* misneachail.
courier *n* teachdaire *m*.
course *n* slighe *m*.
court *n* cùirt *f*. • *v* dèan suirghe.

courtesy n modh f.

courthouse n taigh-cùirte m.

cousin n co-ogha m.

cove n bàgh, camas m.

cover n còmhdach, brat m. • v còmhdaich.

cow n bò f.

coward n gealtaire m.

cowardice n geilt f.

cowherd n buachaille m.

coy adj nàrach.

crab n partan m, crùbag f.

crack n sgàinneadh m. • v sgàin.

cradle n creathail f.

craft n cèaird m; (cunning) seòltachd f; (vessel) bàta m.

craftsman n fear-ceàirde m.

crag n creag f.

cram v dìnn.

crane n crann m.

crannog n crannag f.

cranny n cùil f.

crash v co-bhuail.

craving n miann m/f.

crawl v snàig.

crazy adj às a chiall.

creak v dèan dìosgan.

cream n uachdar m.

crease n filleadh m.

create v cruthaich.

creation n cruthachadh m.

creature n creutair m.

credible adj creideasach.

crèche n ionad-là leanaban m.

credit n creideas m. • v creid.

credit card n cairt-iasaid f.

creditor n fear-fèich m.

creed n creud f.

creel n cliabh m.

cremate v loisg.

crest n cìrean m.

crew n sgioba m/f.

crime n eucoir f.

criminal adj eucoireach. • n eucoireach m.

crimson adj crò-dhearg.

cringe v crùb.

cripple n crioplach m.

crisis n gàbhadh m.

crisp adj brisg; fionnar.

criterion n slat-tomhais m.

critic n sgrùdair m.

critical adj breitheach.

criticise v dèan sgrùdadh.

criticism n breithneachadh m.

croak v dèan gràgail.

crockery npl soitheachan-crèadha.

croft n croit f.

crofter n croitear m.

crook n cromag f; (person) cruc m.

crooked adj cam, crom.

croon v crònaich.

crop n bàrr m. • v beàrr, buain.

cross adj crosta. • n crois f. • v rach tarsaing.

cross-breed n tair-bhrìd m.

cross-examine v ath-cheasnaich.

cross-roads n crois a' rothaid f.

crossword puzzle n tòimh-seachan-tarsainn m.

crotch n gobhal m.

crotchet n (music) dubh-nota m.

crouch v crom.

crow n feannag f.

crowd n sluagh m. • v dòmhlaich.

crowdie n gruth m.

crown n crùn m. • v crùn.

crucible n soitheach-leaghaidh m.

cruciform adj crasgach.

crude adj amh.

cruel adj an-iochdmhor.

cruelty n an-iochdmhorachd m.

cruise n cùrsa mara m.

crumb n criomag f.

crumple v rocaich.

crush v pronn.

crust n plaosg m.

crutch n crasg f.

cry v èigh; guil.

cub n cuilean m.

cube n ciùb m.

cuckoo n cuach m.

cuff n bun-dùirn m.

culprit n ciontach m.

cultivate v àitich.

culture n saothrachadh m; (arts) cultur m.

cup n copan m.

cupboard n preas m.

cupidity n sannt f.

curable adj so-leigheas.

curb v bac.

curdle v binndich.

cure n leigheas m. • v leigheis.

curious adj ceasnachail.

curl n bachlag f. • v bachlaich.

curlew n guilbneach m.

currency n sgaoileadh m; airgead m.

current adj gnàthaichte. • n sruth m.

curse n mallachd f. • v mallaich.

curtain n cùrtair m.

curvature n caime f.

curve v crom.

cushion n pillean m.

custody n cùram m.

custom n àbhaist m.

customary adj àbhaisteach.

cut n gearradh m. • v geàrr.

cutlery n uidheam-ithe f.

cynical adj searbhasach.

cyst n ùthan m.

D

dabble v crath uisge air.

dad n dadaidh m.

daffodil n lus-a-chrom-chinn m.

dagger n biodag f.

daily adj làitheil. • adv gach là.

dainty adj mìn.

dairy n taigh-bainne m.

daisy n neòinean m.

dale n dail f.

dam n dàm m.

damage n dochann m. • v dochainn.

damnable *adj* damaichte.

damnation *n* dìteadh *m*.

damp *adj* tais.

dampen *v* taisich.

dance *n* dannsa *m*. • *v* danns.

dandelion *n* beàrnan-brìde *m*.

dandle *v* luaisg.

danger *n* cunnart *m*.

dangerous *adj* cunnartach.

dappled *adj* ball-bhreac.

dare *v* gabh air.

daring *adj* neo-sgàthach.

dark *adj* dorch.

darken *v* dorchaich.

darkness *n* dorchadas *m*.

darling *n* annsachd, eudail *f*, luaidh *m*.

darn *v* càirich.

dash *v* spealg.

database *n* stòr-dàta *m*.

date *n* ceann-latha *m*; (*fruit*) deit *f*.

daub *v* smeur.

daughter *n* nighean *f*.

daughter-in-law *n* ban-chlia-mhain *f*.

dawn *n* camhanach *f*.

day *n* là *m*.

daylight *n* solas an latha *m*.

daze *v* cuir bho mhothachadh.

dazzle *v* deàrrs.

dead *adj* marbh.

deadlock *n* glasadh *m*.

deadly *adj* marbhtach.

deaf *adj* bodhar.

deafen *v* bodhair.

deafness *n* buidhre *f*

deal *n* cùnnradh *m*. • *v* dèilig.

dealer *n* fear-malairt *m*.

dealing *n* dèiligeadh *m*.

dear *adj* gaolach; (*cost*) daor.

dearness *n* (*cost*) daoire *f*.

dearth *n* gainne *f*.

death *n* bàs *m*.

debar *v* bac.

debase *v* truaill.

debate *n* deasbad *m*. • *v* deasbair.

debit *n* fiach-shuim *f*. • *v* cuir fia-ch-shuim.

debts *npl* fiachan.

decade *n* deichead *m*.

decadent *adj* air claonadh.

decant *v* taom.

decanter *n* searrag ghlainne *f*.

decay *n* crìonadh *m*. • *v* caith.

deceit *n* cealg *f*.

deceive *v* meall, breug.

December *n* An Dùbhlachd.

decency *n* beusachd *f*.

decent *adj* beusach.

deception *n* mealladh *m*.

decide *v* co-dhùin.

deciduous *adj* seargach.

decimal *adj* deicheach.

decision *n* breith *f*.

decisive *adj* cinnteach.

deck *n* bòrd-luinge *m*. • *v* sgia-mhaich.

declaration *n* dearbhadh *m*.

declare *v* cuir an cèill.

decompose *v* lobh.

decorate *v* sgeadaich.

decoration n sgeadachadh m.

decorous adj cubhaidh.

decrease n lùghdachadh m. • v lùghdaich.

decrepit adj breòite.

decry v càin.

dedicate v coisrig.

deduce v tuig.

deduct v beagaich.

deduction n beagachadh m.

deed n gnìomh m; (legal) gnìomhas m.

deep adj domhainn.

deepen v doimhnich.

deer n fiadh m.

deer-forest n frìth f.

deface v mill.

defamation n tuaileas m.

defame v cùl-chàin.

default n dearmad m.

defeat n call m. • v gabh air, faigh buaidh.

defect n easbhaidh f.

defective adj easbhaidheach.

defence n dìon m; leisgeul m.

defenceless adj gun dìon.

defend v dìon.

defensive adj dìona.

defer v cuir air dàil.

deference n ùmhlachd f.

deferment n dàil f.

defiance n dùlan m.

deficiency n dìth m.

deficit n easbhaidh f.

definable adj sonnrachail.

define v sonnraich.

definite adj comharraichte.

definition n comharrachadh m.

deflect v aom.

deform v cuir à cumadh.

deformity n mì-dhealbh m.

defraud v feallaich.

deft adj ealamh.

defy v thoir dùlan do.

degenerate v meath. • adj meathaichte.

degrade v ìslich.

degree n inbhe f; (academic) ceum m; (temp) puing f.

deign v deònaich.

deity n diadhachd f.

dejected adj fo bhròn.

delay n maille f. • v cuir maille air.

delegate n fear-ionaid m.

delegation n luchd tagraidh m.

delete v dubh-às.

deliberate adj mall. • v meòraich.

delicacy n mìlseachd f.

delicate adj fìnealta.

delicious adj ana-bhlasta.

delight v toilich.

delightful adj aoibhneach.

delinquency n ciontachd f.

delinquent adj ciontach.

delirium n breisleach f.

deliver v saor; (baby) asaidich.

delivery n teàrnadh m; post m; (baby) asaid m.

dell n lagan m.

deluge n tuile f.

demand n tagradh m. • v tagair.

demean v ìslich.

demented adj air bhoile.

dementia n troimhe-chèile m.

demerit n lochd m.

democracy n sluagh-fhlaitheas m.

democrat n sluagh-fhlaithear m.

demolish v sgrios.

demon n deamhan m.

demonstrable adj so-dhearbhte.

demonstration n taisbeanadh m.

demote v thoir ceum a-nuas.

demur v cuir teagamh ann.

demure adj stuama.

den n saobhaidh m.

denial n àicheadh m.

denigrate v dèan dìmeas air.

dense adj tiugh; (mind) maol.

density n dlùths m.

dent v dèan lag ann.

dentist n fiaclaire m.

denture n deudach m.

denude v rùisg.

deny v àicheidh.

depart v imich.

department n roinn f.

departure n falbh m.

depend v (on) cuir earbsa ann.

dependence n eisimealachd f.

dependent adj eisimealach.

depict v dealbh.

deplorable adj truagh.

deplore v caoidh.

deportment n giùlan m.

depose v cuir às oifig.

deposit n tasgadh m. • v tasgaich.

depravity n truailleachd f.

depreciate v cuir an dìmeas.

depress v brùth sìos.

depressant n locshlaint-ìsleach-aidh f.

depression n ìsleachadh m.

deprive v toirt air falbh.

depth n doimhneachd f.

depute adj leas-. • v sonnraich.

derelict adj trèigte.

deride v dèan fanaid air.

derision n fanaid f.

derivation n sìolachadh m.

derive v sìolaich.

descend v teirinn.

descent n teàrnadh m.

describe v thoir tuaraisgeul air.

description n tuaraisgeul m.

desert[1] n fàsach m/f.

desert[2] v trèig.

deserve v toill.

design n rùn m; (art) dealbh m.

design v rùnaich; deilbh.

designer n dealbhadair m.

desire n miann m. • v miannaich.

desist v stad.

desk n deasg m.

despair n eu-dòchas m. • v leig thairis dòchas.

desperate adj eu-dòchasach; dam-ainnte.

despicable adj suarach.

despise v dèan tàir air.

despite prep a dh'aindeoin.

dessert n mìlsean m.

destiny n dàn m.

destitute *adj* falamh.

destroy *v* sgrios.

destruction *n* milleadh *m*.

detach *v* dealaich.

detail *n* mion-chùnntas *m*; mion-phuing *f*.

detain *v* cùm air ais.

detect *v* lorg.

detective *n* lorg-phoileas *m*.

determination *n* diongbhaltas *m*.

determine *v* cuir roimh.

determinism *n* cinnteachas *m*.

detest *v* fuathaich.

detestation *n* fuath *m*.

detonate *v* toirm-spreadh.

detour *n* bealach *m*.

detract *v* thoir air falbh.

detriment *n* dolaidh *f*

devalue *v* di-luachaich.

devastate *v* lèir-sgrios.

devastation *n* lèir-sgrios *m*.

develop *v* leasaich; fàs.

development *n* leasachadh *m*.

deviate *v* claon.

device *n* innleachd *f*.

devil *n* diabhal *m*.

devious *adj* seachranach.

devise *v* innlich.

devolve *v* thig fo chùram; (*political*) sgaoil cumhachd.

devolution *n* sgaoileadh-cumhachd *m*.

devotion *n* cràbhadh *m*; teas-ghràdh *m*.

devour *v* sluig.

dew *n* dealt *m*.

dexterity *n* deisealachd *f*.

diagnose *v* breithnich.

diagnosis *n* breithneachadh *m*.

diagonal *adj* trasdanach.

dial *n* aodann *m*. • *v* comharraich àireamh.

diameter *n* meadhan-thrasdan *m*.

diarrhoea *n* a' bhuinneach *f*.

dice *npl* dìsnean.

dictate *v* deachd.

dictionary *n* faclair *m*.

die *v* bàsaich.

diesel *n* dìosail *m*.

diet *n* riaghailt bidhe *f*.

differ *v* eadar-dhealaich.

difference *n* eadar-dhealachadh *m*.

different *adj* air leth.

differentiate *v* diofaraich.

difficult *adj* duilich.

difficulty *n* duilgheadas *m*.

dig *v* cladhaich.

digest *v* cnàmh.

digestible *adj* so-chnàmh.

digit *n* meur *f*; (*number*) meur-àireamh *f*.

digital *adj* meurach.

dignified *adj* urramaichte.

dilate *v* leudaich.

dilemma *n* imcheist *f*.

diligent *adj* dìcheallach.

dilute *v* tanaich.

dim *adj* doilleir; (*person*) mall 'na intinn.

dimension *n* tomhas *m*.

diminish *v* lùghdaich.

dimple *n* tibhre *m*.

din *n* toirm *f*.

dine *v* gabh dìnnear.

dining-room *n* seòmar-bidhe *m*.

dinner *n* dìnnear *f*.

dinner-time *n* tràth-dìnneireach *m*.

dip *n* tumadh *m*. • *v* tum, bog.

diplomacy *n* seòltachd *f*.

dipsomania *n* miann-daoraich *m/f*.

direct *adj* dìreach. • *v* seòl.

direction *n* seòladh *m*; àird *f*.

direction-finder *n* àird-lorgair *m*.

directly *adv* air ball; dìreach.

director *n* fear-stiùiridh *m*.

dirk *n* biodag *f*.

dirt *n* salchar *m*.

dirty *adj* salach.

disability *n* neo-chomas *m*.

disadvantage *n* mì-leas *m*.

disagree *v* rach an aghaidh.

disagreement *n* eas-aonta *f*.

disappear *v* rach à sealladh.

disappoint *v* meall.

disapprove *v* coirich.

disaster *n* mòr-thubaist *f*.

disbelieve *v* na-creid.

disc *n* clàr *m*.

discard *v* cuir dhe.

discerning *adj* tuigseach.

discharge *n* di-luchdachadh *m*. • *v* di-luchdaich; cuir à dreuchd.

disclaim *v* àicheidh.

disclose *v* foillsich.

discomfort *n* anshocair *f*.

disconnect *v* sgaoil.

disconsolate *adj* brònach.

discontented *adj* mì-thoilichte.

discord *n* mì-chòrdadh *m*; (*mus*) dì-chòrda *m*.

discount *n* lasachadh *m*. • *v* lasaich.

discourage *v* mì-mhisnich.

discover *v* nochd; leig ris.

discovery *n* nochdadh *m*.

discrepancy *n* diofar *m*.

discretion *n* cùram *m*.

discriminate *v* (*in favour of*) gabh taobh; (*against*) rach an aghaidh.

discuss *v* deasbair.

discussion *n* deasbaireachd *f*.

disease *n* euslaint *f*.

disembark *v* cuir air tìr.

disengage *v* dealaich.

disentangle *v* fuasgail.

disfavour *n* mì-fhàbhar *m*.

disgrace *n* masladh *m*. • *v* maslaich.

disgraceful *adj* maslach.

disguise *n* breug-riochd *m*. • *v* cuir breug-riochd air.

disgust *n* gràin *f*.

disgusting *adj* gràineil.

dish *n* soitheach *m*.

dish-cloth *n* tubhailt-shoithichean *f*.

dishearten *v* mì-mhisnich.

dishonest *adj* mì-onorach.

dishonesty *n* mì-onair *f*.

dishwasher *n* nigheadair-shoithichean *m*.

disillusion n bristeadh-dùil m.

disinclined adj neo-thoileach.

disinherit v buin còir bhreith o.

disinterested adj neo-fhèin-chuiseach.

disjointed adj an-altaichte.

disk n clàr m.

disk drive n clàr-inneal m.

dislike v mì-thaitneamh.

dislodge v cuir à àite.

disloyal adj neo-dhìleas.

dismal adj dubhach.

dismay n uabhas m.

dismember v spion o chèile.

dismiss v cuir air falbh.

disobedience n eas-ùmhlachd f.

disobey v bi eas-umhail do.

disorder n mì-riaghailt f.

disown v na gabh ri.

disparity n neo-ionnanachd f.

dispel v fògair.

dispensation n riarachadh m.

dispense v riaraich.

dispersal n sgàpadh m.

displace v cuir à àite.

display n foillseachadh m. • v foillsich.

displease v mì-thoilich.

dispose v suidhich.

disprove v breugnaich.

disputatious adj connsachail.

dispute v connsaich.

disqualification n neo-iomchaidheachd f.

disqualify v dèan neo-iomchuidh.

disregard v dèan dìmeas air.

disrepair n droch-chàradh m.

disrespect n eas-urram m.

disrupt v bris, reub.

disruption n briseadh m.

dissatisfaction n mì-thoileachadh m.

dissatisfied adj mì-riaraichte.

dissect v sgrùd; gèarr suas.

dissertation n tràchd f.

disservice n droch-chomain f.

dissimilar adj eu-coltach.

dissipate v sgap.

dissociate v eadar-sgar.

dissolute adj drùiseil.

dissolve v leagh; fuasgail.

dissuade v comhairlich an aghaidh.

distance n astar m, fad m.

distant adj cèin.

distaste n droch bhlas m.

distasteful adj neo-bhlasta.

distil v tarraing.

distiller n grùdaire m.

distillery n taigh-staile m.

distinct adj soilleir.

distinction n eadar-dhealachadh m; (merit) cliù m.

distinctive adj so-aithnichte.

distinguish v eadar-dhealaich.

distort v fiaraich.

distract v buair.

distress n àmhghar m. • v sàraich.

distribute v roinn, compàirtich.

district n ceàrn m.

district nurse n banaltram sgìreachd f.

distrust *v* an-earbsa.

disturb *v* cuir dragh air.

disturbance *n* aimhreit *f*.

disunite *v* eadar-sgar.

disunity *n* eadar-sgaradh *m*.

disuse *n* mì-cleachdeach *m*.

ditch *n* clais *f*.

ditto *adv* an nì ceudna.

ditty *n* luinneag *f*.

dive *v* daoibhig.

diver *n* daoibhear *m*.

diverge *v* iomsgair.

diverse *adj* eugsamhail.

diversify *v* sgaoil.

diversion *n* claonadh *m*; (*pastime*) fearas-chuideachd *f*.

diversity *n* eugsamhlachd *m*.

divert *v* claon.

divide *v* roinn, pàirtich.

dividend *n* earrann *f*.

divination *n* fàistneachd *f*.

divine *adj* diadhaidh. • *v* dèan a-mach.

divisible *adj* so-roinn.

division *n* roinn *f*.

divorce *n* dealachadh pòsaidh *m*. • *v* dealaich ri.

dizzy *adj* tuainealach.

do *v* dèan.

dock[1] *n* port *m*.

dock[2], docken *n* copag *f*.

dockyard *n* doca *m*.

doctor *n* lighiche, doctair *m*; (*academic*) ollamh *m*.

doctrine *n* teagasg *m*.

document *n* sgrìobainn *f*.

documentary *adj* aithriseach.

dodge *v* seachainn.

doe *n* maoiseach *f*.

dog *n* cù *m*.

dogged *adj* doirbh, dùr.

dogmatic *adj* dìorrasach.

dole *n* dòil *m*.

dollar *n* dolair *m*.

domain *n* tighearnas *m*.

domestic *adj* teaghlachail.

domesticate *v* càllaich.

domicile *n* fàrdach *f*.

dominate *v* ceannsaich.

domineer *v* sàraich.

dominion *n* uachdranachd *f*.

donate *v* thoir tabhartas.

donor *n* tabhartaiche *m*.

doom *n* binn *m*. • *v* dìt.

doomsday *n* latha-luain *m*.

door *n* doras *m*.

dope *n* druga, drugaichean *f*.

dose *n* tomhas *m*.

dot *n* puing *f*.

dotage *n* leanabachd na h-aoise *f*.

double *adj* dùbailte. • *n* dùbladh *m*. • *v* dùblaich.

double-bass *n* prò-bheus *m*.

doubt *n* teagamh *m*. • *v* cuir an teagamh.

doubtful *adj* teagmhach.

doubtless *adv* gun teagamh.

dough *n* taois *f*.

dour *adj* dùr.

down *prep* shìos, a-nuas.

downfall *n* tuiteam *m*.

downhill *adv* leis a' bruthach.

downright adv air fad.

downstairs adv shìos staidhre.

downward adj le bruthach.

downwards adv sìos.

dowry n tochradh m.

doze v rach an clò-chadal.

dozen n dusan m.

drag v slaod.

drain n drèana f. • v sìolaidh.

drake n dràc m.

dram n dràm, drama m.

dramatist n dràmaire m.

draught n (drink) tarraing f; (wind) gaoth troimh tholl. f

draughts n dàmais f.

draughtsman n fear-tarraing m.

draw v tarraing; (liquid) deoghail; (art) dèan dealbh.

drawer n drabhair m.

drawing n dealbh m/f.

drawing-pin n tacaid f.

dread n oillt f. • v oilltich.

dreadful adj eagalach.

dream n aisling f. • v bruadair, faic aisling.

dreamer n aislingiche m.

dredge v glan grùnnd.

dregs npl druaip f.

drench v dèan bog-fliuch.

dress v cuir aodach air.

dresser n dreasair m.

dressing n ìoc-chòmhdach m.

dribble v sil; (sport) drioblaig.

drift v siab.

drill v drilich.

drilling platform n clàr-tollaidh m.

drink n deoch f. • v òl, gabh.

drinker n fear-òil m.

drip v snigh.

drive v greas; (car) stiùir.

drivel n briathran gorach mpl, sgudal m.

driver n dràibhear m.

driving licence n cead-dràibhidh m.

drizzle n ciùthran m.

droll adj neònach; èibhinn.

drone n torman m; (pipes) dos m.

droop v searg.

drop n boinne f. • v leig às.

drought n turadh m.

drove n dròbh m.

drover n dròbhair m.

drown v bàth.

drowsy adj cadalach.

drudgery n dubh-chosnadh m.

drug n droga f.

drug addict n tràill-dhrogaichean m.

druggist n drogadair m.

druid n draoidh m.

druidism n draoidheachd f.

drum n druma f.

drum-major n màidseir-druma m.

drummer n drumair m.

drumstick n bioran-druma m.

drunk adj air misg.

drunkard n misgear m.

drunkenness n misg f.

dry adj tioram. • v tiormaich.

dub v dùblaich.

duck¹ n tunnag f.

duck² v tum; crùb.
dud n rud gun fheum m.
due adj dligheach.
duel n còmhrag-dithis f.
duet n òran-dithis m.
dull adj trom-inntinneach; tiugh.
dullness n truime m.
dulse n duileasg m.
duly adv gu riaghailteach.
dumb adj balbh.
dummy n fear-brèige m, breagag f.
dump n òcrach m. • v caith air falbh.
dumpling n turraisg f.
dunce n ùmaidh m.
dung n innear f.
dunghill n dùnan m.
duplicate n dùblachadh m.
duplicity n dùbailteachd f.
durable adj maireannach.
duration n fad m, rè f.

during prep rè.
dusk n duibhre f.
dusky adj ciar.
dust n dust, stùr m. • v glan stùr dhe.
dustbin n biona-stùir m.
Dutch adj Duitseach.
dutiful adj umhail.
duty n dleasdanas m; (customs) diùtaidh m.
duty-free adj saor o dhiùtaidh.
dwarf n troich m.
dwell v tuinich.
dwelling n fàrdach f.
dwindle v crìon.
dye n dath m. • v dath.
dyke n gàradh m.
dynamic adj fiùghantach.
dynamite n dinimit m.
dynasty n rìgh-shliochd m.
dyspepsia n an do-chnàmh m.

E

each adj gach, gach aon. • pron gach aon; an duine.
eager adj dealasach.
eagle n iolair f.
ear n cluas f.
earphone n cluasan m.
earring n cluas-fhail f.
earl n iarla m.
early adj tràth.
earn v coisinn.

earnest adj dùrachdach.
earth n talamh f.
earthenware n soitheach criadha m.
earthly adj talmhaidh.
earthworm n daolag f.
ease n fois f.
easel n dealbh-thaic f.
east n ear, an àirde an ear f.
Easter n Càisg f.

easterly adj an ear.

easy adj furasda.

eat v ith.

eatable adj so-ith.

ebb n tràghadh m. • v tràigh.

eccentric adj iomrallach.

eccentricity n iomrallachd f.

echo n mac-talla m.

eclipse n dubhadh grèine m; (lunar) dubhadh gealaich m.

ecology n eag-eòlas m.

economics n eaconomachd m.

ecomomist n eaconomair m.

economise v caomhain.

economy n eaconomaidh m; banas-taighe m.

ecstasy n àrd-èibhneas m.

ecstatic adj àrd-èibhneach.

ecumenical adj uil-eaglaiseil.

eddy n saobh-shruth m.

edge n oir, iomall m; faobhar m. • v dèan oir.

edgewise adv air oir.

edible adj so-ithe.

edict n reachd m.

edifice n aitreabh m.

edify v teagaisg.

Edinburgh n Dun Eideann.

edit v deasaich.

edition n deasachadh m.

editor n fear-deasachaidh m.

educate v foghlaim.

education n foghlam m.

educational adj oideachail.

effect n buaidh f. • v thoir gu buil.

effective adj buadhach.

effeminate adj boireannta.

effervescent adj bruichneach.

efficacy n èifeachd f.

efficient adj èifeachdach.

effigy n ìomhaigh f.

effluent n sruthadh m.

effort n dìcheall m.

egg n ugh m.

egghead n eanchainn mhòr m.

egotism n fèin-spèis f.

Egypt n An Eiphit f.

eight n ochd.

eighth adj ochdamh.

eighteen n ochd-deug.

eightsome n ochdnar m.

eightsome reel n ruidhle-ochdnar m.

eighty n ochdad.

either conj **either . . . or . . .** an dara cuid . . . no . . . . • adv a bharrachd, nas motha.

ejaculate v cuir a-mach.

eject v tilg a-mach.

elaborate adj saothraichte.

elapse v rach seachad.

elastic adj sùbailte.

elate v tog suas.

elbow n uileann f.

elder n (church) eildear m; (tree) droman m. • adj as/nas sine.

elderly adj sean.

elect v tagh.

election n taghadh.

electioneering n taghadaireachd f.

elector n taghadair m.

electorate n luchd-taghaidh m.

electric adj dealain.

electricity n dealan m.

electrification n dealanachadh m.

electrocute v dealan-marbh.

electronic adj eleactronach.

elegance n grinneas m.

elegant adj grinn.

eleglac adj caointeach.

elegy n tuireadh m.

element n dùil f.

elementary adj bun.

elephant n ailbhean m.

elevate v àrdaich.

eleven n aon.... deug.

eligible adj ion-tagha.

eliminate v geàrr às.

elixir n ìocshlaint f.

elm n leamhan m.

elongate v fadaich.

elope v teich.

eloquence n deas-bhriathrachd f.

else adj/adv eile.

elude v seachainn.

elusive adj èalaidheach.

e-mail n post dealain m.

emancipate v saor.

embalm v splosraich.

embargo n bacadh m.

embark v cuir air bòrd.

embarrass v cuir troimhe chèile.

embarrassment n beag-nàrach-adh m.

embassy n tosgaireachd f.

ember n èibhleag f.

embezzle v dèan maoin-èalach-adh.

emboss v gràbhail.

embrace v iath an glacaibh.

embroider v cuir obair-ghrèis air.

embryo n suth m.

emerald n smàrag f.

emerge v thig an uachdar.

emergency n bàlanaich m.

emigrant n eilthireach m.

emigrate v dèan eilthireachd.

eminent adj àrd.

emit v leig a-mach.

emotion n tòcadh m.

emotional adj tòcail.

emphasis n cudrom m.

emphatic adj làidir.

empire n ìompaireachd f.

empirical adj deuchainneach.

employ v fasdaich.

employee n fear-obrach m.

employer n fastaidhear m.

empty adj falamh.

emulation n strì f.

enable v dèan comasach.

enact v òrdaich.

enamel n cruan m.

enchant v cuir fo gheaṣaibh.

enchantment n draoidheachd f.

enclosure n crò m.

encourage v misnich.

encroach v thig a-steach.

encumbrance n uallach m.

end n deireadh m, crìoch f. • v cuir crìoch air.

endemic adj dùthchasach.

endless *adj* neo-chrìochnach.
endorse *v* cùl-sgrìobh.
endowment *n* bronnadh *m*.
enemy *n* nàmhaid *m*.
energetic *adj* brìoghmhor.
energy *n* brìogh *f*.
enforce *v* co-èignich.
engagement *n* gealladh-pòsaidh *m*.
engine *n* inneal *m*.
engineer *n* innleadair *m*. • *v* innlich.
England *n* Sasainn *f*.
English *n* Beurla *f*.
Englishman *n* Sasannach *m*.
enhance *v* meudaich.
enigma *n* dubhfhacal *m*.
enjoy *v* meal.
enlarge *v* meudaich.
enlighten *v* soillsich.
enlist *v* liostaig.
enormous *adj* uabhasach.
enough *adv* gu leòr.
enquire *v* feòraich.
enrage *v* feargaich.
ensue *v* lean.
ensure *v* dèan cinnteach.
enter *v* rach/thig a-steach.
enterprise *n* iomairt *f*.
enterprising *adj* ionnsaigheach.
entertainer *n* oirfideach *m*.
entertainment *n* aoigheachd *f*.
enthusiasm *n* dìoghras *m*.
entice *v* tàlaidh.
entire *adj* iomlan.
entirely *adv* gu lèir.

entitle *v* thoir còir.
entrance *n* dol a-steach *m*.
entreat *v* guidh.
entrepreneur *n* fear-tionnsgain *m*.
envelope *n* cèis *f*.
environment *n* comhearsnachd *f*; (*ecology*) àrainn-eachd *f*.
envy *n* farmad *m*.
ephemeral *adj* geàrr-shaoglach.
episode *n* tachartas *m*.
epitaph *n* leac-sgrìobhadh *m*.
epoch *n* tùs-aimsir *f*.
equal *adj* seise.
equalise *v* dèan co-ionann; (*game*) ruig an aon àireamh.
equation *n* co-ionannas *m*.
equator *n* meadhan-chearcall na tal-mhainn *m*.
equidistant *adj* co-fhad air falbh.
equinox *n* co-fhreagradh nan tràth *m*.
equip *v* uidheamaich.
equipment *n* uidheam *f*.
equipped *adj* uidheamaichte.
equity *n* ceartas *m*; (*fin*) stoc-roinn *f*.
equivalent *adj* co-ionann.
erase *v* dubh às.
erect *v* tog.
erection *n* togail *m*.
erode *v* meirg.
erotic *adj* drùis-mhiannach.
err *v* rach iomrall.
errand *n* gnothach *m*.
erratic *adj* iomrallach.
error *n* mearrachd *f*.

eruption n brùchdach m.

escalator n streapadan m.

escape n èaladh m. • v teich.

esoteric adj às an rathad.

essay n aiste f.

essence n gnè f.

essential adj riatanach.

establish v suidhich.

estate n oighreachd f.

esteem n meas m.

estimate v meas.

estrange v dèan fuathach.

estuary n inbhir m.

eternal adj bith-bhuan.

eternity n sìorraidheachd f.

ethical adj modhannach.

ethnic adj cinnidheach.

eunuch n cailltearach m.

Europe n An Roinn Eòrpa f.

European adj Eòrpach.

evaporate v deataich.

even adj rèidh. • adv eadhon; fèin.

evening n feasgar m.

event n tuiteamas m.

ever adv aig àm sam bith, idir.

evergreen adj sìor-uaine.

everlasting adj sìorraidh.

evermore adv gu bràth.

every adj gach, na h-uile.

everyday adj làitheil.

everyone pron gach duine.

everything pron gach nì.

evict v fuadaich.

eviction n fuadachadh m.

evidence n fianais f.

evident adj soilleir.

evil adj olc. • n olc m.

ewe n othaisg f.

exact adj pongail.

exact v buin.

exactly adv dìreach.

exaggerate v cuir am meud.

examination n ceasnachadh m.

examine v ceasnaich.

example n eisimpleir m.

excavate v cladhaich.

excavation n cladhach m.

exceed v rach thairis air.

exceedingly adv glè.

excel v thoir bàrr.

excellence n feabhas m.

excellent adj barrail.

except v fàg a-mach. • prep ach a-mhàin; **except for** saor o.

exceptional adj sònraichte.

exchange v malairtich.

exchange rate n co-luach cùinnidh m.

exchequer n stàitchiste f.

exciseman n gàidsear m.

excite v gluais.

excitement n brosnachadh m.

exclaim v glaodh.

exclamation n glaodh m.

exclamation mark n clisg-phuing f.

exclusive adj dlùth.

excrement n cac m.

excrete v cac.

excuse n leisgeul m. • v gabh leisgeul, math.

executive *n* fear-gnìomha *m*.

executor *n* fear-cùraim tiomnaidh *m*.

exercise *n* eacarsaich *f*. • *v* obraich, cleachd.

exertion *n* spàirn *f*.

exhaust *v* falmhaich.

exhaustion *n* traoghadh *m*.

exile *n* fògarrach *m*.

exist *v* bi, bi beò.

existence *n* bith *f*.

exit *n* dol a-mach *m*.

exonerate *v* fìreanaich.

exorbitant *adj* ana-cuimseach.

exotic *adj* coimheach.

expand *v* sgaoil.

expatriate *adj* às-dhùthchach.

expect *v* bi dùil aig.

expedient *adj* coltach.

expedite *v* luathaich.

expedition *n* turas *m*.

expeditious *adj* cabhagach.

expend *v* caith.

expenditure *n* caiteachas *m*.

expensive *adj* cosgail.

experience *n* cleachdadh *m*. • *v* mothaich.

experiment *n* deuchainn *f*.

expert *adj* ealanta. • *n* eòlaiche *m*.

expire *v* analaich; (*die*) bàsaich.

explain *v* mìnich.

explanation *n* mìneachadh *m*.

explicit *adj* fosgailte.

explode *v* spreadh.

exploit *n* euchd *m*. • *v* dèan feum de.

explore *v* rannsaich.

export *n* eas-tharraing *f*. • *v* cuir thairis.

expose *v* nochd.

exposure *n* nochdadh *m*.

express[1] *v* cuir an cèill.

express[2] *adj* luath.

express train *n* luath-thrèana.

expression *n* fiamh *m*.

exquisite *adj* òirdheirc.

extensive *adj* leathann.

exterior *n* taobh a-muigh *m*.

extinct *adj* bàthte.

extinguish *v* smàl.

extinguisher *n* smàladair *m*.

extra *adj* fìor, ro-. • *adv* a bharrachd.

extraordinary *adj* anabarrach.

extravagant *adj* ana-caiteach.

extreme *adj* fìor.

extricate *v* saor.

extrovert *n* duine fosgarra *m*.

exuberance *n* braise.

exuberant *adj* bras.

eye *n* sùil *f*. • *v* seall.

eyesight *n* fradharc *m*.

eyesore *n* cùis mhì-thlachd *f*.

eyrie *n* nead iolaire *m*.

F

fable *n* uirsgeul *m*.

fabric *n* aodach *m*; togalach *m*.

facade *n* aghaidh *f*.

face *n* aghaidh, gnùis *f*.

facet *n* taobh *m*.

facilitate *v* soirbhich.

facilities *npl* goireasan.

fact *n* beart *m*.

factor *n* seumarlan *m*.

factory *n* taigh-cèairde, factaraidh *m*.

faculty *n* comas *m*; (*university*) dàmh *m*.

fad *n* àilleas *m*.

fade *v* searg.

fail *v* dìobair.

failure *n* fàilinn *f*.

faint *adj* fann. • *v* fannaich.

fair *n* fèill.

fairly *adv* an ìre mhath.

fairness *n* maisealachd *f*.

fairway *n* prìomh-raon *m*.

fairy *adj* sìdh. • *n* sìdhiche *m*.

faith *n* creideamh *m*.

faithful *adj* dìleas.

fake *n* rud brèige *m*.

fall *n* tuiteam *m*. • *v* tuit.

fallacy *n* saobh-chiall *f*.

fallow *adj* bàn.

false *adj* meallta.

falsehood *n* breug *f*.

falter *v* lagaich.

fame *n* cliù *m*.

familiar *adj* càirdeil.

familiarise *v* gnàthaich.

family *n* teaghlach *m*.

famine *n* goirt *f*.

famous *adj* ainmeil.

fanatic *n* eudmhoraiche *m*.

fancy *adj* guanach. • *v* smaoinich.

fank *n* faing *f*.

fantastic *adj* ro-iongantach.

fantasy *n* sgeul guaineis *m*.

far *adj* fada, fas às. • *adv* fada, fas às.

fare *n* faradh *m*; biadh *m*.

farewell *n* soraidh *m*.

farm *n* baile-fearainn, tuathanas *m*.

farmer *n* tuathanach *m*.

fart *n* braidhm *m*; tùd *m*.

farther *adv* nas fhaide.

fascinate *v* cuir fo gheasaibh.

fascination *n* geasachd *f*.

fascism *n* faisisteachas *m*.

fashion *n* fasan *m*. • *v* cum.

fashionable *adj* fasanta.

fast *adj* luath; daingeann.

fasten *v* ceangail.

fast food *n* grad-bhiadh *m*.

fastidious *adj* àilleasach.

fat *adj* reamhar. • *n* reamhrachd *m*.

fatal *adj* marbhtach.

fate *n* dàn *m*.

father *n* athair *m*. • *v* bi mar athair.

father-in-law *n* athair-cèile *m*.

fatherly *adj* athaireil.

fathom *v* ruig air.

fatigue *n* sgìos *f*. • *v* sgìthich.

fatuous *adj* baoth.

fault *n* coire *f*.

faultless *adj* neo-chiontach.

faulty *adj* easbhaidheach.

favour *v* bi fàbharach.

favourite *n* annsachd *m/f*.

fawn *n* mang *f*.

fax *n* facs *m*.

fear *n* eagal *m*. • *v* gabh eagal.

fearful *adj* eagalach.

fearless *adj* gun eagal.

feast *n* fèisd *f*, fleadh *m*. • *v* dèan fèist.

feat *n* euchd *m*.

feather *n* ite *f*.

February *n* Feabruari *f*, An Gearran *m*.

federal *adj* feadarail.

fee *n* duais *f*.

feeble *adj* fann.

feed *v* biath.

feel *v* fairich.

feeling *n* faireachdainn *f*.

felicitous *adj* sona.

feline *adj* mar chat.

fellowship *n* companas *m*.

felon *n* slaoightear *m*.

female *adj* boireann, baineann.

feminine *adj* banail.

fence *n* lann. • *v* dùin.

fender *n* dìonadair *m*.

ferment *n* brachadh *m*. • *v* brach.

fermentation *n* brachadh *m*.

fern *n* raineach *f*.

ferret *n* feocallan *m*.

ferry *n* aiseag *f*. • *v* aisig.

ferry-boat *n* bàta-aiseig.

fertile *adj* torach.

fertility *n* torachas *m*.

fertilise *v* toraich.

fervent *adj* dian.

fervour *n* dèine *f*.

fester *v* at.

festive *adj* fleadhach.

fetch *v* faigh.

feu *n* gabhail *m*.

feud *n* falachd *f*.

fever *n* fiabhras *m*.

feverish *adj* fiabhrasach.

few *adj* beag, tearc. • *n* beagan *m*.

fibre *n* snàithleach *m*.

fibrous *adj* snàithlainneach.

fickle *adj* caochlaideach.

fiction *n* uirsgeul *m*.

fiddle *n* fidheall *f*. • *v* dèan fìdhleireachd; foillich.

fiddler *n* fìdhlear *m*.

fidelity *n* dìlseachd *f*.

field *n* achadh *m*.

field-glasses *n* prosbaig *f*.

field-mouse *n* luch-fheòir *f*.

fierce *adj* garg.

fierceness *n* gairge *f*.

fiery *adj* teinnteach.

fifteen *n* còig-deug.

fifth *adj* còigeamh.

fifty *n* leth-cheud.

fiftieth *adj* leth-cheudamh.

fig *n* fiogais *f*.

fight *n* còmhrag *f*. • *v* còmhraig.

figure *n* dealbh *m*; figear *m*.

file *n* eighe *f*; (*documents*) còmhlachadh *m*. • *v* liòmh; còmhlaich.

filial *adj* macail.

fill *v* lìon.

fillet *v* colpaich.

filly *n* loth *m/f*.

film-star *n* reul film *m*, reultag film *f*.

filter *n* sìolachan *m*. • *v* sìolaidh.

filth *n* salchar *m*.

filthy *adj* salach.

final *adj* deireannach.

finalise *v* thoir gu crìch.

finance *n* maoineachas *m*. • *v* maoinich.

financier *n* maoiniche *m*.

find *v* faigh, lorg.

fine[1] *adj* grinn.

fine[2] *n* ùnnlagh *m*. • *v* leag ùnnlagh.

finery *n* rìomhachas *m*.

finger *n* meur, corrag *f*.

fingernail *n* ìne *f*.

finish *n* crìoch *f*. • *v* crìochnaich.

fir *n* giuthas *m*.

fire *n* teine *m*. • *v* cuir 'na theine.

fire-arm *n* airm-theine *m*.

fire-escape *n* staidhre èalaidh *f*.

fire-proof *adj* teine-dhìonach.

fireside *n* teallach *m*.

firewood *n* fiodh connaidh *m*.

firm[1] *adj* teann.

firm[2] *n* companaidh *f*.

first *adj* a'chiad. • *adv* (*time*) an toiseach; (*sequence*) air toiseach.

first aid *n* ciad-fuasgladh *m*.

first-born *n* ciad-ghin *m*.

firth *n* caol *m*.

fiscal *adj* fioscail.

fish *n* iasg *m*. • *v* iasgaich.

fisher *n* iasgair *m*.

fishing *n* iasgaireachd *f*.

fishing-line *n* driamlach *m*.

fishing rod *n* slat-iasgaich *f*.

fishy *adj* mar iasg; neònach.

fist *n* dòrn *m*.

fit[1] *adj* freagarrach.

fit[2] *n* taom *m*.

five *adj/n* còig.

fix *v* dèan teann; suidhich.

fixture *n* rud socraichte *m*.

fizz *n* copraich *f*.

flabby *adj* plamach.

flag *n* bratach *f*.

flagrant *adj* follaiseach.

flagstone *n* leac *f*.

flair *n* liut *m*.

flake *n* bleideag *f*.

flame *n* lasair *f*.

flannel *n* flannain *f*.

flap *n* cleitearnach *m*. • *v* crath.

flare *n* lasair-bhoillsg *m*.

flash *n* lasair *f*. • *v* boillsg.

flask *n* searrag *f*.

flat[1] *adj* còmhnard; (*mus*) maol, flat.

flat[2] *n* còmhnard *m*; flat *m*.

flatten *v* laigh ri; (*mus*) maolaich.

flatter *v* dèan sodal.

flattery n sodal m.

flautist n cuisleannach m.

flavour n blas m. • v blasaich.

flea n deargann f.

fleece n rùsg m. • v rùisg.

fleecy adj rùsgach.

fleet n cabhlach m.

fleeting adj siùbhlach.

flesh n feòil f.

fleshy adj sultmhor.

flex n fleisg f.

flexible adj so-lùbadh.

flicker v priob.

flight n itealadh m.

flimsy adj tana.

flinch v clisich.

flint n ailbhinn f.

flippant adj beadaidh.

flit v èalaidh; (house) dèan imrich.

float v snàmh.

flock n treud m.

flood n tuil f. • v còmhdaich le uisge.

floodlight n tuil-sholas m.

floor n ùrlar m. • v cuir ùrlar ann.

floppy disk n clàr sùbailte m.

floral adj flùranach.

flounder n leòbag f.

flour n flùr m.

flourish v fàs gu math; beartaich.

flow v ruith.

flower n blàth, flùr m.

fluctuate v atharraich.

fluency n fileantachd f.

fluent adj fileanta.

fluid adj silteach. • n lionn m.

flush v fàs dearg; (toilet) sruth-laich.

fluster v cuir gu cabhaig.

flute n cuisle chiùil f.

fly[1] n cuileag f, (fishing) maghar m.

fly[2] v theirig air iteig.

fly[3] adj carach.

foal n searrach m.

foam n cop m. • v cuir cop dhe.

focus n cruinn-ionad m; fòcas m. • v faigh cruinn-shealladh.

fodder n fodar m.

foetus n toircheas m.

fog n ceò m/f.

foggy adj ceòthach.

foil v cuir casg air.

fold n buaile f. • v cuir an crò.

folded adj fillte.

foliage n duilleach m.

folk n muinntir f.

folk-song n mith-òran m.

folk-tale n mith-sgeul m.

folklore n beul-aithris f.

follow v lean.

folly n amaideachd f.

fond adj dèidheil.

fondle v cniadaich.

food n biadh m.

fool n amadan m. • v thoir an car à.

foolproof adj do-mhillte.

foolish adj gòrach.

foot n cas, troigh f.

footpath n frith-rathad m.

footwear n caisbheart f.

for *prep* air; a chionn; an àite; do bhrìgh; ri; gu; fad; do.

forage *v* solair.

forbid *v* toirmisg.

forbidding *adj* gruamach.

force *n* neart *m*. • *v* co-èignich.

forceps *n* teanchair *m*.

ford *n* àth *m*.

fore *adj* toisich.

forearm *n* ruighe *f*.

forecast *n* roimh-aithris *f*. • *v* roimh-aithris.

forefather *n* sinnsear *m*.

forefinger *n* sgealbag *f*.

forego *v* fàg.

foreground *n* roimh-ionad *m*.

forehead *n* bathais *m*.

foreign *adj* gallda, coimheach.

foreigner *n* Gall, coigreach *m*.

foreknow *v* roimh-aithnich.

foreknowledge *n* roimh-aithne *f*.

foremost *adj* prìomh.

forerunner *n* roimh-ruithear *m*.

foresail *n* seòl-toisich *m*.

foresee *v* faic roimh làimh.

foresight *n* roimh-shealladh *m*.

forest *n* coille *f*.

forester *n* forsair *m*.

forestry *n* forsaireachd *f*.

foretaste *n* roimh-bhlasad *m*.

foretell *v* roimh-innis.

forever *adv* a chaoidh.

forewarn *v* cuir air earalas.

foreword *n* roimh-ràdh *m*.

forge *v* dèan goibhneachd.

forger *n* fallsaidhear *m*.

forget *v* dìochuimhnich.

forgetful *adj* dìochuimhneach.

forgetfulness *n* dìochuimhne *f*.

forgive *v* thoir mathanas.

forgotten *adj* air dìochuimhne.

fork *n* greimire, forc *m*. • *v* fàs gòbhlach.

forlorn *adj* aonaranach.

form *n* cumadh *m*. • *v* dealbh, cum.

formal *adj* dòigheil, foirmeil.

formality *n* deas-ghnàth *m*.

format *n* cruth *m*.

formidable *adj* cumhachdach.

formula *n* foirmle *f*.

formulate *v* riaghailich.

fornicate *v* dèan strìopachas.

fornication *n* strìopachas *f*.

forsake *v* cuir cùl ri.

forsaken *adj* trèigte.

fort *n* daingneach *f*, dùn *m*.

forth *adv* a-mach.

forthwith *adv* gun dàil.

fortitude *n* cruadal *m*.

fortnight *n* cola-deug *f*.

fortuitous *adj* tuiteamach.

fortunate *adj* fortanach.

fortune *n* sealbh *m*.

fortuneteller *n* fiosaiche *m*.

forty *adj/n* ceathrad.

forward *adj* iarrtach. • *adv* air adhart.

forwards *adv* air adhart.

fossil *n* fosail *f*.

foster *v* altrum.

foster-sibling *n* co-alta *m*.

foster-father n oide m.

foster-mother n muime f.

foul¹ adj breun.

foul² n fealladh m.

found v stèidhich.

foundation n stèidh f.

founder¹ n fear-stèidheachaidh f.

founder² v theirig fodha.

foundling n faodalach m.

fountain n fuaran m.

four adj/n ceithir; (persons) cea-thrar.

foursome n ceathrach f.

fourteen adj/n ceithir-deug.

fourteenth adj ceathramh deug.

fourthly adv sa' cheathramh àite.

fowl n eun m.

fox n sionnach m.

fraction n bloigh f.

fracture n bristeadh m.

fragile adj brisg.

fragment n fuigheall m.

fragrant adj cùbhraidh.

frail adj lag.

frailty n laige f.

frame n cèis f.

France n An Fhraing f.

frank adj faoilidh.

frank v (stamp) saor.

frantic adj air bhoile.

fraternal adj bràithreil.

fraud n foill f.

freak n tuiteamas m.

freckles npl breacadh-seunain m.

freckled adj breac-bhallach.

free adj saor; an asgaidh.

freedom n saorsa f.

freelance adj neo-cheangailte.

freemason n saor-chlachair m.

free-range adj saor-thogta.

free trade n saor-mhalairt f.

free will n saor-thoil f.

freeze v reòdh.

freezer n reodhadair m.

freight n luchd m.

French adj Frangach. • n Fraingis f.

frenzy n boile f.

frequency n tricead m.

frequent adj tric. • v tadhail.

fresh adj (air) fionnar; (food) ùr.

fret v luaisg.

fretful adj frionasach.

friar n bràthair-bochd m.

friction n suathadh m.

Friday n Dihaoine m.

friend n caraid m, bana-charaid f.

friendliness n càirdeas m.

friendly adj càirdeil.

fright n eagal m.

frighten v cuir eagal air.

frightful adj oillteil.

frigid adj fuar.

frill n grinneas m.

frisky adj mireagach.

frivolity n faoineas m.

frivolous adj faoin.

fro adv air ais.

frock n froca m.

frog n losgann m.

from prep o, bho, à.

front n aghaidh f.

front-door n doras-mòr m.
frontier n crìoch f.
frost n reothadh m.
frostbitten adj reo-sheargte.
frosty adj (frozen) reòta.
frown n gruaim f.
frugal adj glèidhteach.
frugality n glèidhteachd f.
fruit n meas m.
fruity adj measach.
frustrate v mill dùil.
fry v ròsd.
frying pan n aghann f.
fuck v rach air muin.
fuel n connadh m.
fugitive n fògarrach m.
fulfil v coilion.
fulfilment n coilionadh m.
full adj làn.
full-grown adj aig làn fhàs.
full stop n stad phuing f.
full-time adj làn-aimsireach.

fumble v làimhsich gu cearbach.
fun n spòrs f.
function n dreuchd f.
function key n (comput) inchair-gnìomha f.
fundamental adj bunaiteach.
funeral n adhlacadh m.
funny adj sùgach, èibhinn.
fur n bian m.
furnish v uidheamaich.
furniture n àirneis f.
furrow n clais f.
furry adj molach.
further, furthermore adv rud eile, a bhàrr air sinn.
fury n cuthach m.
fuse n leagadh m.
fusty adj malcaidh.
futile adj dìomhain.
futility n dìomhanas m.
future adj ri teachd. • n àm ri teachd m.

G

gable n stuadh f.
gadget n uidheam f.
Gael n Gaidheal m.
Gaelic adj/n Gàidhlig.
gaiety n cridhealas m.
gaily adv gu cridheil.
gain v buannaich.
gale n gaoth mhòr f.
gallant adj basdalach.

gallery n lobhta m.
galley n birlinn f.
gallon n galan m.
gallop v luath-mharcaidh.
Galloway n A'Ghall-Ghaidheal-tachd f.
gallows n croich f.
galore adv gu lèor.
gamble v iomair air gheall.

gambler n cèarraiche m.

gambling n cèarrachas m.

game n cluiche f; (meat) sitheann f.

gamekeeper n geamair m.

gander n gànradh m.

gang n buidheann f.

gannet n sùlaire m.

gaol n prìosan m.

gap n beàrn m.

gape v spleuchd.

garage n garaids f.

garbage n fuighleach m.

garble v cuir às a riochd.

garden n lios m.

gardener n gàirnealair m.

garland n blàth-fhleasg f.

garlic n creamh m.

garment n bad aodaich m.

garron n gearran m.

garrulity n goileam m.

garrulous adj cabach.

garter n gartan m.

gas-cooker n cucair-gas m.

gas fire n teine gas m.

gash n gearradh m.

gasp v plosg.

gastronomic adj sòghail.

gastronomy n sòghalachd f.

gate n geata m.

gather v cruinnich.

gathering n cruinneachadh m.

gaudy adj basdalach.

gauge n tomhas m.

gaunt adj lom.

gawky adj sgleòideach.

gay adj sùnndach; (sexuality) co-sheòrsach.

gaze v dùr-amharc.

gear n (car) gèar m.

gem n seud m.

gender n gnè f.

genealogical adj sloinnnteachail.

genealogist n sloinntear m.

genealogy n sloinntearachd f.

general adj coitcheann.

generalise v ginearalaich.

generally adv am bitheantas.

generation n àl m; linn m.

generator n gineadair m.

generic adj gnèitheach.

generosity n fialaidheachd m.

generous adj fial.

genetic adj ginteil.

genial adj coibhneil.

genitals npl buill gineamhainn.

genius n sàr-ghin m.

genteel adj suairce.

gentle adj ciùin.

gentleman n duine uasal m.

gentlewoman n bean uasal f.

gentry npl uaislean.

genuine adj fìor.

geography n cruinn'-eòlas m.

geological adj geòlâch.

geologist n geòlaiche m.

geology n geòlas m.

geometry n geoimeatras m.

germ n bitheag f.

German n Gearmailt f. • adj Gearmailteach.

Germany *n* A' Ghearmailt *f*.

germinate *v* ginidich.

gestation *n* torrachas *m*.

gesture *n* gluasad *m*.

get *v* faigh, coisinn.

ghastly *adj* oillteil.

ghost *n* taibhse *m/f*, bòcan *m*.

ghostly *adj* taibhseil.

giant *adj* ana-mhòr. • *n* famhair *m*.

gibber *v* dèan goileam.

gibe *n* sgeig *f*.

giddy *adj* guanach.

gift *n* tiodhlac *m*.

gifted *adj* tàlantach.

gigantic *adj* fuamhaireil.

gild *v* òraich.

gill *n* giùran *m*.

gin *n* sine *f*; (*trap*) ribe *f*.

gingerbread *n* aran-crì *m*.

gipsy *n* giofag *f*.

giraffe *n* sioraf *m*.

girdle *n* greideal *f*.

girl *n* caileag, nighean *f*.

girth *n* giort *f*.

give *v* thoir.

glaciation *n* eighreachadh *m*.

glacier *n* eighre-shruth *m*.

glad *adj* toilichte.

glance *n* grad-shealladh *m*. • *v* grad-amhairc.

gland *n* fàireag *f*.

glare *n* deàrrsadh *m*.

Glasgow *n* Glaschu *f*.

glass *n* glainne *f*.

glassy *adj* glainneach.

gleam *v* soillsich.

glean *v* dìoghlam.

glee *n* mire *f*.

glen *n* gleann *m*.

glib *adj* cabanta.

glide *v* gluais.

glimmer *n* fann-sholas *m*.

glister *v* deàrrs.

glitter *n* lainnir *f*.

gloaming *n* fionnaraigh *f*.

global *adj* domhanta.

global warming *n* blàthachadh na cruinne *m*.

globe *n* cruinne *f*.

gloom *n* duibhre *f*.

gloomy *adj* doilleir.

glory *n* glòir *f*.

glossy *adj* lìomharra.

glove *n* miotag *f*.

glow *n* luisne *f*. • *v* luisnich.

glower *v* seall fo na mùgan.

glue *n* glaodh *m*.

glum *adj* gruamach.

glutton *n* craosaire *m*.

gluttony *n* craos *m*.

gnash *v* gìosg.

gnaw *v* creim.

go *v* falbh, imich, theirich, rach, gabh.

goal *n* crìoch *f*; gòil *m*.

goalie *n* fear-bàire *m*.

goalpost *n* post-bàire *m*.

goat *n* gobhar *m*.

goblin *n* bòcan *m*.

god *n* dia *m*.

goddess *n* ban-dia *f*.

going n falbh m.

gold n òr m.

golden adj òir, òrach.

golf n goilf m.

good adj math, deagh.

goodbye interj slàn leat; beannachd leat.

goodness n mathas m.

goodwill n gean math m.

goods npl bathar m; (possessions) cuid f.

goose n gèadh f.

gooseberry n gròiseid f.

gore v sàth.

gorge¹ n clais-mhòr f.

gorge² v lion craos.

gorgeous adj greadhnach.

gorse n conasg m.

gory adj gaorrach.

gospel n soisgeul m.

gossip n goistidh m. • v bi a' gobaireachd.

govern v riaghail.

government n riaghaltas m.

gown n gùn m.

grab v gabh grèim air.

grace n gràs m; (prayer) altachadh m; (manner) loinn m. • v sgeadaich.

grace-note n nota-altaidh f.

graceful adj maiseach.

gracious adj gràsmhor.

grade n ceum m.

gradient n àrdachadh m.

gradual adj beag is beag.

gradually adv beag is beag.

graduate n fear-ceuma m.

graduation n ceumnachadh m.

graft n nòdachadh m. • v nòdaich; (toil) saothraich.

grain n gràinne f.

gralp n gràpa m.

granary n sìol-lann f.

grand adj mòr, uasal.

grandchild n ogha m.

grandeur n mòrachd m.

grandfather n seanair m.

grandmother n seanmhair f.

granite n clach-ghràin f.

grant n tabhartas m.

granular adj cnapach.

grape n fìon-dearc f.

grapefruit n seadag f.

grapple v greimich.

grasp n grèim m. • v dèan grèim air, glac.

grass n feur m.

grassy adj feurach.

grate n cliath-theine f.

grate v sgrìob.

grateful adj taingeil.

grater n sgrìoban m.

gratitude n taingealachd f.

gratuity n tiodhlac m.

grave¹ adj stòlda.

grave² n uaigh f.

gravel n grinneal m.

gravestone n leac-uaghach f.

graveyard n cladh m.

gravity n iom-tharraing f.

graze¹ v (browse) feuraich.

graze² v (scrape) suath.

grease n saill f. • v crèisich.

greasy adj crèiseach.

great adj mòr; àrd.

greatness n mòrachd f.

Greece n A' Ghreig f.

Greek adj Greugach. • n Greugais f.

greed n sannt m.

greedy adj sanntach.

green adj uaine.

greenness n uainead m.

greet v fàiltich.

greeting n fàilte f.

gregarious adj greigheach.

grey adj glas, liath.

grey-haired adj liath.

grid n cliath f.

griddle n greideal f.

grief n mulad m.

grieve v cràidh.

grill v grìosaich.

grilse n bànag f.

grim adj gnù.

grimace n mùig m.

grin n braoisg f. • v cuir braosg air.

grind v meil.

gristle n maothan m.

grit n grian m.

grizzled adj grìsfhionn.

groan n cnead m. • v dèan cnead.

groceries n bathair grosaireach m.

groin n loch-bhlèin f.

groove n clais f.

grope v rùraich.

gross¹ adj dòmhail.

gross² n dà dhusan deug m.

grotesque adj mì-nàdurrach.

ground n grùnnd m. • v socraich.

group n còmhlan m.

grouse¹ n (bird) eun-fhraoich m.

grouse² n (grumble) gearan m.

grove n doire m.

grovel v snàig.

grow v fàs, meudaich.

growl n dranndan m. • v dèan dranndan.

growth n fàs m.

grudge n diomb m. • v talaich.

grumble v gearain.

grunt n gnòsail f. • v dèan gnòsail.

guarantee n barrantas m.

guard n faire f, (individual) freiceadan m. • v dìon.

guardian n (tutor) taoitear m.

guess n tomhas m. • v tomhais.

guest n aoigh m.

guide n fear-treòrachaidh m. • v treòraich.

guided missile n urchair thrèoraichte f.

guillemot n eun dubh an sgadain m.

guilt n ciont m.

guilty adj ciontach.

gulf n camas m.

gully n gil f.

gulp n slugadh m. • v sluig.

gum n càireas.

gumption n ciall f.

gun n gunna m.

gunwale n beul-mòr m.

gurgle n glugan m.
gust n oiteag f.
gusto n cridhealas m.

gusty adj stoirmeil.
gut n caolan m.

H

habit n cleachdadh m; (monk) earradh m.
habitual adj gnàthach.
hack v geàrr.
haddock n adag f.
haft n cas m.
hag n cailleach f.
haggis n taigeis f.
haggle v dèan còmhstri mu phrìs.
hailstones npl clachan-meallain.
hair n falt m.
hairy adj molach.
half n leth m.
half-bottle n leth-bhotal m.
half-way adj letheach-slighe.
hall n talla m/f.
Hallowe'en n Oidhche Shamhna f.
hallucination n mearachadh m.
halo n fainne f.
halt v stad.
halter n aghastar m.
halve v roinn 'na dhà leth.
ham n hama m.
hamlet n clachan m.
hammer n òrd m. • v buail le òrd.
hamper¹ n bascaid bidhe f.
hamper² v bac.
hand n làmh, cròg f. • v sìn.

handbag n poca làimhe m.
handful n dòrlach m.
handicap n bacadh m.
handkerchief n neapaigear f.
handle n làmh, cas f. • v làimhsich.
handshake n crathadh làimhe m.
handsome adj eireachdail.
handwoven adj làmh-fhighte.
handy adj deas.
hang v croch.
hangover n ceann daoraich m.
happen v tachair.
happening n tachartas m.
happiness n sonas m.
happy adj sona.
harass v sàraich.
harbour n cala, acarsaid m. • v gabh ri.
hard adj cruaidh.
hard disk n clàr cruaidh m.
harden v cruadhaich.
hardihood n cruadal m.
hardly adv gann.
hardship n cruaidh-chàs m.
hardware n cruaidh-bhathar m; (comput) bathar cruaidh m.
hare n maigheach f.
hare-brained adj gaoitheanach.

harm *n* cron *m*. • *v* dèan cron air.
harmful *adj* cronail.
harmless *adj* neo-chronail.
harmonic *adj* co-cheòlach.
harmonious *adj* co-chòrdach.
harmonise *v* ceòl-rèim.
harmony *n* co-sheirm *m*.
harp *n* clàrsach *f*.
harper *n* clàrsair *m*.
Harris *n* Na Hearadh.
Harris tweed *n* clò na Hearadh *m*.
harrow *v* cliath.
harsh *adj* garg.
harshness *n* gairge *f*.
hart *n* damh-fèidh *m*.
harvest *n* buain *f*.
haste *n* cabhag *f*.
hasten *v* greas.
hasty *adj* cabhagach.
hat *n* ad *f*.
hatch *n* gur *m*; (*ship*) saidse *f*.
hatchet *n* làmh-thuagh *f*.
hate *n* fuath *m*. • *v* fuathaich.
hateful *adj* fuathach.
hauteur *n* àrdan *m*.
haughty *adj* àrdanach.
haul *v* tarraing.
haunch *n* leis *f*.
haunt *v* tathaich.
have *v* bi aig; seilbhich; (*eat, etc*) gabh; (*have to*) feum.
hawk *n* seabhag *m/f*.
hawser *n* taod *m*.
hawthorn *n* sgitheach *m*.
hay *n* feur, feur caoin *m*.
haystack *n* goc, tudan *m*.

haze *n* ceò *m*.
hazy *adj* ceòthach.
he *pron* e.
head *n* ceann *m*.
headmaster *n* maighstir-sgoile *m*.
headmistress *n* bana-mhaighstir-sgoile *f*.
headache *n* cràdh-cinn *m*.
header *n* buille-cinn *f*.
headland *n* rubha *m*.
headlight *n* solas-mòr *m*.
headquarters *n* prìomh-àros *m*.
headstrong *adj* ceann-làidir.
headway *n* adhartas *m*.
heady *adj* bras.
heal *v* leighis.
healer *n* slànaighear *m*.
health *n* slàinte *f*.
healthy *adj* slàn.
heap *n* tòrr *m*. • *v* cruach.
hear *v* cluinn, èisd.
hearer *n* fear-èisdeachd *m*.
hearing *n* claisneachd *f*.
hearing-aid *n* inneal-claistinn *m*.
hearsay *n* iomradh *m*.
hearse *n* carbad-mharbh *m*.
heart *n* cridhe *m*.
hearten *v* misnich.
hearth *n* teinntean *m*.
hearty *adj* sùnndach.
heat *n* teas *m*. • *v* teasaich.
heater *n* uidheam teasachaidh *f*.
heathen *n* pàganach *m*. • *adj* pàganta.
heather *n* fraoch *m*.

heathery *adj* fraochach.
heave *n* togail *f*. • *v* tarraing.
heaven *n* nèamh *m*.
heavenly *adj* nèamhaidh.
heaviness *n* truime *f*.
heavy *adj* trom.
Hebrides *n* Innse Gall.
heckle *v* tras-cheusnaich.
hedge *n* callaid *f*.
hedgehog *n* gràineag *f*.
heed *n* aire *m*. • *v* thoir aire.
heedful *adj* faicilleach.
heedless *adj* neo-aireach.
heel *n* sàil *f*.
heifer *n* agh *f*.
height *n* àirde *f*.
heighten *v* àrdaich.
heir *n* oighre *m*.
heiress *n* ban-oighre *f*.
helicopter *n* helicoiptear *m*.
hell *n* ifrinn, iutharn *f*.
help *n* cuideachadh *m*. • *v* cuidich.
helpful *adj* cobhaireach.
hem *n* faitheam *m*.
hemisphere *n* leth-chruinne *m*.
hen *n* cearc *f*.
hence *adv* às a seo.
henceforth *adv* o seo a-mach.
her *pron* i, ise. • *poss adj* a, aice.
herald *n* teachdaire *m*.
herb *n* lus *m*.
herbal *adj* lusragach.
herd *n* treud, buar *m*. • *v* buachaillich.
herdsman *n* buachaille *m*.
here *adv* seo. an seo.

hereafter *n* an ath shaogal *m*.
hereby *adv* le seo.
hereditary *adj* dùthchasach.
heredity *n* dùchas *m*.
heresy *n* saobh-chreideamh *m*.
heritage *n* oighreachd *f*.
hermit *n* aonaran *m*.
hero *n* curaidh, laoch *m*.
heroic *adj* gaisgeach.
heroine *n* bana-ghaisgeach *f*.
heron *n* corra-ghritheach *f*.
herring *n* sgadan *m*.
herring-gull *n* faoileag *f*.
herself *pron* ise, i fhèin.
hesitate *v* bi an imcheist.
hesitation *n* imcheist *f*.
hiccup *n* aileag *f*.
hide *v* ceil.
hideous *adj* gràineil.
hiding-place *n* àite-falaich *m*.
high *adj* àrd; mòr; urramach.
high-frequency *adj* àrd-tricead.
Highland *adj* Gaidhealach.
Highlander *n* Gaidheal *m*.
Highlands *n* A'Ghaidhealtachd *f*.
highlight *v* leig cudthrom air.
high-minded *adj* ard-intinneach.
high-powered *adj* mòr-chumhachdach.
high tide *n* muir-làn *m/f*.
highway *n* rathad-mòr *m*.
hike *v* bi a'heidhceadh.
hill *n* cnoc *m*.
hillock *n* cnocan, sìthean *m*.
hillside *n* leathan *m*.
hilly *adj* cnocach.

hilt *n* dòrn *m*.

himself *pron* e fhèin.

hind *n* eilid *f*.

hinder *v* bac.

hinge *n* bann *m*.

hint *n* sanas *m*.

hip *n* cruachann *f*.

hire *v* fasdaidh.

hire purchase *n* cìs-cheannach *m*.

his *pron* a. • *poss adj* a, aige.

hiss *v* siosarnaich.

historian *n* eachdraiche *m*.

historical *adj* eachdraidheil.

history *n* eachdraidh *f*.

hit *n* buille *f*. • *v* buail.

hither *adv* an seo.

hive *n* sgeap *f*.

hoard *n* ulaidh *f*. • *v* taisg.

hoar-frost *n* liath-reodhadh *m*.

hoarse *adj* tùchanach.

hoarseness *n* tùchadh *m*.

hobby *n* cur-seachad *m*.

hobnail *n* tacaid *f*.

hoe *n* todha *m*. • *v* todhaig.

Hogmanay *n* Callain, Oidhche Challain *f*.

hold *v* cùm.

hole *n* toll *m*.

holiday *n* saor-là *m*.

hollow *n* còs *m*.

hollowness *n* falamhachd *m*.

holly *n* cuileann *m*.

holy *adj* naomh.

homage *n* ùmhlachd *f*.

home *n* dachaigh *f*. • *adv* dhachaigh.

home rule *n* fèin-riaghladh *m*.

homesick *adj* cianalach.

homesickness *n* cianalas *m*.

homespun *adj* dachaigheil.

homosexual *adj* co-sheòrsach.

honest *adj* onorach.

honesty *n* onair *f*.

honey *n* mil *f*.

honeymoon *n* mìos nam pòg *f*.

honeysuckle *n* iadh-shlat *f*.

honour *n* onair *f*; urram *m*. • *v* onaraich.

hood *n* cochall *m*.

hoof *n* iongna *f*.

hook *n* dubhan *m*.

hooked *adj* crom.

hooligan *n* ùpraidiche *m*.

hoot *v* goir.

hop *n* sìnteag *f*. • *v* dèan sìnteag.

hope *n* dòchas *m*. • *v* tha dùil aig.

hopeful *adj* dòchasach.

hopeless *adj* eu-dòchasach.

horizon *n* fàire *f*.

horizontal *adj* còmhnard.

horn *n* adharc *f*; (*musical instrument, drink*) còrn *m*.

hornet *n* connspeach *f*.

horoscope *n* reul-shealladh *m*.

horrible *adj* oillteil.

horrid *adj* dèisinnneach.

horror *n* uamhann *m*.

horse *n* each *m*.

horseman *n* marcaiche *m*.

horseshoe *n* crudha *m*.

hose *n* (*sock*) osan *m*; (*pipe*) plob *f*.

hospitable *adj* fial.

hospital n taigh-eiridinn m.
hospitality n aoigheachd f.
host n fear-taighe m; sluagh m.
hostage n bràigh m.
hostess n bean-taighe f.
hostile adj nàimhdeil.
hostility n nàimhdeas m.
hot adj teth.
hotel n taigh-òsda m.
hour n uair f.
hourly adv gach uair.
house n taigh m. • v thoir taigh do.
household n teaghlach m.
hover v fo-luaimnich.
how adv ciamar?; dè cho?
however adv co-dhiù.
howl n donnal m. • v dèan donnal.
huddle v còmhlaich.
hug v glac teann.
hull n cochall m.
hum n srann f. • v dèan torman.
human adj daonna.
humane adj caomh.
humanity n daonnachd f.
humankind n an cinne daonna m.
humble adj umhal. • v ùmhlaich.
humid adj tais.

humorist n fear àbhachdach m.
humorous adj àbhachdach.
humour[1] n àbhachd f.
humour[2] v toilich.
hump n croit f.
hundred adj/n ceud.
hundredth adj ceudamh.
hunger n acras m.
hungry adj acrach.
hunt n sealg m. • v sealg.
hunter n sealgair m.
hurricane n doinnean f.
hurry n cabhag f. • v luathaich.
hurt n dochann m. • v goirtich.
hurtful adj cronail.
husband n fear-pòsda, cèile m.
hush v sàmhaich.
hut n bothan m.
hybrid n cros-chineal m.
hydro-electric adj dealan-uisgeach.
hydro-electricity n dealan-uisge m.
hygiene n slàinteachas m.
hymn n laoidh m.
hypocrisy n breug-chràbhadh m.
hypocrite n breug-chràbaiche m.
hysterical adj reachdail.
hysterics npl reachd f.

I

I pron mi; mise.
Ice n deigh f.
Iceberg n cnoc-eighre m.

Ice-cream n reòiteag f.
Icicle n caisean-reòta m.
Icing n còmhdach-siùcair m.

icy *adj* reòta.
idea *n* beachd-smuain *f*.
ideal *adj* sàr. • *n* sàr-beachd *m*.
identical *adj* ionann.
identification *n* aithneachadh *m*.
identify *v* dearbh-aithnich.
identity *n* dearbh-aithne *f*.
idiom *n* gnathas-cainnt *m*.
idiot *n* amadan *m*.
idle *adj* dìomhain.
idleness *n* dìomhanas *m*.
idler *n* leisgean *m*.
idol *n* iodhal *m*.
if *conj* ma, nan, nam.
if not *conj* mur.
ignite *v* cuir teine ri.
ignition *n* adhnadh *m*.
ignominious *adj* nàr.
ignorance *n* aineolas *m*.
ignorant *adj* aineolach.
ignore *v* leig le.
ill *adj* tinn.
ill-health *n* euslainte *f*.
illegal *adj* neo-laghail.
illegality *n* mì-laghalachd *f*.
illegible *adj* do-leughadh.
illegitimate *adj* dìolain.
illiterate *adj* neo-litireach.
illness *n* tinneas *m*.
illogical *adj* mì-reusanta.
illuminate *v* soilleirich.
illumination *n* soillseachadh *m*.
illusion *n* mealladh *m*.
illusory *adj* meallach.
illustrate *v* dealbhaich.
illustrator *n* dealbhadair *m*.

ilustrious *adj* ainmeil.
image *n* ìomhaigh *f*.
imaginable *adj* so-smuainich.
imaginary *adj* mac-meanmnach.
imagination *n* mac-meanmainn *m*.
imagine *v* smaoinich.
imbecile *n* lethchiallach *m*.
imbibe *v* òl.
imbue *v* lìon.
imitate *v* dèan atharrais air.
imitation *n* atharrais *f*.
immaculate *adj* fìorghlan.
immaterial *adj* neo-chorporra; coma.
immature *adj* an-abaich.
immaturity *n* an-abaichead *m*.
immediate *adj* ciad.
immediately *adv* gun dàil.
immense *adj* an-mhòr.
immerse *v* cuir fodha.
immigrant *n* inn-imriche *m*.
immigration *n* inn-imrich *f*.
imminent *adj* gus teachd.
immodest *adj* mì-nàrach.
immoral *adj* mì-bheusach.
immorality *n* mì-bheus *f*.
immortal *adj* neo-bhàsmhor.
immortality *n* neo-bhàsmhorachd *f*.
immunise *v* dìon bho ghalar.
immunity *n* saorsa *f*; dìon *m*.
imp *n* spruis.
impair *v* mill.
impalpable *adj* do-fhaireach-dainn.

Impart *v* compàirtich.
Impartial *adj* ceart-bhreitheach.
Impassable *adj* do-shiubhal.
Impassive *adj* socair.
Impatience *n* mì-fhoighidinn *f.*
Impatient *adj* mì-fhoighidneach.
Impede *v* bac.
Impediment *n* bacadh *m.*
Impel *v* greas.
Impenetrable *adj* do-inntrig.
Imperative *adj* òrduigheach.
Imperceptible *adj* do-mhoth-aichte.
Impersonal *adj* neo-phearsanta.
Impersonate *v* pearsonaich.
Impertinence *n* mì-mhodh *f.*
Impertinent *adj* mì-mhodhail.
Impervious *adj* do-ruighinn.
Impetuous *adj* cas, bras.
Impetus *n* dèine *f.*
Impinge *v* buail.
Implacable *adj* gamhlasach.
Implement *n* inneal *m.*
Implement *v* thoir gu buil.
Implicate *v* cuir an sàs.
Implication *n* ribeadh *m.*
Implicit *adj* fillte.
Implore *v* aslaich.
Imply *v* ciallaich.
Impolitic *adj* neo-sheòlta.
Import *n* brìgh *f*; (*goods*) badhar o chèin *m.* • *v* thoir a-steach badhar.
Importance *n* cudrom *m.*
Important *adj* cudromach.
Impose *v* cuir air.

Impossibility *n* nì do-dhèanta *m.*
Impossible *adj* do-dhèanta.
Impostor *n* mealltair *m.*
Impotence *n* eu-comas *m.*
Impotent *adj* eu-comasach.
Impoverish *v* dèan bochd.
Impracticable *adj* do-dhèanta.
Impregnable *adj* do-ionnsaighe.
Impressive *adj* drùidhteach.
Imprison *v* cuir am prìosan.
Improbability *n* mì-choltas *m.*
Improbable *adj* mì-choltach.
Improper *adj* neo-iomchuidh.
Improve *v* leasaich.
Improvement *n* leasachadh *m.*
Improvident *adj* neo-fhreas-dalach.
Imprudent *adj* neo-chùramach.
Impudence *n* dànachd *f.*
Impulsive *adj* spreigearra.
Impure *adj* neòghlan.
Impute *v* cuir às leth.
In *prep* an, ann an. • *adv* ann; a-steach, a-staigh.
In-shore *adj* cladaich.
Inability *n* neo-chomas.
Inaccurate *adj* neo-chruinn.
Inadequate *adj* uireasach.
Inadvertent *adj* neo-aireach.
Inane *adj* faoin.
Inarticulate *adj* gagach.
Inasmuch as *conj* aig a'mheud 's a.
Incarnate *adj* san fheòil.
Incense¹ *n* tùis *f.*
Incense² *v* feargaich.

incest *n* col *m*.
incestuous *adj* colach.
inch *n* òirleach *f*.
inclement *adj* an-iochdmhor.
inclination *n* aomadh *m*.
incline *v* aom.
include *v* cuir san àireamh.
incognito *adv* gu dìomhair.
income *n* teachd-a-steach *m*.
income tax *n* càin-teachd-a-steach *f*.
incomparable *adj* gun choimeas.
incompatible *adj* neo-fhreagarrach.
incomplete *adj* neo-choileanta.
incomprehensible *adj* do-thuigsinn.
inconvenience *n* neo-ghoireasachd *f*.
inconvenient *adj* mì-ghoireasach.
incorrect *adj* mearachdach.
increase *n* meudachadh *m*. • *v* meudaich; rach am meud.
incredible *adj* do-chreidsinn.
incredulous *adj* às-creideach.
incriminate *v* ciontaich.
incubate *v* guir.
incur *v* bi buailteach do.
incurable *adj* do-leigheas.
indebted *adj* an comain.
indecent *adj* mì-chuibheasach.
indeed *adv* gu dearbh.
indelible *adj* do-sgriosta.
indemnify *v* theirig an urras air.
indent *v* eagaich.

independence *n* neo-eisimeileachd *f*.
independent *adj* neo-eisimeileach.
index *n* clàr-amais *m*. • *v* clàraich.
indicate *v* comharraich.
indifferent *adj* coma.
indigestion *n* cion-meirbhidh *m*.
indignant *adj* diombach.
indignation *n* diomb *m*.
indiscreet *adj* neo-chrìonna.
indiscretion *n* neo-chrìonnachd *f*.
individual *adj* air leth.
individual *n* urra *f*.
indoor *adj* a-staigh.
indulge *v* leig le.
indulgent *adj* bàigheil.
industrial *adj* tionnsgalach.
industrious *adj* gnìomhach.
industry *n* (*abstract*) saothair *f*; gnìomhachas *f*.
inedible *adj* do-ithe.
inept *adj* baoth.
inequality *n* neo-ionnanachd *f*.
inert *adj* marbhanta.
inexcusable *adj* neo-leisgeulach.
inexpensive *adj* saor.
inexperienced *adj* neo-eòlach.
inexplicable *adj* do-mhìneachadh.
inextricable *adj* do-fhuasgladh.
infallible *adj* do-mhearachdach.
infant *n* naoidhean *m*.
infantile *adj* leanabail.
infantry *n* cois-shluagh *m*.

Infect v cuir galar air.
Infection n galar-gabhail m.
Inferior adj ìochdarach.
Infertile adj mì-thorrach.
Infest v claoidh.
Infinitesimal adj beag-bìodach.
Infirm adj anfhann.
Inflammable adj so-lasadh.
Inflate v sèid.
Inflation n (money) at cùinnidh m.
Inflict v leag peanas air.
Influence n buaidh f. • v treòraich.
Influenza n fliù f.
Inform v innis.
Informal adj neo-fhoirmeil.
Information n fiosrachadh m.
Information technology n teicneolas fiosrachaidh m.
Infrequent adj ainmig.
Infringe v bris.
Ingenious adj innleachdach.
Ingenuous adj fosgarra.
Ingot n uinge f.
Ingredient n tàthchuid f.
Inhabit v àitich.
Inhabitable adj so-àiteachadh.
Inhabitant n fear-àiteachaidh m.
Inhale v tarraing anail.
Inherit v faigh mar oighreachd.
Inhibit v cùm air ais.
Inhibition n urchall m.
Inhospitable adj neo-fhialaidh.
Inhuman adj mì-dhaonna.
Initial adj ciad. • n ciad litir f.
Inject v ann-steallaich.

Injection n ann-stealladh m.
Injure v ciurr.
Injurious adj cronail.
Injury n ciurradh m.
Ink n dubh m.
Inland adj a-staigh san tìr.
Inlet n caolas m.
Inn n taigh-òsda m.
Innate adj dualach.
Inner adj as fhaide a-staigh.
Innkeeper n òsdair m.
Innocent adj neo-chiontach.
Innovate v ùr-ghnàthaich.
Innovation n ùr-ghnàthachadh m.
Innovator n ùr-ghnàthadair m.
Innuendo n fiar-shanas m.
Inoculate v cuir a' bhreac air.
Inquire v feòraich.
Inquiry n ceasnachadh m.
Inquisitive adj faighneachail.
Insane adj air chuthach.
Insanitary adj mì-shlàinteil.
Insanity n cuthach m.
Insect n meanbh-fhrìde f.
Insecure adj neo-thèarainte.
Inseparable adj do-sgaradh.
Insert v cuir a-steach.
Inside prep am broinn. • adv air an taobh a-staigh.
Insincere adj neo-onorach.
Insipid adj neo-bhlasda.
Insist v cùm air.
Insolvency n bristeadh m.
Insolvent adj briste.
Insomnia n bacadh cadail m.
Inspect v sgrùd.

inspection *n* sgrùdadh *m*.
instal *v* cuir an dreuchd.
instalment *n* earrann *f*.
instance *n* eisimpleir *m*.
instant *adj* grad. • *n* tiota *m*.
instead *prep* an àite. • *adv* an àite sin.
instil *v* teagaisg.
instinct *n* dùchas *m*.
instinctive *adj* dùchasach.
institute *n* stèidheachadh *m*.
institution *n* stèidheachadh *m*.
instrument *n* inneal *m*, beart *f*.
insular *adj* eileanach.
insulate *v* dealaich.
insult *n* tàmailt *f*. • *v* tàmailtich.
insurance *n* urras *m*.
insurance policy *n* poileasaidh urrais *m*.
insure *v* faigh urras air.
intact *adj* slàn.
integrity *n* ionracas *m*.
intellect *n* inntinn *f*.
intellectual *adj* inntleachdail.
intelligence *n* tuigse *f*.
intelligible *adj* so-thuigsinn.
intend *v* cuir roimh.
intense *adj* teann.
intensify *v* teinnich.
intensity *n* dèine *f*.
intention *n* rùn *m*.
intentional *adj* a dh'aon rùn.
intercede *v* dèan eadar-ghuidhe.
intercept *v* ceap.
intercourse *n* co-chomann *m*; (*sexual*) co-ghineadh *m*.

interest *n* ùidh *f*.
interesting *adj* ùidheil.
interfere *v* buin ri.
internal *adj* san leth a-staigh.
international *adj* eadar-nàiseanta.
driver *n* dràibhear *m*.
internet *n* eadarlìon *m*.
interpret *v* mìnich.
interpreter *n* fear-mìneachaidh *m*.
interrupt *v* cuir casg air.
interruption *n* casgadh *m*.
intertwine *v* eadar-thoinn.
intervene *v* thig eadar.
intervention *n* eadar-ghabhail *m*.
interview *n* agallamh *m*. • *v* agallaich.
intestine *n* greallach *f*.
intimacy *n* dlù-chaidreamh *m*.
intimate *adj* dlù-chaidreach.
into *adv* a-steach do; ann an.
intonation *n* guth-cheòl *m*.
intricate *adj* eadar-fhighte.
intrigue *n* cluaineireachd *f*. • *v* dèan cluaineireachd.
intrinsic *adj* gnèitheach.
introduce *v* cuir an aithne.
introduction *n* cur an aithne.
intrude *v* brùth a-steach.
intruder *n* bruthaiche-steach *m*.
intuition *n* imfhios *m*.
invalid¹ *adj* neo-bhrìgheach.
invalid² *adj* (*ill*) tinn. • *n* euslainteach *m*.
invariable *adj* neo-chaochlaideach.

invent v innlich.
invention n innleachd f.
inventor n tionnsgalair m.
inventory n cùnntas m.
Inverness n Inbhir Nis.
invert v cuir bun-os-cionn.
invest v èid; (*money*) cuir an seilbh.
invisible adj do-fhaicsinneach.
invitation n cuireadh m.
invite v iarr.
invoice n maoin-chlàr m.
involuntary adj neo-shaor-thoileach.
involve v gabh a-steach.
inward adv a-staigh.
inwards adv a-steach.
Ireland n Eirinn f.
Irish adj Eireannach.
irksome adj buaireasach.
iron n iarann m. • adj iarrain. • v iarnaich.
ironic adj loronta.
irony n loronas m.

irrational adj eu-cèillidh.
irregular adj mì-riaghailteach.
irrelevant adj nach buin ri.
irreverent adj eas-urramach.
irrigate v uisgich.
irrigation n uisgeachadh m.
irritable adj crosda.
irritation n frionas m.
island n eilean m.
islander n eileanach m.
Islay n Ile f.
isolated adj air leth.
issue n ceist f; (*descendants*) sliochd m.
isthmus n aoidh f.
it pron e, i.
Italian adj Eadailteach.
Italy n An Eadailt f.
itch n tachas m.
itchy adj tachasach.
itinerary n cùrsa m.
its pron aige, aice.
itself pron e fhèin, i fhèin.
ivory n ìbhri f.

J

jab n briogadh m. • v briog.
jacket n seacaid f.
jacobite adj seumasach.
jagged adj eagaich.
jail n carcair m.
jam n silidh m; (*traffic*) dòmhlachd m.

jamb n ursainn f.
jangle v dèan gleadhraich.
janitor n dorsair m.
jar n sileagan m.
jargon n goileam m.
jaundice n a' bhuidheach f.
jaunt n cuairt f.

jaunty adj sgeilmeil.

jaw n giall f.

jawbone n peirceall m.

jealous adj eudmhor.

jealousy n eud m.

jeans npl dìnichean.

jeer v mag.

jelly n slaman-milis m.

jellyfish n muir-tiachd m.

jerkin n còta-geàrr m.

jersey n geansaidh m.

jest n abhcaid f.

jester n cleasaiche m.

jet plane n diet-itealan m.

jettison v tilg a-mach.

jetty n cidhe m.

jewel n seud m.

jib[1] n dioba f.

jib[2] v cuir stailc ann.

jig n port-cruinn m.

jilt v trèig.

job n car-òibre, gnothach m.

jockey n marcach m.

jog v put; (run) dèan dabhdail.

join v ceangail.

joiner n saor m.

joinery n saorsinneachd f.

joint adj coitcheann. • n alt m; spòld m.

jointed adj altach.

jointly adv le chèile.

joke n fealla-dhà f.

jollity n cridhealas m.

jolly adj cridheil.

jolt n crathadh m. • v crath.

jostle v brùth.

jot n pong m.

journal n leabhar-latha; pàipear làith–eil m.

journalism n naidheachdas m.

journalist n naidheachdair m.

journey n turas m, cuairt f.

jovial adj fonnmhor.

jowl n giall f.

joy n aoibhneas m.

joyful adj aoibhneach.

joyfully adv gu h-aoibhinn.

jubilant adj lùthghaireach.

jubilee n àrd-fhèill f.

judge n britheam m. • v thoir breith.

judgment n breitheanas m.

judicial adj dligheil.

judicious adj geur-chuiseach.

jug n siuga f.

juggle v dèan cleasachd.

jugular adj sgòrnanach.

juice n sùgh m.

juicy adj sùghmhor.

July n Iuchar m.

jump n leum m. • v leum.

jumper n leumadair m; siumpar m.

junction n ceangal m.

June n An t-Og-mhìos m.

jungle n dlùth-fhàsach m.

junior adj às òige; (rank) iar-.

juniper n aiteann m.

junk n truilleis m.

junket, junketing n cuirm f.

juror n fear/bean diùraidh m/f.

just adj còir. • adv dìreach; air èiginn.

justice n còir f.
justifiable adj reusanta.
justification n fìreanachadh m.
justify v fìreanaich.

jut v seas a-mach.
juvenile adj òganta.
juxtapose v cuir ri chèile.

K

kail n càl m.
keel n druim m.
keen[1] adj geur.
keen[2] v caoin.
keenness n gèire f.
keep n daingneach f. • v cùm, glèidh.
keeping n glèidheadh m.
keepsake n cuimhneachan m.
kelp n ceilp f.
kennel n taigh-chon m.
kerb n cabhsair m.
kernel n eitean m.
kettle n coire m.
key n iuchair f; (mus) gleus f.
keyboard n meur-chlàr f.
keystone n clach-ghlasaidh f.
kick n breab m. • v breab.
kid n meann m.
kidnap v goid air falbh.
kidney n dubhag f.
kill v marbh.
killer n marbhaiche m.
kilogram n cile-gram m.
kilometre n cilemeatair m.
kilowatt n cileavat m.
kilt n fèileadh, fèileadh beag m.

kin n cinneadh m.
kind[1] adj coibhneil.
kind[2] n gnè f.
kindle v las, fad.
kindly adj bàigheil.
kindred adj dàimheil.
kindred n muinntir f.
king n rìgh m.
kingdom n rìoghachd m.
kinsfolk npl luchd-dàimh.
kinsman n caraid m.
kinswoman n bana-charaid f.
kiosk n ciodhosg f.
kipper n ciopair m.
kiss n pòg f. • v pòg.
kit n trusgan m.
kitbag n màileid f.
kitchen n cidsin m.
kite n clamhan m; (model) iteileag f.
kitten n piseag m.
knack n liut f.
knapsack n aparsaig f.
knave n slaightear m.
knead v fuin.
knee n glùn f.
kneecap n failmean m.

kneel *v* sleuchd.

knickers *npl* drathars.

knife *n* sgian *f.*

knight *n* ridire *m.*

knighthood *n* ridireachd *m.*

knit *v* figh.

knitter *n* figheadair *m.*

knitting needle *n* bior-fighe *m.*

knob *n* cnap *m.*

knock *n* buille *f.* • *v* buail.

knoll *n* tolm *m.*

knot *n* snaidhm *m.* • *v* snaidh-mich.

knotted, knotty *adj* snaidh-meach.

know *v* aithnich; tuig; bi eòlach air.

knowing *adj* eòlach.

knowingly *adv* gu h-eòlach.

knowledgeable *adj* fiosrach.

knuckle *n* rùdan *m.*

kyle *n* caol *m.*

L

label *n* bileag *f.*

labial *adj* liopach.

laboratory *n* deuchainn-lann *f.*

laborious *adj* deacair.

labour *v* saothraich.

labourer *n* oibriche *m.*

labyrinth *n* ioma-shlighe *f.*

lace¹ *n* lios *f.*

lace² *n* barrall *f.* • *v* (*shoe, etc*) dùin.

lacerate *v* reub.

laceration *n* reubadh *m.*

lack *n* easbhaidh *f.* • *v* bi a dh'eas-bhaidh.

lad, laddie *n* gille *m.*

ladder *n* fàradh *m.*

ladle *n* liagh *f.*

lady *n* bean-uasal *f.*

ladybird *n* an daolag dhearg-bhreac *f.*

ladylike *adj* bainndidh.

lair *n* saobhaidh *f.*

laird *n* tighearna *m.*

lake *n* linn *f*, loch *m.*

lamb *n* uan *m*; (*roast*) uainfheòil *m.*

lame *adj* bacach.

lameness *n* crùbaiche *f.*

lament *n* cumha *m.*

lament *v* caoidh.

lamentable *adj* tùrsach.

lamp *n* làmpa *m.*

lance *v* leig fuil.

lancet *n* lannsa *f.*

land *n* tìr, dùthaich *f.* • *v* rach air tìr.

landholder *n* fear-fearainn *m.*

landing *n* ceann staidhre *m*; (*of aeroplane*) laighe *m.*

landing strip *n* raon-laighe *m.*

landlady *n* bean-an-taighe *f.*

landlocked *adj* tìr-dhruidte.
landmark *n* comharradh *m*.
landscape *n* dealbh tìre *m/f*.
landslide *n* beum-slèibhe *m*.
landward *adv* gu-tìr.
lane *n* lònaid *f*.
language *n* cànan *m*; (*speech*) cainnt *f*.
languish *v* fannaich.
lanky *adj* fada caol.
lantern *n* lanntair *m*.
lap[1] *n* uchd *m*.
lap[2] *v* sùgh.
lapel *n* liopaid *f*.
lapse *n* mearachd *f*. • *v* sleamhna-ich.
lapwing *n* currcag *f*.
larceny *n* braide *f*.
larch *n* learag *f*.
lard *n* blonag *f*.
larder *n* preas-bidhe *m*.
large *adj* mòr.
lark *n* uiseag *f*.
lass, lassie *n* nighean *f*.
last[1] *adj* deireannach, mu dheir-eadh. • *adv* mu dheireadh.
last[2] *v* mair.
lasting *adj* maireannach.
late *adj* anmoch.
lately *adv* o chionn ghoirid.
lateness *n* fadalachd *m*.
latent *adj* dìomhair.
lather *n* cop *m*. • *v* dèan cop.
Latin *n* Laideann *f*.
latitude *n* leud *m*; (*line*) domhan-leud *m*.

latter *adj* deireannach.
laugh *n* gàire *m*. • *v* dèan gàire.
laughter *n* gàireachdaich *f*.
launch *v* cuir air bhog.
laurel *n* labhras *m*.
lavatory *n* taigh-failcidh, taigh beag *m*.
lavish *adj* sgapach. • *v* sgap.
law *n* lagh, reachd *m*.
law-suit *n* cùis lagha *f*.
lawful *adj* laghail.
lawn *n* rèidhlean *m*.
lawyer *n* fear-lagha *m*.
laxative *n* purgaid *f*.
lay *v* càirich, cuir, leag sìos.
lay-by *n* far-rathad *m*.
layer *n* filleadh *m*.
layman *n* neo-chlèireach *m*.
laziness *n* leisge *f*.
lazy *adj* leisg.
lead[1] *n* luaidhe *m/f*.
lead[2] *n* (*dog*) iall *f*. • *v* treòraich.
leaden *adj* luaidhe.
leader *n* ceannard *m*.
leaf *n* duilleag *f*.
leafy *adj* duilleagach.
league *n* co-cheangal *m*; (*sport*) lìg *m*.
leak *v* leig a-steach.
leaky *adj* ao-dìonach.
lean[1] *adj* caol.
lean[2] *v* leig do thaic air.
leap *v* leum.
leap-year *n* bliadhna-leum *f*.
learn *v* ionnsaich.
learner *n* neach-ionnsachaidh *m*.

lease n gabhail m/f.
least adj as lugha.
leather n leathar m.
leave n fòrladh m. • v fàg, trèig.
lecher n drùisire m.
lecherous adj drùiseil.
lecture n òraid f. • v teasgaig.
ledge n oir m.
ledger n leabhar-cùnntais m.
lee, lee-side n taobh an fhas-
gaidh m.
leech n deala f.
leek n cainneann m.
leet n (list) ciad-thaghadh m.
left n an taobh ceàrr m.
left hand n làmh chlì f.
left-handed adj ciotach.
leg n cas f.
legacy n dìleab f.
legalise v dèan laghail.
legend n fionnsgeul f.
legendary adj fionnsgeulach.
legibility n so-leughtachd f.
legible adj so-leughadh f.
legislate v dèan lagh.
legitimate adj dligheach.
leisure n suaimhneas m.
leisurely adj athaiseach.
lemon n liomaid f.
lend v thoir an iasad.
lender n iasadaiche m.
length n fad m.
lengthen v cuir am fad.
lengthwise adv air fhad.
lenient adj tròcaireach.
lenition n sèimheachadh m.

lens n lionsa f.
Lent n Carghas m.
leper n lobhar m.
leprechaun n luchraban m.
less adj nas lugha.
lessen v lùghdaich.
lesson n leasan m.
lest conj air eagal gu.
let¹ n bacadh m; (house) n gabhail
m/f.
let² v leig; thoir air ghabhail.
lethal adj bàsmhor.
letter n litir f.
letter-box n bocsa-litrichean m.
lettuce n leiteis f.
level adj còmhnard.
level n còmhnard m. • v dèan
còmhnard.
lever n luamhan m.
lewd adj draosda.
lewdness n draosdachd f.
Lewis n Leòdhas m.
liability n buailteachd f.
liable adj buailteach.
liar n breugaire m.
libel v dèan cliù-mhilleadh.
liberal adj pailt-làmhach.
Liberal n Liberaileach m.
librarian n leabhar-lannaiche m.
library n leabhar-lann f.
licence n cead m.
license v ceadaich.
lichen n crotal m.
lick v imlich.
lid n ceann m.
lie¹ v laigh.

lie¹ n breug f. • v innis breug.

life n beatha f.

lifeboat n bàta-teasairginn m.

lifestyle n seòl-beatha m.

lifeguard n freiceadan m.

lift n (*elevator*) àrdaichear m. • v tog.

light¹ adj aotrom; suarach; guanach; soilleir.

light² n solas m. • v las.

light-headed adj gog-cheannach.

lighten v deàlraich.

lighthouse n taigh-solais m.

lightness n aotromachd m.

lightning n dealanach m.

like¹ adj coltach. • n samhail f.

like² v is toigh le.

liken v samhlaich.

likeness n coltas m.

likewise adv mar an ceudna.

limb n ball m.

lime n aol m; (*fruit*) teile f.

limestone n aol-chlach f.

lime tree n teile f.

limit n crìoch m. • v cuir crìoch ri.

limited adj (*Ltd*) earranta.

limp¹ adj bog.

limp² n ceum m. • v bi crùbach.

limpet n bàirneach f.

linden tree n teile f.

line¹ n loidhne f; streath f.

line² v lìnig.

lineage n linn, sliochd m.

lineal adj dìreach.

linear adj streathach.

linen n anart m.

linger v gabh ùine.

linguist n cànanaich m.

link n tinne f. • v co-cheangail.

links npl machair goilf f.

linnet n breacan-beithe m.

lion n leòghann m.

lioness n ban-leòghann f.

lip n bile f.

liquefy v leagh.

liquid adj lionnach. • n lionn m.

liquidate v glan air falbh.

lisp n liotachas m. • v bi liotach.

list n liosta f, (*items*) clàr-ainm f. • v liostaig; cuir sìos.

listen v èisd.

listener n fear-èisdeachd m.

listless adj coma; gun smior.

literacy n litireachd f.

literal adj litireil.

literate adj litir-foghlaimte.

literature n litreachas m.

litre n liotair m.

litter n treamsgal m; (*young*) cuain m. • v dèan treamsgal; beir.

little adj beag.

littoral n cladach m.

liturgy n ùrnaigh choitcheann f.

live¹ adj beò.

live² v bi beò.

livelihood n teachd-an-tìr m.

lively adj beothail.

liver n adha m.

livid adj dùghorm.

lizard n laghairt m.

load n luchd m. • v luchdaich.

loaf n buileann f, lof m/f.

loan *n* iasad *m*.

loath *adj* aindeonach.

loathe *v* fuathaich.

loathing *n* gràin *f*.

loathsome *adj* gràineil.

lobster *n* giomach *m*.

lobster-pot *n* cliabh-ghiomach *f*.

local *adj* ionadail.

locality *n* àite *m*.

locate *v* cuir 'na àite.

loch *n* loch *m*.

lock[1] *n* glas *f*. • *v* glais.

lock[2] *n* (*hair*) dual *m*

locket *n* glasag-mhuineil *f*.

locksmith *n* gobha-ghlasan *m*.

lodge *n* taigh-gheata *m*. • *v* suidhich; gabh còmhnaidh.

lodger *n* lòisdear *m*.

loft *n* lobhta *m*.

log *n* sgonn *m*.

logic *n* ealain reusanachaidh, loidig *f*.

logical *adj* loidigeach.

loiter *v* dèan màirneal.

loll *v* seas ri taic.

London *n* Lunnainn.

lone *adj* aonarach.

loneliness *n* aonaranachd *f*.

long[1] *adj* fada; buan.

long[2] *v* miannaich.

long ago *adv* o chionn fhada.

long-term *adj* fad-ùineach.

longevity *n* fad-shaoghalachd *f*.

longing *n* miann *m*.

longitude *n* domhan-fhad *m*.

long-suffering *adj* fad-fhulangach.

long-wave *adj* fad-thonnach.

long-winded *adj* fad-anaileach.

look *n* fiamh *m*; sùil *f*. • *v* seall, amhairc; **look for** sir.

looking-glass *n* sgàthan *m*.

loop *n* lùb *f*.

loophole *n* fosgladh *m*.

loose *adj* sgaoilte. • *v* fuasgail.

lop *v* sgath.

lop-sided *adj* leathoireach.

lord *n* tighearna, morair *m*.

lore *n* oilean *m*.

lorry *n* làraidh *f*.

lose *v* caill.

loser *n* fear a chaill *m*.

loss *n* call *m*.

lost *adj* air chall.

lotion *n* cungaidh *f*.

lottery *n* crannchur *m*.

loud *adj* labhar.

loudness *n* faram *m*.

loudspeaker *n* glaodhaire *m*.

lounge *n* seòmar-searraidh *m*. • *v* seàrr.

lour, lower *v* (*face*) bi an gruaim.

louse *n* mial *f*.

lousy *adj* mialach.

lout *n* burraidh *m*.

love *n* gaol, gràdh *m*.

lovely *adj* àlainn.

lover *n* leannan *m*.

lovesick *adj* tinn le gaol.

loving *adj* gràdhach.

low *adj* ìosal.

lower¹ v ìslich.

lower² see **lour**.

lowest adj as ìsle.

Lowland adj Gallda.

Lowlands n A' Ghalltachd f.

lowly adj iriosal.

loyal adj dìleas.

loyalty n dìlse f.

lubricate v lìomh.

lucid adj soilleir.

luck n fortan m.

lucky adj fortanach.

lucrative adj buannachail.

ludicrous adj amaideach.

luggage n treallaich f.

lukewarm adj meadh-bhlàth.

lull v cuir a chadal.

lullaby n òran tàlaidh m.

luminous adj deàlrach.

lump n meall m.

lumpy adj meallanach.

lunacy n cuthach m.

lunar adj gealachail.

lunch n ruisean m.

lung n sgamhan m.

lurch¹ n sitheadh m.

lurch² v dèan sitheadh.

lure n mealladh m. • v meall, buair.

lurid adj cròn.

lurk v falaich.

luscious adj sòghmhor.

lust n ana-miann m.

lustre n deàlradh m.

lusty adj sultmhor.

luxuriant adj fàsmhor.

luxurious adj sòghail.

luxury n sògh m, n sòghalachd f.

lyre n cruit f.

lyric n liric f.

M

mace n cuaille suaicheantais m.

machine n inneal m.

machinery n innealradh. m.

mackerel n rionnach m.

magazine n iris f.

magic adj draoidheil. • n draoi-dheachd f.

magician n draoidh m.

magistrate n bàillidh m.

magnet n clach-iùil f.

magnification n meudachadh m.

magnificence n greadhnachas m.

magnificent adj òirdheirc.

magnify v meudaich.

magnitude n meudachd m.

magpie n pioghaid f.

maid n maighdeann f.

mail n litrichean pl; post m. • v cuir sa' phost.

mail order n òrdugh tron phost m.

main adj prìomh.

mainland n tìr-mòr m.

mainly *adv* anns a' mhòr-chuid.

maintain *v* glèidh.

maintenance *n* glèidheadh *m*.

majestic *adj* flathail.

majesty *n* mòrachd *f*.

major *adj* as motha. • *n* màidsear *m*.

make *v* dèan, dealbh; **make to do** thoir air; **make towards** dèan air. • *n* dèanamh *m*.

maker *n* dealbhadair *m*.

make-up *n* rìomhadh *m*.

making *n* dèanamh *m*.

male *adj* fireannach. • *n* fireannach *m*.

malevolence *n* gamhlas *m*.

malice *n* mì-rùn *m*.

malicious *adj* mì-runach.

malign *v* càin.

malignant *adj* millteach; (*med*) aillseach.

mallet *n* fairche *m*.

malt *n* braich *f*.

maltster *n* brachadair *m*.

maltreat *v* droch ghrèidh.

mam, mammy *n* mam, mamaidh *f*.

mammal *n* sineach *m*.

man *n* duine, fear *m*.

manage *v* stiùir.

manageable *adj* so-riaghladh.

management *n* riaghladh *m*.

manager *n* manaidsear *m*.

manageress *n* bana-mhanaidsear *f*.

mane *n* muing *f*.

manful *adj* duineil.

manger *n* prasach *f*.

mangle *v* reub.

manhood *n* fearalas *m*.

maniac *n* dearg amadan *m*.

manifest *v* taisbein.

manifestation *n* foillseachadh *m*.

manifesto *n* gairm-fhollaiseach *f*.

manipulate *v* oibrich.

mankind *n* cinne-daonna *m*.

manner *n* modh *m/f*.

mannerism *n* magaid *f*.

mannerly *adj* modhail.

manners *npl* modh *m/f*.

manse *n* mansa *m*.

mansion *n* taigh-mòr *m*.

mantelpiece *n* breus *m*.

manual *adj* làmhach. • *n* leabhar-tuairisgeil *m*.

manufacture *v* saothraich.

manure *n* mathachadh *m*. • *v* mathaich.

manuscript *n* làmh-sgrìobhainn *m*.

many *adj* mòran; iomadh. • *n* mòran, tòrr *m*.

map, *n* map *m*.

mar *v* mill.

marble *n* màrmor *m*.

March *n* Am Màrt *m*.

march *n* màrsail *f*. • *v* dèan màrsail.

mare *n* làir *f*.

marijuana *n* a' bhang *f*.

marine *adj* mara.

mariner *n* maraiche *m*.

maritime *adj* fairgeach.

mark *n* comharradh *m*.

market *n* fèill *f*, margadh *m/f*.

marketable *adj* a ghabhas reic.

maroon *v* cuir air eilean uaigneach.

marquee *n* puball *m*.

marriage *n* pòsadh *m*.

marriageable *adj* aig aois pòsaidh.

married *adj* pòsda.

marry *v* pòs.

marshy *adj* bog, fèitheach.

marten *n* taghan *m*.

martial *adj* gaisgeanta.

martyr *n* martarach *m*.

marvel *n* iongnadh *m*. • *v* gabh iongnadh.

marvellous *adj* iongantach.

mascot *n* suaichnean *m*.

masculine *adj* fireannta.

mash *v* pronn.

mask *n* aghaidh choimheach *f*.

mason *n* clachair *m*.

masonry *n* clachaireachd *m*.

mass *n* tomad *m*; meall *m*; (*church*) aifreann *m*.

massacre *n* casgradh *m*. • *v* casgair.

massage *n* suathadh *m*.

massive *adj* tomadach.

mast *n* crann *m*.

master *n* maighstir *m*.

masterly *n* ealanta *m*.

masterpiece *n* euchd *m*.

masturbate *v* brod.

mat *n* brat *m*.   ʼ

match *n* lasadair *m*; seise *m*. • *v* freagair.

matchless *adj* gun choimeas.

mate *n* cèile *m*; (*ship*) meite *m*; (*chess*) clos *m*. • *v* cuir clos air.

material *n* stuth *m*.

maternal *adj* màithreil.

maternity *n* màthaireachd *f*.

mathematics *n* eòlas matamataic.

matins *npl* maidnean.

matrimony *n* dàimh-pòsaidh·*m/f*.

matter *n* stuth *m*; brìgh *f*; gnothach *m*.

mattress *n* leabaidh-lòchdrach *f*.

mature *adj* abaich.

maul *v* pronn.

mavis *n* smeòrach *f*.

maw *n* goile *f*.

maximum *n* os-mheud *m*.

May *n* A' Mhàigh *f*; An Cèitean *m*.

may *v* faod.

May Day *n* Là-Bealltainn.

maze *n* ioma-shlighe *f*.

me *pron* mi, mise.

meadow *n* lòn *m*.

meagre *adv* gann.

meagreness *n* gainne *f*.

meal *n* min *f*; (*repast*) biadh *f*.

mealy *adj* mar mhin.

mean[1] *adj* suarach.

mean[2] *n* cuibheasachd *f*.

mean[3] *v* ciallaich.

meaning *n* ciall *f*.

means *npl* comas *m*; seilbhean *fpl*.

meantime *adv* an dràsda.

measles *n* a' ghriùthlach *f*.

measurable *adj* a ghabhas tomhas.

measure *v* tomhais. • *n* tomhas *m*.

measurement *n* tomhas *m*.

meat *n* feòil *f*.

mechanic *n* meicnic *m*.

mechanism *n* meadhan *m*.

medal *n* bonn *m*.

meddle *v* buin ri.

mediate *v* rèitich.

mediation *n* eadraiginn *f*.

mediator *n* eadar-mheadhanair *m*.

medical *adj* lèigh.

medicinal *adj* ìocshlainteach.

medicine *n* eòlas-leighis; ìocshlaint *m*.

medieval *adj* meadhan-aoiseil.

mediocre *adj* meadhanach.

meditate *v* beachd-smuainich.

meditation *n* beachd-smuaineachadh *m*.

medium *n* meadhan *m*.

medium-wave *adj* meadhanthonnach.

meek *adj* macanta.

meekness *n* macantas *m*.

meet *v* coinnich.

meeting *n* coinneachadh *m*; (*official*) coinneamh *f*.

megalith *n* tursa *m*.

melancholy *adj* dubhach.

melancholy *n* leann-dubh *m*.

mellifluous *adj* mealach.

mellow *adj* tlàth.

melodious *adj* fonnmhor.

melody *n* binneas *m*; fonn *m*.

melon *n* meal-bhucan *m*.

melt *v* leagh.

member *n* ball *m*.

member of parliament *n* ball-pàrla-maid *m*.

membership *n* ballrachd *f*.

memento *n* cuimhneachan *m*.

memoir *n* tràchdas *m*; beatha-aisneis *m*.

memorable *adj* ainmeil.

memorise *v* cùm air mheomhair.

memory *n* cuimhne *f*.

mend *v* càraich.

menstrual *adj* mìosach.

menstruation *n* fuil-mìos *f*.

mental *adj* inntinneil.

mention *v* ainmich.

menu *n* cairt-bidhe *f*.

merchant *n* ceannaiche *m*.

mercy *n* tròcair *m*.

mere *adj* a-mhain.

merely *adv* a-mhain.

merge *v* rach an aon.

merit *n* luach *m*.

mermaid *n* maighdeann-mhara *f*.

merriment *n* aighear *m*.

mess *n* truidhleis *f*.

message *n* teachdaireachd *f*.

messenger *n* teachdaire *m*.

metal *n* meatailt *f*.

metallic *adj* meatailteach.

meteor *n* dreag *f*.

meter *n* inneal-tomhais *m*.

method n dòigh f.

metre n meatair m; (verse) rann-aigh-eachd m.

mettle n smioralachd f.

microbe n bitheag f.

microwave oven n àmhainn mheanbh-thonn f.

mid adj eadar-mheadannach.

middle n meadhan m.

middle-aged adj leth-shean.

midge n meanbh-chuileag f.

midnight n meadhan-oidhche m.

midwife n bean-ghlùine f.

might n cumhachd m.

migrate v dèan imrich.

mild adj ciuin.

mile n mìle f.

military adj cogail.

milk n bainne m. • v bleoghain.

milky adj bainneach.

mill n muileann m/f.

millennium n am mìle-bliadhna m.

miller n muillear m.

million n millean m.

mime n mìm f.

mimicry n atharrais f.

mince n mions m.

Minch n An Cuan Sgìth.

mind n inntinn f.

mind v thoir an aire; cuimhnich.

mine[1] n mèinne f.

mine[2] poss pron agam; leam.

mineral adj mèinneach. • n mèinnearach m.

mingle v measgaich.

miniature n meanbh-dhealbh m/f.

minister n ministear m. • v fritheil.

minor n neach fo làn-aois m. • adj beag, as lugha.

minstrel n oirfideach m.

minus prep as aonais; mìonas.

minute[1] adj meanbh.

minute[2] n mionaid f.

minx n aigeannach f.

miracle n mìorbhail f.

mirage n mearachadh-sùla m.

mirror n sgàthan m.

misapprehension n mì-thuig-sinn f.

misbehaviour n droch-ghiùlan m.

miscarriage n asaid anabaich f.

mischief n aimhleas m.

mischievous adj aimhleasach.

misdeed n dò-bheart f.

miser n spìocaire m.

miserable adj truagh.

misinterpret v mì-bhreithnich.

misogyny n fuath-bhan m.

Miss n A' Maighdeann, A' Mh f.

miss v rach iomrall; ionndrainn.

missing adj a dhìth.

missionary n misionairidh m.

mist n ceò m.

mistake v mì-aithnich.

Mister n Maighstir, Mgr m.

mistletoe n an t-uil-ìoc m.

mistress n bana-mhaighstir f; coileapach f.

misty adj ceòthach.

misunderstand v mì-thuig.

mite n fineag f.

mix v measgaich.

mixture n measgachadh m.

moan n gearan m. • v gearain.

mob n gràisg f.

mobile phone n fòn shiubhail f.

mock v mag.

model n cumadh m. • v deilbh.

moderate adj stuama.

moderation n stuaim m.

modern adj ùr, nodha.

modernise v ùraich.

modest adj nàrach.

modesty n beusachd f.

moist adj tais, bog.

moisten v taisich.

mole[1] n famh f.

mole[2] (spot) ball-dòrain m.

molest v cuir dragh air.

mollify v maothaich.

mollusc n maorach m.

moment n tiota m.

momentary adj grad-ùineach.

momentous adj cudromach.

monarch n monarc m.

monastery n mannachain f.

Monday n Diluain m.

money n airgead m.

monitor n foillsear m.

monk n manach m.

monkey n muncaidh m.

monopoly n lèir-shealbhachd f.

monotony n aon-ghuthachd f.

monster n uilebheist m.

month n mìos m/f.

monthly adj mìosach.

monument n carragh f.

mood n gleus m.

moody adj gruamach.

moon n gealach f.

moor[1] n mòinteach f.

moor[2] v tilg acair.

moral n beus f.

morale n misneach f.

morality n deagh bheusachd f.

more adv tuilleadh. • n tuilleadh m.

moreover adv a thuilleadh.

morning n madainn f.

mortal adj bàsmhor.

mosquito n còrr-mhial m.

moss n còinneach f.

most adj as mò. • n a' mhòr chuid m.

mostly adv mar as trice.

moth n leòman m.

mother n màthair f.

mother-in-law n màthair-cèile f.

motherly adj màithreil.

motion n gluasad m.

motive n adhbhar m.

motor n motair m.

motorist n motairiche m.

motto n facal-suaicheantais m.

mould n molldair m.

mouldy adv cloimh-liathach.

moult v tilg fionnadh.

mound n tom m.

mountain n beinn f, meall m.

mountaineer n streapaiche m.

mourn v caoidh.

mourning n bròn m.
mouse n luch f.
moustache n stais f.
mouth n beul m.
mouth-music n port-a-beul m.
mouthful n balgam m.
move v gluais; luaisg; imich.
mow v geàrr.
Mrs n A' Bhean, A' Bh f.
much adv mòran.
muck n salchar m.
mud n poll m.
muddle n troimhe-chèile f.
muddy adj eabarach.
mug n muga f.
Mull n Muile f.
multiple adj ioma-sheòrsach.
multiply v meudaich.
mumble v dèan brunndail.
mumps n an tinneas-plocach m.
murder n mort m.
murderer n mortair m.
murmur n monmhor m.
muscle n fèith f.

museum n taigh-tasgaidh m.
mushroom n balgan-buachrach m.
music n ceòl m.
musical adj ceòlmhor.
musical instrument n inneal ciùil m.
mussel n feusgan m.
must v feum, 's èiginn, 's fheudar.
muster n cruinneachadh m.
mutation n mùthadh m.
mute adj balbh.
mutilate v ciorramaich.
mutiny n ceannairc f.
mutton n feòil caorach f.
mutual adj aontachail.
my pron mo, m', agam.
myself pron mi fhìn.
mysterious adj dìomhair.
mystery n dìomhaireachd f.
mystical adj fàidheanta.
myth n miotas m.
mythical adj miotasach.
mythology n miotas-eòlas m.

N

nag v dèan dranndan.
nail n tarrag f.
naive adj soineannta.
naked adj lomnochd.
name n ainm m. • v ainmich.
nap n dùsal m.
narrate v aithris.

narrative n aithris m.
narrow adj cumhang.
nasal adj srònach.
nasty adj truaillidh.
nation n nàisean m.
national adj nàiseanta.
nationalism n nàiseantachd f.

nationalist n nàiseantach m.
nationality n dùthchas m.
native adj gnèitheach. • n gnàth-fhear m.
natural adj nàdurrach.
nature n nàdur m.
naughty adj dona.
nausea n dèistinn f.
nauseous adj sgreamhail.
nautical adj seòlaidh.
navel n imleag f.
neap-tide n conntraigh f.
near adj faisg.
near-sighted adj geàrr-fhradharcach.
nearly adv faisg air. • adv (conj) cha mhòr (nach).
neat adj grinn.
necessary adj riatanach.
necessity n èiginn; aimbeart f.
neck n amhach f.
need n feum m. • v feum.
needle n snàthad f.
needy adj feumach.
negative adj àicheanach.
neglect v dèan dearmad.
negligent adj dearmadach.
negotiate v dèan gnothach ri.
neighbour n nàbaidh m.
neither adv/conj/pron cha mhò.
nephew n mac peathar m.
nerve n fèith-mhothachaidh f; (cheek) aghaidh f.
nest n nead m.
Netherlands n An Isealtir f.
net n lìon m.

nettle n feanntag f.
neutral adj neo-phàirteil.
never adv a chaoidh, gu brath.
nevertheless adv gidheadh.
new adj ùr, nuadh.
New Year n A' Bhliadhna Ur f.
news n naidheachd f.
next adj an ath.
nice adj gasta.
niche n oisinn f.
nickname n farainm m.
niece n nighean peathar f.
night n oidhche f.
nightingale n spideag f.
nil n neo-ni m.
nine adj/n naodh, naoi.
nineteen adj naodh-deug.
ninety adj naochad.
ninth adj naodhamh.
nip n teumadh m; (whisky) tè bheag m.
nipple n sine f.
noble adj uasal, flathail.
nod n cromadh m.
noise n fuaim m.
noisy adj fuaimneach.
nominate v ainmich.
non-stop adj gun stad.
nonconformity n neo-aontachd f.
nonsense n amaideas m.
noon n meadhan-latha m.
nor conj no, nas mò.
normal adj gnàthach.
normally adv an cumantas.
north adj tuath. • n tuath m, an àirde tuath f.

northeast n ear-thuath m.
northern adj tuathach.
northwest n iar-thuath m.
nose n sròn f.
note n nota f. • v thoir fa-near.
notebook n leabhar-notaichean m.
nothing n neo-ni m.
notice n sanas, fios m. • v thoir fa-near.
notify v thoir fios do.
nuclear adj niuclasach.
nuclear waste n sgudal niuclasach m.

numb adj meilichte; (cold) air lathadh.
number n àireamh f; mòran f. • v cùnnt, àir.
numeral n cùnntair m.
numerous adj lìonmhor.
nurse n banaltram f. • v altraim.
nursery n plannd-lann f; sgoil-àraich f.
nursing home n taigh-altraim m.
nut n cnò f.
nutshell n plaosg-cnotha m.

O

oak n darach m.
oar n ràmh m.
oatcake n bonnach coirce m.
oath n bòid f.
oatmeal n min-choirce f.
obdurate adj rag-mhuinealach.
obedience n ùmhlachd f.
obey v gèill do.
object[1] n adhbhar m.
object[2] v cuir an aghaidh.
objection n gearan m.
oblige v cuir mar fhiachaibh air; (help) cuir fo chomain.
oblique adj siar.
oblivion n dìochuimhne f.
oboe n òboidh f.
obscene adj drabasda.
obscenity n drabasdachd f.

observant adj aireil.
observe v amhairc.
obsession n beò-ghlacadh m.
obsolete adj bho fheum.
obstinate adj rag-mhuinealach.
obstinacy n rag-mhuinealas m.
obvious adj follaiseach.
occasion n fàth; cothrom m.
occasional adj corra.
occult adj dìomhair.
occupancy n seilbh f.
occupy v gabh sealbh.
ocean n cuan m, fairge f.
octagon n ochd-shliosach f.
octave n ochdad m.
October n Octòber, An Dàmhair m.
octopus n ochd-chasach m.

ocular adj sùl, shùilean.

odd adj còrr.

ode n duanag f.

odour n boladh m.

of prep de, dhe, a.

off adv dheth, às, air falbh. • prep de, dhe, o, bhàrr, a-mach bho.

offence n oilbheum m.

offend v dèan oilbheum do.

offer n tairgse f.

office n oifis f; gnothach f; dreuchd f.

officer n oifigeach m.

officious adj bleideil.

often adv tric; adv gu tric.

ogle v caog.

oil n ola f. • v olaich.

oil-field n ola-raon m.

oil-rig n crann-ola m.

oily adj uilleach.

ointment n ol-ungaidh f.

old adj aosda, sean.

old-fashioned adj sean-fhasanta.

omen n manadh m.

ominous adj droch-fhàistinneach.

omit v fàg às.

on adv air. • prep air.

once adv uair.

one adj aon. • n a h-aon m.

onion n uinnean m.

only adj aon. • adv a-mhàin. • conj ach.

onward adv air adhart.

ooze v sil.

open adj fosgailte. • v fosgail.

opening n fosgladh m.

operation n gnìomhachd m; (surgical) opairèisean m.

opinion n barail f.

opponent n nàmhaid m.

opportune adj tràthail.

opportunity n cothrom m.

oppose v cuir an aghaidh.

opposite prep fa chomhair.

oppress v claoidh.

oppressive adj fòirneartach.

optic adj fradharcach.

optimism n soirbh-dhùil f.

optimistic adj soirbh-dhùileach.

or conj no, air neo.

oral adj troimhn bheul.

orange adj orainds.

orator n cainntear m.

orbit n reul-chuairt f.

orchard n ubhalghort m.

ordain v socraich.

order n òrdugh m. • v òrdaich.

ordinary adj gnàthaichte.

ore n mèinn f.

organ n ball m; orghan m.

organic adj innealach.

organise v eagraich.

organiser n fear-eagraidh m.

orgasm n reachd f.

orgy n ruitearachd f.

oriental adj earach.

origin n tùs, bun m.

originality n bun-mhèinn f.

originate v tàrmaich.

Orkney n Arcaibh.

ornithology n eun-eòlas m.

orphan n dìlleachdan m.
osprey n iolair-uisge f.
ostensible adj a-rèir-coltais.
ostrich n oistric f.
other pron eile.
otherwise adv air modh eile.
otter n dòbhran m.
ought v bu chòir (dhomh, etc).
ounce n ùnnsa m.
our pron ar, ar n-.
ours pron ar ..... -ne, againne, leinne.
ourselves pron sinn fhèin.
out adv a-muigh.
out-of-date adj às an fhasan.
outdo v buadhaich air.
outlaw n fear-cùirn m.
outrage n sàrachadh m.
outright adv gu buileach. • adj dearg.
outside adv a-muigh.
outskirts n iomall m.
outspoken adj fosgarra.
outward adj faicsinneach.

outwit v thoir an car às.
oven n àmhainn f.
over prep os cionn; thairis air. • adv (here) a-null; (there) a-nall.
overall adv thar a chèile.
overboard adv thar bòrd.
overcharge v cuir tuilleadh 's a' chòir.
overflow n cur thairis m. • v tar-shruth.
overnight adj ri linn oidhche.
overrrule v cuir fo smachd.
overseas adv thall thairis.
overtake v beir air.
overtime n seach-thìm f.
overturn v cuir bun-os-cionn.
overweight adj ro-throm.
owe v bi fo fhiachaibh.
owl n comhachag f.
own pron fèin, fhèin.
owner n fear-seilbhe m.
oxter n achlais f.
oyster n eisir m.

P

pace n ceum m. • v ceumnaich.
pacifism n sìochantas m.
pacifist n sìochantair m.
pack v paisg.
packet n pacaid f.
pact n cùmhnant f.
pad n pada f.
paddle v pleadhagaich.
paddling n plubraich f.

padlock n glas-chrochaidh f.
page n duilleag f; (boy) pèidse m.
pageant n taisbeanadh m.
pain n pian f.
painful adj piantach.
painless adj neo-phiantach.
paint n peant m. • v peant.
painting n dealbh m.
pair n càraid f.

palace n lùchairt f.

palate n bràighe-beòil m.

pale adj bàn. • v bànaich.

pallid adj bàn.

palm n bas f.

pamper v dèan peata dhe.

pan n pana f.

pancake n foileag f.

pane n gloinne f.

panic n clisgeadh m.

pant v plosg.

pantry n seòmar-bìdh m.

pants npl pantaichean.

papal adj pàpanach.

paper n pàipear m.

parable n cosamhlachd f.

paradise n pàrras m.

paradox n frith-chosamhlachd f.

paragraph n earran sgrìobhaidh f.

parallel adj co-shìnteach.

paralysis n pairilis m.

parapet n uchd-bhalla m.

parcel n parsail m.

pardon n mathanas m. • v math.

parent n pàrant m.

parish n sgìre f.

park n pàirce f.

Parliament n Parlamaid f.

parody n sgig-athrais f.

parrot n pearraid f.

parsimonious adj splòcach.

parsley n peirsill f.

part¹ n cuid f.

part² v dealaich.

partake v com-pàirtich.

participate v com-pàirtich.

particle n gràinean m.

particular adj àraidh.

parting n dealachadh m.

partition n roinneadh m; (wall) cailbhe m.

partly adv ann an cuid; gu ìre bhig.

partner n companach m.

partridge n cearc-thomain m.

party n cuideachd f; pàrtaidh f.

pass¹ n bealach m.

pass² v gabh seachad; (sport) pasaig.

passable adj cuibheasach.

passage n turas m; (in building) trannsa f.

passion n boile f.

passionate adj dìoghrasach.

passive resistance n aghaidheachd fhulangach f.

passivity n fulangachd m.

passport n cead dol thairis m.

past adj seachad. • n an t-àm a dh'fhalbh m.

pastry n pastra f.

pasture n feurach m. • v feuraich.

pat v slìob.

patch n tùthag f.

paternal adj athaireil.

path n ceum m, slighe f.

pathetic adj tiamhaidh.

patience n foighidinn f.

patient n euslainteach m. • adj foighidneach.

patrimony n dualchas m.

patronymic n ainm sinnsireil m.

pattern n pàtran m.
paunch n maodal f.
pause n stad m. • v fuirich.
paw n spòg f.
pawn[1] n pàn m.
pawn[2] v thoir an geall.
pay n pàigheadh m. • v pàigh.
pea n peasair f.
peace n sìth, fois f.
peaceful adj sìothchail.
peach n pèitseag f.
peak n stùc f, binnean m.
pear n peur f.
pearl n neamhnaid f.
peat n mòine f; (single) fad m.
peat-stack n cruach-mhònach f.
pebble n dèideag f.
peck v pioc.
pectoral adj uchdail.
peculiar adj àraid.
pedal n troighean m.
pedantry n rag-fhoglam m.
peddle v reic.
pedestrian n coisiche m.
pee v dèan mùn.
peel n rùsg m. • v ruisg.
peep n caogadh m. • v caog.
peevish adj dranndanach.
peewit n curracag f.
pelt v caith 'air.
pen n peann m.
penalty n peanas m.
penance n aithridh f.
pending adj ri thighinn.
penetrate v drùidh.
peninsula n leth-eilean m.

penis n bod m.
penny n peighinn f.
pension n peinnsean m.
pensioner n fear-peinnsein m, bean peinnsein f.
people n sluagh, poball m.
pepper n piobair m.
perceive v tuig, mothaich.
per cent adv sa' ceud.
perch n spiris f. • v rach air spiris.
percolator n sìolachan m.
percussion n faram m.
perennial adj maireannach.
perfect adj foirfe. • v dèan foirfe.
perform v coimhlion.
perfume n cùbhrachd f.
perhaps adv is dòcha, ma dh' fhaoite.
period n cuairt f.
perish v faigh bàs.
perishable adj neo-sheasmhach.
permanence n maireannachd f.
permanent adj buan.
permissive adj ceadachail.
permit n bileag-cead f. • v ceadaich.
perpendicular adj dìreach.
perquisite n frith-bhuannachd f.
persecute v geur-lean.
persevere v lean air.
persistent adj leanailteach.
person n neach m.
personal adj pearsanta.
persuade v cuir ìmpidh air.
persuasion n ìmpidheachd f.
pertinent adj iomchuidh.

peruse *v* leugh.

perverse *adj* claon.

pervert *n* claonair *m*.

pessimist *n* fear gun dòchas *m*.

pest *n* plàigh *f*.

pestle *n* plocan *m*.

pet *n* peata *m*.

petition *n* iarrtas *m*. • *v* aslaich.

petrol *n* peatroil *m*.

petticoat *n* còta-bàn *m*.

pew *n* suidheachan *m*.

phantom *n* faileas *m*.

pheasant *n* easag *f*.

phenomenon *n* iongantas *m*.

philosopher *n* feallsanach *m*.

philosophy *n* feallsanachd *f*.

phlegmatic *adj* ronnach.

phone *n* fòn *m*. • *v* fòn.

phosphorescence *n* teine-ghea-lan *m*.

photograph *n* dealbh *m*.

phrase *n* abairt *m*.

physical *adj* fisiceach; corporra.

piano *n* piàno *m*.

pianist *n* cluicheadair piàno *m*.

pibroch *n* pìobaireachd, ceòl-mòr *f*.

pick *v* tagh.

pickle *v* saill.

Pict *n* Cruithneach *m*.

picture *n* dealbh *m*.

picturesque *adj* àillidh.

pie *n* pai *m*.

piece *n* pìos *m*.

pier *n* ceadha *m*.

pierce *v* toll.

pig *n* muc *f*.

pigeon *n* calman *m*.

pigsty *n* fail muice *f*.

pile *v* cruach.

pilfer *v* dèan braide.

pilgrim *n* eilthireach *m*.

pill *n* pile *f*.

pillar *n* carragh *f*.

pillow *n* cluasag *f*.

pilot *n* pìleat *m*. • *v* treòraich.

pimple *n* plucan *m*.

pin *n* dealg *f*.

pinch *v* fàisg.

pine *n* giuthas *m*.

pink *adj* pinc.

pipe *n* pìob *f*.

piper *n* pìobaire *m*.

pirate *n* spùinneadair mara *m*.

piss *n* mùn *m*. • *v* mùin.

pistol *n* daga *m*.

pitch *n* bìth *f*; (*mus*) àirde *f*; (*field*) raon-cluiche *m*.

pitiful *adj* truacanta.

pittance *n* suarachas *m*.

pity *n* truas *m*. • *v* gabh truas de.

place *n* àite *m*. • *v* suidhich.

placidity *n* ciùineachd *f*.

plague *v* plàighich.

plaice *n* lèabag-mhòr *f*.

plaid *n* breacan *m*.

plain *adj* còmhnard; soilleir.

plait *n* figheachan *m*.

plan *n* innleachd, plana *f*. • *v* innlich.

planet *n* planaid *f*.

plank *n* clàr *m*.

plant *n* luibh *m*. • *v* cuir.

plantation n planntachadh m.

plaster n sglàib f; plàsd m.

plastic adj plastaic; coineallach.
• n plastaic f.

plate n truinnsear m.

plateau n àrd-chlàr m.

plausible adj beulach.

play v cluich.

player n fear-cluiche m; cleas-aiche m.

plead v tagair.

pleasant adj taitneach.

please v toilich, riaraich, taitinn, còrd.

pleasure n tlachd f.

pleat n pleat f.

plenty adv gu leòr.

plenty n pailteas m.

plight n cor m.

plod v saothraich.

plot n goirtean m; (scheme) cuil-bheart f.

plough n crann m. • v treabh.

plug n plucan m.

plum n plumas m.

plumb v feuch doimhneachd.

plump adj sultmhor.

plunder n cobhartach m. • v spùinn.

plunge v tum.

plural adj iolra.

plus prep agus.

poach v poidsig.

poacher n poidsear m.

pocket n pòcaid f.

poem n dàn m.

poet n bàrd m.

poetry n bàrdachd f.

point v comharraich.

poison n puinnsean m.

police n poileas m.

polish n lìomh f.

polite adj modhail.

pollute v truaill.

pompous adj mòrchuiseach.

pond n linne f.

pony n pònaidh m.

pool n linne f.

poor adj bochd.

Pope n am Pàpa m.

popular adj coiteanta.

population n sluagh m.

porch n sgàil-thaigh m.

porridge n lite f.

port n port m.

portable adj so-ghiùlan.

portion n earrann f.

Portugal n A' Phortagail f.

positive adj cinnteach.

possess v sealbhaich.

possible adj comasach.

possibly adv is dòcha.

post v cuir air falbh.

postal order n òrdugh-puist m.

postcard n cairt-phostachd f.

postcode n còd-puist m.

postman n posta m.

post office n oifis a' phuist f.

pot n poit f.

potato n buntàta m.

pottery n crèadhadaireachd f.

pound n pùnnd m.

pour v dòirt; (*rain*) sil.

powder n fùdar m.

power n cumhachd f.

power station n stèisean dealain m.

practicable adj so-dhèanamh.

practice n cleachdadh m.

practise v cleachd.

praise n moladh m. • v mol.

prank n cleas m.

prawn n muasgan-caol m.

pray v guidh.

prayer n guidhe f.

preach v searmonaich.

precarious adj cugallach.

precaution n roi-chùram m.

precentor n fear togail fuinn m.

precious adj prìseil.

precipitous adj cas.

precise adj pongail.

precocious adj roi-abaich.

predatory adj creachach.

predict v roi-innis.

predominant adj buadhach.

preface n roi-ràdh m.

prefer v is fheàrr (leam, etc).

pregnant adj trom.

prehistoric adj roi-eachdraidheil.

prejudice n claon-bhàigh f.

preliminary adj tòiseachail.

premises n aitreabh m.

premonition n roi-fhiosrachadh f.

prepare v ullaich.

preposterous adj mì-reusanta.

prescription n riaghailt-lèigh f.

presence n làthaireachd f.

present[1] n an t-àm tha làthair m

present[2] n (*gift*) tiodhlac m. • v thoir do.

presently adv an ceart uair.

president n ceann-suidhe m.

press release n aithris-naidheachd f.

pretence n leigeil air m.

pretend v leig air.

pretty adj brèagha.

prevailing adj buadhach.

previously adv roimh làimh.

prey n creach f. • v creach.

price n prìs f.

prick v stuig.

prickly adj biorach.

pride n àrdan m.

priest n sagart m.

prim adj frionasach.

primary school n bun-sgoil f.

primitive adj tùsach.

primrose n sòbhrach f.

prince n prionnsa m.

print v clò-bhuail.

printer n (*comput*) clò-bhualadair m.

print-out n lethbhreac clo-bhuailte m.

private adj uaigneach.

privilege n sochair f.

prize n duais f.

probable adj coltach.

probably adv is dòcha.

probity n treibhdhireas m.

problem n ceist f.

problematic adj ceisteach.

process n cùrsa m.

proclaim v èigh.

procurator fiscal n fioscail m.

prod v stob.

produce n toradh m. • v thoir gu cinneas.

producer n riochdaire m.

profession n dreuchd f.

professor n proifeasair m.

profit n buannachd f. • v tairbhich.

profound adj domhainn.

profuse adj pailt.

program(me) n prògram m.

programming language n cànan-prògramaidh m.

progress n imeachd f; piseach f.

prohibit v toirmisg.

prolific adj torrach.

prominent adj faicsinneach.

promise n gealladh m. • v geall.

promontory n rubha m.

prompt adj deas.

pronoun n riochdair m.

pronounce v fuaimnich.

proof n dearbadh m.

prop v cùm suas.

proper adj iomchuidh.

property n seilbh f.

prophesy v fàisnich.

proportion n co-rèir m.

proprietor n sealbhadair m.

propulsion n sparradh m.

prose n rosg m.

prosecute v dlù-lean.

prosper v soirbhich.

prostitute n strìopach f.

prostrate adj sleuchdte.

protect v dìon.

protection n dìon m.

protest v tog casaid.

Protestant adj Pròsdanach.

proud adj uaibhreach.

prove v dearbh.

proverb n seanfhacal m.

provide v solair.

province n roinn f.

provocation n buaireadh m.

provoke v buair.

provost n pròbhaist m.

prow n toiseach m.

prowl v èalaidh.

prude n leòmag f.

prudent adj glic.

prune v sgath.

pry v lorgaich.

psalm n salm m.

psalter n salmadair m.

psychic adj anamanta.

ptarmigan n tàrmachan m.

pub n taigh-seinnse m.

public adj follaiseach.

publicity n follaiseadh m.

public relations n dàimh phoblach f.

publish v foillsich.

pudding n marag; mìlsean f.

puddle n lòn m.

puffin n buthaid m.

pull v tarraing.

pulpit n cùbaid f.

pulse n cuisle f.

pump n pumpa m; bròg-dannsa f.

punctual *adj* pongail.
puncture *n* tolladh *m*.
punish *v* peanasaich.
punishment *n* peanasachadh *m*.
pupil *n* sgoilear *m*; (*eye*) clach na sùla *m*.
puppy *n* cuilean *m*.
pure *adj* fiorghlan.
purge *v* glan.
purity *n* glaine *f*.
purple *adj* còrcair.
purse *n* sporan *m*.

pursue *v* lean.
pursuer *n* fear-tòire *m*.
pursuit *n* tòir *f*.
push *n* bruthadh *m*. • *v* brùth.
pussy cat *n* piseag *f*.
put *v* cuir, suidhich.
putrid *adj* grod.
putt *v* amas.
puzzle *n* imcheist. • *v* cuir an imcheist, bi an imcheist.
pylon *n* paidhleon *m*.
pyramid *n* biorramaid *f*.

Q

quack *v* dèan gàgail.
quaint *adj* neònach.
qualification *n* feart *m*.
qualify *v* ullaich.
quality *n* gnè *f*.
quantify *v* àirmhich.
quarrel *n* còmhstri *m*. • *v* connsaich.
quarrelsome *adj* connspaideach.
quarry *n* cuaraidh *m*; creach *m*. • *v* cladhaich.
quarter *n* ceathramh *m*; (*season*) *n* ràith *f*.
quartz *n* èiteag *f*.
quaver *n* crith *f*; (*mus*) *n* caman *m*.
queasy *adj* sleogach.
queen *n* ban-rìgh *f*.
quell *v* smachdaich.
quench *v* bàth.
quern *n* brà *f*.

question *n* ceist *f*. • *v* ceasnaich.
question-mark *n* comharradh ceiste *m*.
queue *n* ciudha *f*.
quibble *v* car-fhaclaich.
quick *adj* bras, luath.
quicksand *n* beò-ghainmheach *f*.
quiet *adj* sàmhach.
quiet *n* sàmhchair *m*.
quieten *v* sàmhaich.
quilt *n* cuibhrig *m*.
quirk *n* car *m*.
quit *v* fàg.
quite *adv* gu tur, gu lèir; gu math.
quiver[1] *n* balg-shaighead *m*.
quiver[2] *v* dèan ball-chrith.
quiz *n* ceasnachadh *m*.
quotation *n* luaidh *m*; (*price*) luach *m*.
quote *v* luaidh; thoir mar ùghdarras.

R

rabbit *n* coineanach *m*.

rabid *adj* cuthachail.

race *n* rèis *f*, (*human*) cinneadh *f*.

racism *n* cinneadachd *f*.

racket *n* gleadhraich *f*.

radiant *adj* lainnireach.

radiate *v* deàlraich.

radiator *n* rèididheator *m*.

radical *adj* bunasach.

radio *n* rèidio *m*.

raffle *n* crannchur-gill *m*.

raft *n* ràth *m*.

rafter *n* taobhan *m*.

rag *n* luideag *f*.

rage *n* boile *f*.

raid *n* ruaig *f*.

railway *n* rathad-iarainn *m*.

rain *n* uisge *m*; frasachd *f*. • *v* sil, dòirt.

rainbow *n* bogha-frois *m*.

rainy *adj* frasach.

raise *v* àrdaich, tog.

rake *v* ràc.

ram *n* reithe *m*.

ram *v* spàrr.

rambler *n* fear-fàrsain *m*.

rampant *adj* sùrdagach.

rancid *adj* breun.

random *adj* tuaireamach.

range *n* sreath *m*. • *v* siubhail.

rank *n* inbhe *f*; sreath *m/f*.

rankle *v* feargaich.

ransom *n* èirig *f*. • *v* fuasgail.

rapacious *adj* gionach.

rape *n* toirt air èiginn *f*. • *v* èignich.

rapidity *n* braise *f*.

rare *adj* tearc.

rarity *n* annas *m*.

rash[1] *n* broth *m*.

rash[2] *adj* dàna.

raspberry *n* subh-craoibh *m*.

rat *n* ratan *m*.

rate *n* luach *m*; ràta *f*.

rather *adv* rudeigin.

ravage *v* sgrios.

rave *v* bi air bhoile.

raven *n* fitheach *m*.

ravenous *adj* clocrach.

raw *adj* amh.

razor *n* ealtainn *f*.

reach *n* ruigheachd *f*. • *v* ruig.

read *v* leugh.

reader *n* leughadair *m*.

readily *adv* gu rèidh.

readiness *n* ullamhachd *f*.

ready *adj* ullamh.

real *adj* fìor.

realise *v* tuig.

reality *n* fìrinn *f*.

really *adv* gu dearbh.

reap *v* buain.

rear *n* deireadh *m*.

reason *n* reusan *m*.

rebate n lùghdachadh m.

rebel n reubalach m. • v dèan ar-a-mach.

rebuff n diùltadh m.

rebuild v ath-thog.

recall v cuimhnich air.

recede v rach air ais.

receive v gabh.

recent adj ùr.

recently adv o chionn ghoirid.

reception n fàilteachadh m.

receptive adj so-ghabhail.

recession n ìsleachadh m.

recipe n modh m.

reciprocal adj malairteach.

recital n aithris; (mus) ceadal f.

reckless adj neo-chùramach.

reckon v cùnnt.

reclaim v ath-leasaich.

recline v sìn.

recognise v aithnich.

recommend v cliùthaich.

reconcile v rèitich.

reconnoitre v feuch.

record n cùnntas m; clàr m. • v sgrìobh; clàraich.

recover v faigh air ais; fàs nas fheàrr.

recovery n faotainn air ais f; fàs nas fheàrr m.

recreation n cur-seachad m.

rectify v ceartaich.

rector n ceannard m, reactor m.

recur v tachair a-rithist.

red adj dearg; ruadh.

redeem v ath-cheannaich.

redirect v ath-sheòl.

redouble v dùblaich.

reduce v ìslich.

redundant adj anbharra.

reed n cuilc f; (mus) ribheid f.

reef n sgeir f.

reel n ruidhle m; (thread) piorna f.

refer v cuir gu.

referee n breitheamh, reaf m.

reference n iomradh m; teistean-as m.

refill v ath-lìon.

refit v ath-chàirich.

reflect v tilg air ais; (think) smaoinich.

reform n leasachadh m. • v ath-leasaich.

refrain n luinneag f.

refresh v ùraich.

refreshment n ùrachadh m; deoch f.

refuge n tèarmann m.

refund v ath-dhìol.

refusal n diùltadh m.

refuse v diùlt.

refute v breugnaich.

regard n suim f. • v gabh suim ann.

register n clàr m.

regret n duilchinn f. • v bi duilich.

regulate v riaghlaich.

rehearsal n ath-aithris f.

rehearse v ath-aithris.

reign v rìoghaich.

reimburse v ath-phàigh.

rein n srian f.

reinforce v ath-neartaich.
rejoice v dèan aoibhneas.
relate v innis.
related adj (akin) càirdeach.
relation n caraid m, ban-charaid f.
relative adj dàimheach.
relax v lasaich.
release v cuir ma sgaoil.
relent v taisich.
relentless adj neo-thruacanta.
relevant adj a' buntainn ri.
reliable adj earbsach.
relic n fuidheall m.
relief n furtachd f.
relieve v furtaich.
religion n diadhachd f.
relish n tlachd f. • v gabh tlachd de.
reluctant adj aindeonach.
rely v earb.
remain v fuirich.
remains npl fuidhleach m; (human) duslach m.
remark n facal m. • v thoir fanear.
remarkable adj suaicheanta.
remedy n leigheas m.
remember v cuimhnich.
remind v cuimhnich do.
reminiscence n cuimhneachadh m.
remorse n agartas-cogais m.
remorseful adj cogaiseach.
remote adj iomallach.
renaissance n ath-bheothachadh m.

rend v srac.
renew v nuadhaich.
rent n sracadh m; (fee) màl m. • v gabh air mhàl.
repair n càireadh m. • v càirich.
repay v ath-dhìol.
repeat v aithris.
repel v tilg air ais.
replace v cuir an àite.
replay v ath-chluich.
replete adj làn.
reply n freagairt f. • v freagair.
report v thoir iomradh.
representative n riochdaire m.
reprieve n stad-bhreith f.
reprimand n casaid f.
reprisal n èirig f.
reproach v cronaich.
reproduce v gin.
reproduction n gintinn m; mac-samhlachadh m.
reptile n pèist f.
republic n poblachd f.
reputation n cliù m.
request n iarrtas m. • v iarr.
rescue n fuasgladh m. • v fuasgail.
research v rannsaich.
researcher n neach-rannsachaidh m.
resent v gabh tàmailt dhe.
resentment n doicheall m.
reserve n tasgadh m. • v caomhain.
reservoir n tasgadh-uisge m.
residence n ionad-còmhnaidh m.

resign v thoir suas, gèill.
resistance n strì f.
resolute adj gramail.
resonant adj glòrach.
resource n goireas m.
respect n urram m. • v thoir urram do.
respectable adj measail.
respectful adj modhail.
respective adj àraidh.
respite n anail f.
responsibility n cùram m.
responsive adj freagairteach.
rest n fois f; (mus) clos m. • v gabh fois.
restaurant n taigh-bidhe m.
restful adj sàmhach.
restless adj mì-fhoisneach.
restore v thoir air ais.
restrict v grab.
result n buil f.
retain v cùm.
reticent adj tosdach.
retire v rach air chluainidh, leig dreuchd dhe.
retirement n cluaineas m.
retreat v teich.
retribution n ath-dhìoladh m.
return n tilleadh m. • v till.
reveal v nochd.
revelation n taisbeanadh m.
revenge n dìoghaltas m.
reverend adj urramach.
reverent adj iriosal.
review v ath-bheachdaich.
revise v ath-sgrùd.

revival n dùsgadh m.
revive v dùisg.
revolve v iom-chuartaich.
reward n duais f. • v dìol.
rheumatic adj lòinidheach.
rheumatism n lòinidh m/f.
rhubarb n rùbarb m.
rhyme n comhardadh m. • v dèan rann.
rib n aisean f.
ribbon n rioban m.
rice n rus m.
rich adj beairteach.
riddle n tòimhseachan m; ruideal f.
ride v marcaich.
rider n marcaiche m.
ridge n druim m.
ridiculous adj amaideach.
right adj ceart; (hand) deas. • n ceartas m; dlighe f. • v cuir ceart.
rigid adj rag.
rigour n cruas m.
rim n oir m.
rind n rùsg m.
ring n fàinne m/f; cearcall m. • v seirm.
rinse v sgol.
ripe adj abaich.
ripen v abaich.
ripple n luasgan m.
rise v èirich.
risk n cunnart m. • v feuch.
rival n co-dheuchainniche m. • adj còistritheach.
rivalry n còmhstri f.

river *n* abhainn *f*.

rivulet *n* sruthan *m*.

road *n* rathad *m*, slighe *f*.

roam *v* rach air fàrsan.

roar *n* beuc *m*. • *v* beuc.

roast *v* ròist.

rob *v* spùinn, spùill.

robber *n* spùilleadair *m*.

robbery *n* goid *f*.

robe *n* fallaing *f*.

robin *n* brù-dhearg *m*.

rock[1] *n* carraig *f*.

rock[2] *v* luaisg.

rod *n* slat *f*.

roe *n* earba, ruadhag *f*; (*fish*) glasag *f*.

rogue *n* slaoightear *m*.

roll *n* rolla *f*. • *v* fill.

romance *n* romansachd *f*; (*tale*) ròlaist *m*.

romantic *adj* romansach.

roof *n* mullach *m*.

rook *n* ròcas *m*.

room *n* seòmar, rùm *m*.

roomy *adj* farsaing.

root *n* freumh *m*.

rope *n* ròpa, ball *m*.

rosary *n* paidirean *m*.

rose *n* ròs *m*.

rosy *adj* ruiteach.

rot *n* grodadh *m*.

rotten *adj* grod.

rough *adj* garbh, molach.

round *adj* cruinn. • *adv* mun cuairt.

rouse *v* dùisg.

rout *n* ruaig *f*.

routine *n* gnàth-chùrsa *m*.

row *n* (*rank*) sreath *m/f*; (*fight*) sabaid *f*.

rowan *n* caorann *f*.

rower *n* ràmhaiche *m*.

rub *v* suath.

rubbish *n* salchar, brusgar *m*.

rudder *n* stiùir *f*.

rude *adj* borb.

rue *v* crean.

rueful *adj* dubhach.

ruffian *n* brùid *f*.

rug *n* bràt-urlair *m*.

ruin *n* sgrios *m*; (*house*) làrach *m*.

rule *n* riaghailt *f*. • *v* riaghail.

rumble *v* dèan rùcail.

rummage *v* rannsaich.

rumour *n* fathann *m*.

run *v* ruith.

runnel *n* srùlag *f*.

rural *adj* dùthchail.

rush *v* brùchd.

rushes *npl* luachair *f*.

rust *n* meirg *f*.

rut *n* clais *f*, (*animal*) dàmhair *f*.

ruthless *adj* neo-thruacanta.

S

sabbath n sàbaid f.

sack[1] n poca m.

sack[2] v sgrios; cuir à obair.

sacred adj naomh.

sacrifice n ìobairt f. • v ìobair.

sad adj brònach.

sadden v dèan brònach.

saddle n dìollaid f.

sadness n bròn, mulad m.

safe adj sàbhailte.

safety n tèarainteachd f.

saffron n cròch m.

sag v tuit.

sagacious adj geurchuiseach.

sail n seòl m. • v seòl.

sailor n seòladair m.

saint n naomh m.

sake n sgàth m.

salad n sailead m.

sale n reic m.

saleable adj so-reic.

saliva n seile m.

sallow adj lachdann.

salmon n bradan m.

salmon trout n bànag f.

salt n salann m.

salt-cellar n saillear m.

salutary adj slàinteil.

salute v fàiltich.

salvage n tàrrsainn m.

same adj ionann, ceudna.

sameness n co-ionannachd.

sample n samhla m.

sanctify v naomhaich.

sanctuary n comraich f.

sand n gainmheach f.

sandstone n clach-ghainmhich f.

sandy adj gainmheil.

sane adj ciallach.

sapling n faillean m.

sapphire n gorm-leug f.

sarcasm n searbhas m.

sarcastic adj searbh.

satanic adj diabhlaidh.

satchel n màileid f.

satellite n saideal m.

satiate v sàsaich.

satin n sròl m.

satire n aoir f.

satirical adj aoireil.

satirist n èisg f.

satisfaction n sàsachadh m.

satisfied adj sàsaichte.

satisfy v sàsaich.

Saturday n Disathairne m, Sathairne f.

sauce n sabhs m.

saucepan n sgeileid f.

saucer n sàsar m.

sausage n ìsbean m.

save v sàbhail.

saved adj saorte.

savour v feuch blas.

savoury adj blasda.

saw n sàbh m. • v sàbh.

say v abair.

saying n ràdh, facal m.

scald v sgàld.

scale n cothrom m; (fish) lann m; (mus) sgàla m.

scaly adj lannach.

scalp n craiceann a' chinn m.

scan v sgrùd.

scandal n sgainneal m.

scandalise v sgainnealaich.

scandalous adj maslach.

scanty adj gann.

scar n leòn m.

scarce adj tearc.

scare v cuir eagal air.

scarecrow n bodach-ròcais m.

scarf n stoc m.

scatter v sgap.

scattering n sgapadh m.

scene n sealladh m.

scent n fàileadh m.

scented adj cùbhraidh.

sceptical adj às-creideach.

scheme n innleachd f.

school n sgoil f.

schoolmaster n maighstir-sgoile m.

schoolmistress n bana-maigh-stir-sgoile f.

science n saidheans m.

scientific adj saidheansail.

scissors n siosar f.

scold v troid.

scone n bonnach m, sgona f.

scorch v dadh.

score v cuir; sgrìob.

scorn n tàir f.

scornful adj tàireil.

Scotland n Alba f.

Scottish adj Albannach.

scour v nigh.

scourge v sgiùrs.

scout n beachdair m.

scowl v bi fo ghruaim.

scrape n sgrìob f.

scratch n sgròbadh m. • v sgròb.

scream n sgreuch m. • v sgreuch.

scree n sgàirneach f.

script n sgrìobhadh m.

scroll n rolla f.

scrotum n clach-bhalg m.

scrub v nigh.

scruple n teagamh m.

scrupulous adj teagmhach.

scuffle n tuasaid f.

sculptor n deilbhear m.

sculpture n deilbheadh m.

scythe n speal f. • v speal.

sea n muir m/f, cuan m, fairge f.

seagull n faoileag f.

seal n ròn m; (official) seula m. • v seulaich.

sea level n àirde-mara f.

seaport n longphort m.

sear v crannaich.

search n lorg m. • v lorg, rann-saich.

seashore n cladach m.

season n ràith f.

seasonable adj tràthail.

seaweed n feamainn f.

second adj dara.

secondary adj dàrnach.

secondary school *n* àrd-sgoil *f*.

second-hand *adj* ath-dhìolta.

secondly *adv* anns an dara h-àite.

secrecy *n* cleith *f*.

secret *adj* dìomhair. • *n* rùn.

secretary *n* rùnaire *m*, banrùnaire *f*.

secretive *adj* ceilteach.

secretly *adv* gun fhiosda.

sect *n* dream *m*.

secular *adj* saoghalta.

secure *adj* seasgair. • *v* glais, glac.

security *n* dìon *m*.

seduce *v* truaill.

seduction *n* truailleadh *m*.

see *v* faic, seall, amhairc.

seed *n* sìol *m*. • *v* sìolaich.

seeing *n* lèirsinn *f*.

seek *v* iarr.

seer *n* fiosaiche *m*.

seize *v* glac, cuir làmh ann.

seldom *adv* gu tearc.

select *v* tagh.

self *pron* fèin, fhèin, fhìn.

self-interest *n* fèin-bhuannachd *f*.

selfish *adj* fèineil.

sell *v* reic.

semiquaver *n* leth-chaman *m*.

semitone *n* leth-phong *m*.

senate *n* seanadh *m*.

send *v* cuir.

senile *adj* seantaidh.

senior *adj* as sine.

sensation *n* mothachadh *m*.

sense *n* ciall *f*.

senseless *adj* gun chiall.

sensible *adj* ciallach.

sensitive *adj* mothachail.

sensual *adj* feòlmhor.

sensuous *adj* ceudfaidheach.

sentence *n* rosg-rann *m*; (*law*) binn *f*.

sentimental *adj* maoth-inntinneach.

separate *v* dealaich.

separation *n* dealachadh *m*.

September *n* September *m*; An t-Sultuine *f*.

septic *adj* seaptaic.

sepulchral *adj* tuamach.

sequence *n* leanmhainn *m*.

serene *adj* soinneanta.

sergeant *n* seàirdeant *m*.

series *n* sreath *m*.

serious *adj* suidhichte.

serpent *n* nathair *f*.

serrated *adj* eagach.

servant *n* seirbheiseach *m*.

serve *v* riaraich, fritheil.

service *n* seirbheis *f*; dleasnas *m*.

serviceable *adj* feumail.

session *n* seisean *m*.

set *v* suidhich, cuir.

setter *n* cù-luirg *m*.

settle *v* socraich.

settlement *n* suidheachadh; tuineachadh *m*.

seven *adj* seachd. • *n* (*people*) seachdnar.

seventeen *n* seachd-deug.

seventh *adj* seachdamh.

seventy *n* seachdad, trì fichead 's a deich.

sever *v* sgar.

severe *adj* cruaidh.

severity *n* cruas *m*.

sew *v* fuaigh.

sewage *n* giodar *m*.

sewing *n* fuaigheal *m*.

sex *n* gnè *f*, sex *m*.

sextet *n* ceòl-sianar *m*.

sexual intercourse *n* co-ghineadh *m*.

shade *n* sgàil *f*. • *v* sgàil.

shadow *n* faileas *m*.

shady *adj* dubharach.

shaggy *adj* molach.

shallow *adj* tana; faoin.

sham *adj* mealltach.

shame *n* nàire *f*. • *v* nàraich.

shameful *adj* nàr.

shape *n* cumadh *m*. • *v* cum, dealbh.

shapely *adj* cuimir.

share *n* roinn *f*. • *v* roinn, pàirtich.

shark *n* siorc *m*.

sharp *adj* geur.

sharpen *v* geuraich.

sharpness *n* gèire *f*.

shave *v* beàrr.

shawl *n* seàla *f*.

she *pron* i, ise.

shear *v* rùsg.

shearing *n* rùsgadh *m*.

sheath *n* truaill *f*.

shed[1] *n* bothan *m*.

shed[2] *v* dòirt.

sheep *n* caora *f*.

sheep-dog *n* cù-chaorach.

sheet *n* duilleag *f*.

shelling *n* àirigh *f*.

shelf *n* sgeilp *f*; (*rock*) sgeir *f*.

shellfish *n* maorach *m*.

shelter *n* dìon *m*.

shepherd *n* cìobair *m*.

sheriff *n* siorraidh *m*.

Shetland *n* Sealtainn *m*.

shield *n* sgiath *f*. • *v* dìon.

shine *v* deàlraich.

shinty *n* iomain *f*.

shinty stick *n* caman *m*.

ship *n* long *f*.

shipwreck *n* long-bhriseadh *m*.

shire *n* siorrachd *f*.

shirt *n* lèine *f*.

shiver *v* crith.

shoal *n* bogha; sgaoth *m*.

shock *n* sgannradh *m*. • *v* criothnaich.

shoe *n* bròg *f*.

shoelace *n* barrall *f*.

shoemaker *n* greusaiche *m*.

shoot *v* tilg, loisg; (*grow*) fàs.

shop *n* bùth *f*.

shore *n* tràigh *f*.

short *adj* goirid.

shortage *n* dìth *m*.

shorten *v* giorraich.

shortly *adv* a dh' aithghearr.

short-sighted *adj* geàrr-sheallach.

shorts *npl* briogais ghoirid *f*.

short-wave n geàrr-thonnach m.

shot n urchair f.

shoulder n gualainn f.

shout n glaodh m.

shove n putadh m. • v put.

show v seall.

shower n fras f.

shred n mìr m.

shriek n sgread m.

shrimp n carran m.

shrink v seac.

shrub n preas m.

shudder v criothnaich.

shuffle v tarraing; (cards) measgaich.

shut v druid, dùin. • adj dùinte.

shy adj sochaireach.

sick adj tinn.

sickness n tinneas m.

side n taobh m.

sidelong adv air fhiaradh.

sideways adv an comhair a thaoibh.

siege n sèisd f.

sieve n criathar m.

sigh v leig osna.

sight n sealladh m; lèirsinn f.

sign n comharradh m.

signature n ainm m.

significant adj brìgheil.

signpost n post-seòlaidh m.

silence n sàmhchair f, tosd m.

silent adj tosdach.

silk n sìoda m.

sill n sòlla f.

silly adj gòrach.

silver n airgead m.

similar adj coltach.

simple adj sìmplidh.

simplify v sìmplich.

simultaneous adj còmhla.

sin n peacadh m. • v peacaich.

since conj a chionn is gu. • prep o, bho, o chionn.

sincere adj onorach.

sing v seinn, gabh òran.

singer n seinneadair m.

single adj singilte; gun phòsadh.

singular adj sònraichte.

sinister adj droch thuarach.

sink n since f. • v cuir fodha; rach fodha.

sip v gabh balgam.

sister n piuthar f.

sister-in-law n piuthar-chèile f.

sit v suidh.

sitting room n seòmar-suidhe m.

six adj sia. • n (people) sianar.

sixteen adj/n sia-deug m.

sixty adj/n trì-fichead, seasgad.

size n meud m.

skate[1] n bròg-spèilidh f. • v spèil.

skate[2] n (fish) sgait f.

skeleton n cnàimhneach m.

skerry n sgeir f.

sketch n tarraing f.

ski v sgithich.

skid v sleamhnaich.

ski-lift n àrdaichear-ski m.

skill n sgil m.

skim v thoir uachdar dhe.

skin n craiceann m. • v feann.

skinny *adj* caol.

skip *v* leum.

skirmish *n* arrabhaig *f*.

skirt *n* sgiort *f*.

skull *n* claigeann *m*.

sky *n* adhar *m*.

Skye *n* An t-Eilean Sgitheanach *m*.

skylark *n* uiseag *f*.

slam *v* thoir slàr do.

slander *n* sgainneal *m*.

slant *n* claonadh *m*. • *v* claon.

slap *n* sgailc *f*.

slash *v* geàrr.

slate *n* sglèat *m*.

slaughter *n* marbhadh *m*.

slave *n* tràill *f*.

sledge *n* càrn-slaoid *m*.

sleek *adj* slìom.

sleep *n* cadal *m*.

sleepy *adj* cadalach.

sleet *n* flin *m*.

sleeve *n* muinchill *m*.

slice *n* sliseag *f*.

slide *v* sleamhnaich.

slip *n* tuisleadh *m*. • *v* tuislich.

slipper *n* slapag *f*.

slippery *adj* sleamhainn.

slit *n* sgoltadh *m*.

slogan *n* sluagh-ghairm *f*.

slope *n* leathad *m*.

sloven *n* luid *f*.

slovenly *adj* luideach.

slow *adj* slaodach.

slowness *n* slaodachd *f*.

slur *n* tàir *f*; (*speech*) slugadh *m*.

sly *adj* carach.

smack *n* sglais *f*.

small *adj* beag.

smart *adj* tapaidh.

smattering *n* bloigh eòlais *m*.

smear *v* smiùr.

smell *n* fàileadh *m*. • *v* feuch fàileadh.

smile *n* snodha-gàire *m*. • *v* dèan snodha-gàire.

smith *n* gobha *m*.

smoke *n* ceò *m*. • *v* smocaig.

smoky *adj* ceòthach.

smooth *adj* mìn.

smoothe *v* mìnich.

smother *v* mùch.

smoulder *v* cnàmh-loisg.

smuggle *v* dèan cùl-mhùtaireachd.

smuggler *n* cùl-mhùtaire *m*.

snack *n* blasad bìdh *m*.

snake *n* nathair *f*.

snatch *v* glac.

sneak *v* snàig.

sneer *v* dèan fanaid.

sneeze *v* dèan sreothart.

sniff *n* boladh *m*. • *v* gabh boladh.

snipe *n* naosg *m*.

snivel *v* smùch.

snob *n* sodalan *m*.

snooze *n* norrag *f*.

snore *v* dèan srann.

snout *n* soc *m*.

snow *n* sneachd *m*. • *v* cuir sneachd.

snowdrift *n* cith *m*.

snug *adj* còsach.

snuggle v laigh dlùth ri.
so adv cho; mar seo; mar sin.
soak v drùidh.
soap n siabann m.
soapy adj làn siabainn.
sober adj stuama; sòbair.
sociable adj cuideachdail.
socialism n sòisealachd f.
society n comann m.
sock n socais f.
sod n fòid f.
soft adj bog.
soften v bogaich.
softness n buige f.
software n bathar bog m.
soil n ùir f. • v salaich.
solar adj na grèine.
soldier n saighdear m.
sole n bonn na coise m; (fish) lèabag m.
solemn adj sòlaimte.
solicit v aslaich.
solicitor n fear-lagha m.
solid adj teann.
solidarity n dlùthachd f.
solitude n uaigneas m.
solo n òran aon-neach m.
soloist n òranaiche m.
soluble adj so-sgaoilte.
solve v fuasgail.
solvent adj comasach air pàigheadh.
some pron cuid, feadhainn; pàirt.
somebody n cuideigin m.
somehow adv air dòigh air choreigin.

something n rudeigin m.
sometime adv uaireigin.
sometimes adv air uairibh.
somewhere adv an àiteigin.
son n mac m.
son-in-law n cliamhainn m.
soon adv a dh' aithghearr.
sophisticated adj ionnsaichte.
sordid adj suarach.
sore n creuchd m. • adj goirt.
sorrow n bròn m.
sorry adj duilich.
sort n seòrsa m. • v seòrsaich.
soul n anam m.
sound n fuaim m. • v seirm, seinn.
soup n eanraich f, n brot m.
sour adj geur.
south adj/n deas f.
southerly adj/adv deas, à deas.
sow n cràin f.
space n rùm m.
space probe n taisgealadh fànais m.
spacious adj farsaing.
Spain n An Spàinn f.
spaniel n cù-eunaich m.
Spanish n Spàinnis f.
spare v caomhainn.
spark n sradag f.
sparkle v lainnrich.
spawn v sìolaich.
speak v bruidhinn.
spear n sleagh f.
special adj àraidh.
species n seòrsa m.
spectacles npl speuclairean.

spectre n tannasg m.

speech n cainnt f; òraid f.

speed n luas m.

speed v luathaich.

spell v litrich.

spend v caith.

spider n damhan-allaidh m.

spill v dòirt.

spin v snìomh.

spine n cnàimh-droma f.

spinning wheel n cuibhle-shnìomh f.

spirit n spiorad m.

spirited adj misneachail.

spit v tilg smugaid.

spite n gamhlas m.

splendid adj greadhnach.

split v sgoilt.

spoil v mill.

spoon n spàin f.

sporran n sporan m.

sport n spòrs f.

spot n ball m.

spouse n cèile m.

spreadsheet n duilleag-cleithe f.

spree n daorach f.

Spring n earrach m.

spring n fuaran m; leum m.

spume n cathadh-mara m.

spur v spor.

spy n beachdair m.

squalid adj sgreamhail.

squall n sgal m.

square adj ceithir-cheàrnach. • n ceàrnag f.

squash v brùth.

squat adj cutach.

squeak n blog m.

squirrel n feòrag f.

squirt v steall.

stable[1] adj bunailteach.

stable[2] n stàball m.

stag n damh m.

stair n staidhre f.

stale adj cruaidh; goirt.

stalk n gas f.

stallion n àigeach m.

stammer v bruidhinn gagach.

stamp n stampa f; (embossing) stàmpa f.

stand v seas, stad.

standstill n stad m.

star n rionnag, reul f; prìomh act-air f.

starboard n deasbhòrd m.

stare v spleuchd.

starfish n crosgan m.

starry adj rionnagach.

start v clisg; (motor) cuir a dhol.

starvation n goirt f.

state[1] n staid f; (country) stàit f.

state[2] v cuir an cèill.

station n stèisean m.

statue n ìomhaigh f.

stature n àirde f.

stave n earran f, cliath f.

stay n stad m. • v fuirich.

steak n staoig f.

steal v goid.

steam n toit f.

steel n stàilinn f.

steep adj cas.

steer *v* stiùir.

step *n* ceum *m*.

sterile *adj* seasg.

stern[1] *adj* cruaidh.

stern[2] *n* deireadh *m*.

stick[1] *n* maide *m*.

stick[2] *v* sàth; (*adhere*) lean.

stiffen *v* ragaich.

still[1] *adv* fhathast; an dèidh sin.

still[2] *n* poit-dhubh *f*.

sting *n* gath *m*. • *v* guin.

stink *n* tòchd *m*.

stir *v* gluais.

stitch *n* grèim *m*.

stocking *n* stocainn *f*.

stomach *n* stamag *f*.

stone *n* clach *f*.

stool *n* stòl *m*.

stop *v* stad.

store *v* stòir.

storehouse *n* taigh-stòir *m*.

stork *n* corra bhàn *f*.

storm *n* doineann, stoirm *f*.

stormy *adj* stoirmeil.

story *n* sgeul *m*.

stove *n* stòbha *f*.

straight *adj* dìreach.

strain[1] *n* teannachadh *m*; (*mental*) uallach.

strain[2] *v* teannaich; (*filter*) sìolaidh.

strange *adj* iongantach.

stranger *n* coigreach *m*.

strath *n* srath *m*.

straw *n* connnlach *f*.

strawberry *n* subh-làir *m*.

streaky *adj* stiallach.

stream *n* sruth *m*.

street *n* sràid *f*.

strength *n* neart *m*.

stretch *v* sìn.

strict *adj* teann.

stride *n* sìnteag *f*.

strike *v* buail; (*work*) rach air stailc.

string *n* sreang *f*; teud *f*.

stringed *adj* teudaichte.

stroke *v* slìog.

stroll *v* siubhail.

strong *adj* làidir.

struggle *n* gleac *m*. • *v* gleac.

stubble *n* asbhuain *f*.

stubborn *adj* rag.

stuff *n* stuth *m*.

stupid *adj* baoghalta.

sturdy *adj* bunanta.

sty *n* fail mhuc *f*.

stye *n* leamhnagan *m*.

style *n* modh *m*.

stylish *adj* baganta.

subject *adj* umhal, fo smachd. • *v* ceannsaich.

sublime *adj* òirdheirc.

submit *v* gèill.

subside *v* traogh.

subsidy *n* còmhnadh *m*.

substance *n* stuth *m*; brìgh *f*.

substitute *v* cuir an ionad.

subtle *adj* seòlta.

subtract *v* thoir o.

succeed *v* soirbhich; lean.

successful *adj* soirbheachail.

such *adj/pron* a leithid de, den t-seòrsa.

suck *v* deoghail.

suckle *v* thoir cìoch.

sudden *adj* grad.

suddenly *adv* gu h-obann.

sue *v* tagair.

suffer *v* fuiling.

sufferer *n* fulangaiche *m*.

sufficient *adj* leòr.

sugar *n* siùcar *m*.

suggest *v* mol, comhairlich.

suicide *n* fèin-mhort *m*.

suit *n* deise *f*. • *v* freagair.

suitable *adj* freagarrach.

sum *n* àireamh, suim *f*.

summer *n* samhradh *m*.

summit *n* mullach *m*.

summon *v* gairm.

sun *n* grian *f*.

sunbathe *v* blian.

Sunday *n* Di-Dòmhnaich *m*, Là na Sàbaid *m*.

sunny *adj* grianach.

sunrise *n* èirigh na grèine *f*.

sunset *n* laighe na grèine *m*.

supernatural *adj* os-nàdurrach.

superstition *n* saobh-chràbadh *m*.

supper *n* suipear *f*.

supple *adj* sùbailte.

supply *v* sòlaire ù.

support *v* cùm taic ri.

suppose *v* saoil.

suppress *v* cùm fodha.

supreme *adj* sàr.

sure *adj* cinnteach.

surely *adv* gun teagamh.

surface *n* uachdar *m*.

surge *v* brùchd.

surgeon *n* làmh-leigh *m*.

surgery *n* (*doctor's*) ionad doctair *m*.

surly *adj* iargalta.

surname *n* sloinneadh *m*.

surplus *n* còrr *m*.

surprise *n* iongnadh *m*. • *v* cuir iongnadh air.

surprising *adj* neònach.

surrender *n* gèilleadh *m*.

surround *v* cuartaich.

survive *v* mair beò.

suspect *v* cuir an amharas.

suspend *v* croch.

suspense *n* teagamh *m*.

suspension bridge *n* drochaid croch-aidh *f*.

suspicious *adj* amharasach.

swallow[1] *v* sluig.

swallow[2] *n* gòbhlan-gaoithe *m*.

swamp *n* fèith *f*.

swan *n* eala *f*.

swarm *v* sgaothaich.

swear *v* mionnaich.

sweat *n* fallas *m*. • *v* cuir fallas dhe.

swede *n* (*neep*) snèip *f*.

Sweden *n* An t-Suain *f*.

sweep *v* sguab.

sweet *adj* milis.

sweeties *npl* siùcairean.

sweetheart *n* eudail *f*; leannan *f*.

swim *v* snàmh.

swimming pool *n* amar-snàimh *m*.

swing *n* dreallag *f*.

switch *n* suidse *f*.

sword *n* claidheamh *m*.

symbol *n* samhla *m*.

symbolic *adj* samhlachail.

sympathetic *adj* co-mhothachail.

sympathise *v* co-mhothaich.

syringe *n* steallaire *m*.

syrup *n* siorap *f*.

system *n* riaghailt *f*.

T

table *n* bòrd; clàr *m*.

tablet *n* pile *f*; clàr *m*.

tacit *adj* gun bhruidhinn.

taciturn *adj* dùinte.

tack *n* tacaid *f*.

tacket *n* tacaid *f*.

tacksman *n* fear-baile *m*.

tadpole *n* ceann-pholan *m*.

tail *n* earball *m*.

taint *v* truaill.

take *v* gabh, thoir.

tale *n* sgeulachd *f*.

talent *n* tàlann *m*.

talk *v* bruidhinn.

tall *adj* àrd.

tame *adj* calla. • *v* callaich.

tangle *n* sàs *m*; (*seaweed*) stamh *m*.

tanker *n* tancair *m*.

tantalise *v* tog dòchas.

tap *n* goc *m*.

taper *v* dèan caol.

tapestry *n* grèis-bhrat *m*.

target *n* targaid *f*.

tart[1] *adj* searbh.

tart[2] *n* pithean *m*.

task *n* obair *f*.

taste *v* blais.

tasty *adj* blasta.

tawny *adj* lachdann.

tawse *n* stràic *m*.

tax *v* leag cìs.

tea *n* teatha, tì *f*.

teach *v* teasgaig.

teacher *n* fear-teagaisg, tìdsear *m*.

teach-in *n* seisean connsachaidh *m*.

teacup *n* cupan teatha *m*.

team *n* sgioba *m/f*.

tear *n* deur *m*; (*rip*) sracadh *m*.

tease *v* farranaich.

tedious *adj* liosda.

teenager *n* deugaire *m*.

telephone *n* fòn, teilefon *m*.

television *n* teilebhisean *m*.

tell *v* innis.

temper *n* nàdur *m*.

temperament *n* càil *f*.

temperature *n* teodhachd *f*.

tempest *n* doineann *f*.

temple *n* teampall *m*.

temporary adj sealach.

tempt v buair.

ten adj/n deich; (persons) deich-near.

tenacious adj leanailteach.

tenant n fear-aonta m.

tender adj maoth.

tennis n cluich-cneutaig f.

tent n teanta f.

tenth n an deicheamh earrann f.

term n teirm f; briathar m.

tern n steàrnan m.

terrier n abhag f.

terrorism n oillteachas m.

test n deuchainn f.

testament n tiomnadh m.

testicle n magairle m, clach f.

than conj na.

thank v thoir taing.

thanks npl tapadh leat, tapadh leibh; taing f.

thankful adj taingeil.

that adj/pron sin, ud, siud. • conj gu, chum. • adv a chionn, do bhrìgh.

thatch n tughadh m.

thaw v dèan aiteamh.

the art an, am, a', na, na h-, nan.

theft n meirle m.

their pron an, am, aca.

them pron iad, iadsan.

themselves pron iad fhèin.

then adv an sin; an dèidh sin; a-rèist.

thence adv às a sin.

theory n beachd m.

therapy n leigheas m.

there adv an sin, an siud.

thereby adv le sin.

therefore adv uime sin.

these pron iad seo.

they pron iad, iadsan.

thick adj tiugh.

thief n meirleach m.

thigh n sliasaid f.

thin adj tana.

thing n nì, rud m.

think adj smaoinich.

third adj treas.

thirst n pathadh m. • v bi pàiteach.

thirteen adj/n trì-deug.

thirty adj/n trìthead.

this pron seo.

thistle n cluaran m.

thorny adj driseach.

those pron iad sin.

though conj ge, ged.

thought n smaoin f.

thousand adj/n mìle.

thrash v slaic; (corn) buail.

threat n bagairt f.

threaten v bagair.

three adj/n trì; (persons) triùir.

thrilling adj gaoireil.

throat n amhach f.

through prep tre, troimh, trìd.

throw v tilg.

thrush n smeòrach m.

thumb n òrdag f.

thunder n tàirneanach m.

thunderous adj torranach.

Thursday n Diardaoin m.

thus *adv* mar seo.

ticket *n* bileag *f*.

ticking *n* diogadaich *f*.

tide *n* seòl-mara *m*.

tidy *v* sgioblaich.

tiger *n* tìgeir *m*.

till *prep* gu, gus, gu ruig.

tiller *n* ailm *f*.

time *n* ùine, aimsir *f*.

timely *adj* an deagh àm.

timeous *adj* an deagh àm.

tinker *n* ceàrd *m*.

tiny *adj* crìon.

tipsy *adj* froganach.

tired *adj* sgìth.

tiresome *adj* sgìtheachail.

title *n* tiotal *m*.

to *prep* do, gu, chun, ri, aig, an aghaidh.

toad *n* muile-mhàg *f*.

toast *v* òl deoch-slàinte; tostaig.

tobacco *n* tombaca *m*.

today *adv* an-diugh.

together *adv* le chèile, còmhla.

toilet *n* taigh-beag *m*; sgeadach-adh *m*.

tomb *n* tuam *m*.

tomorrow *adv* a-màireach.

tone *n* fonn *m*; tòna *f*.

tongue *n* teanga *m*.

tonight *adv* a-nochd.

too *adv* cuideachd.

tool *n* inneal *m*.

tooth *n* fiacail *f*.

top *n* mullach, uachdar *m*.

torch *n* leus *m*.

torrent *n* bras-shruth *m*.

tortoise *n* sligeanach *m*.

Tory *n* Tòraidh *m*.

toss *v* luaisg.

total *adj* iomlan.

touch *v* bean do, suath ann.

tough *adj* righinn.

tour *n* turas *m*.

tourists *npl* luchd-turais.

towards *prep* a chum.

tower *n* tùr *m*.

town *n* baile *m*.

toy *n* dèideag *f*.

trace *v* lorg.

track *v* lorg.

trade *n* malairt *f*.

tradition *n* beul-aithris *m*; tradis-ean *m*.

train *n* trèana *f*; (*retinue*) muinntir *f*. • *v* àraich.

traitor *n* fear-brathaidh *m*.

trance *n* neul *m*.

transfer *v* thoir thairis.

transient *adj* diombuan.

translate *v* eadar-theangaich.

transmitter *n* crann-sgaoilidh *m*.

transparent *adj* trìd-shoilleir.

trap *n* ribe *f*. • *v* rib.

travel *n* siubhal *m*. • *v* siubhail.

tray *n* sgàl *m*.

treasure *n* ionmhas *m*. • *v* taisg.

treat *n* cuirm *f*. • *v* riaraich.

tree *n* craobh *f*.

tremor *n* crith *f*.

trespass *n* cionta *m*; peacadh *m*. • *v* rach thar chrìochan.

trews *npl* triubhas *m*.

trial *n* deuchainn *f*.

tribe *n* treubh *f*, sliochd *m*.

tributary *n* leas-abhainn *f*.

trick *n* car *m*.

trim *adj* cuimir.

trip *v* tuislich.

triumph *n* gàirdeachas *m*.

triumph *v* thoir buaidh.

trivial *adj* suarach.

trot *v* dèan trotan.

trouble *n* dragh *f*. • *v* cuir dragh air.

trousers *n* briogais *f*.

trout *n* breac *m*.

true *adj* fìor.

trump card *n* buadh-chairt *f*.

trust *n* earbsa *f*. • *v* earb à.

truth *n* fìrinn *f*.

try *v* feuch; cuir gu deuchainn.

tub *n* balan *m*.

Tuesday *n* Dimàirt *m*.

tumble *v* tuit, leag.

tumult *n* iorghail *f*.

tune *n* fonn, port *m*. • *v* gleus.

tuneful *adj* fonnmhor.

tup *n* reithe *m*.

turf *n* sgrath, fòd *f*.

turn *v* tionndaidh; cuir air falbh.

turtle *n* turtur *f*.

tutor *n* (*guardian*) taoitear *m*.

tweak *v* teannaich.

tweed *n* clò *m*.

twelfth *adj* dara-deug.

twelve *adj/n* dà-deug.

twentieth *adj* ficheadamh.

twenty *adj/m* fichead.

twice *adv* dà uair.

twilight *n* eadar-sholas *m*.

twin *n* leth-aon *m*.

twist *v* toinn.

two *adj/n* dà; (*persons*) dithis.

two-faced *adj* beulach.

typical *adj* dualach.

typography *n* clò-bhualadh *m*.

tyrant *n* aintighearna *m*.

tyro *n* foghlamaiche *m*.

U

udder *n* ùth *m*.

ugliness *n* grànndachd *f*.

ugly *adj* grànnda.

ulcer *n* neasgaid *f*.

ultimate *adj* deiridh.

umbrella *n* sgàilean *m*.

unable *adj* neo-chomasach.

unaccustomed *adj* neo-chle-achdte.

unanimous *adj* aon-inntinneach.

unarmed *adj* neo-armaichte.

unavoidable *adj* do-sheachanta.

unaware *adj* gun fhios.

unbolt *v* thoir an crann de.

uncle *n* bràthair-athar, bràthair-màthar *m*.

uncomfortable *adj* anshocrach.

uncommon *adj* neo-gnàthach.

unconditional *adj* gun chùmh-nantan.

uncork *v* às-àrcaich.

unction *n* ungadh *m*.

undecided *adj* neo-chinnteach.

under *prep* fo.

undergo *v* fuiling.

underground *adj* fo thalamh.

underneath *adv* fodha. • *prep* fo.

understand *v* tuig.

underwear *n* fo-aodach *m*.

undeserved *adj* neo-thoillteanach.

undistinguished *adj* neo-chomharraichte.

undisturbed *adj* neo-bhuairte.

undo *v* fuasgail.

unemployed *adj* dìomhain, gun obair.

unequal *adj* neo-ionnan.

uneven *adj* corrach.

unexpected *adj* gun dùil.

unfair *adj* mì-cheart.

unfinished *adj* neo-chrìochnaichte.

unfold *v* fosgail.

unfriendly *adj* neo-chàirdeil.

unfurl *v* sgaoil.

ungrateful *adj* mì-thaingeil.

uniform *n* culaidh *f*.

unimportant *adj* neo-chudromach.

uninhabited *adj* neo-àitichte.

union *n* aonadh *m*.

unique *adj* air leth.

unit *n* aonad *m*.

unity *n* aonachd *f*.

universal *adj* coitcheann.

universe *n* domhan *m*.

university *n* oilthigh *m*.

unless *conj* mur, mura.

unlike *adj* neo-choltach.

unload *v* thoir an luchd dhe.

unmask *v* leig ris.

unmusical *adj* neo-cheòlmhor.

unnecessary *adj* neo-fheumail.

unoccupied *adj* bàn.

unpack *v* fosgail.

unpardonable *adj* gun leisgeul.

unpleasant *adj* mì-thaitneach.

unpopular *adj* neo-ionmhainn.

unpremeditated *adj* gun roismuain.

unproductive *adj* neo-thorrach.

unreal *adj* neo-fhìor.

unreasonable *adj* mì-reusanta.

unrest *n* aimhreit *f*.

unripe *adj* an-abaich.

unsafe *adj* mì-shàbhailte.

unsatisfactory *adj* mì-shàsail.

unsightly *adj* duaichnidh.

unsuccessful *adj* mì-shealbhar.

unsuitable *adj* neo-iomchuidh.

untidy *adj* luideach.

untie *v* fuasgail.

until *adv* gu, gus, gu ruig.

unto *prep* do, gu.

unused *adj* neo-chleachdte.

unusual *adj* neo-àbhaisteach.

unwanted *adj* gun iarraidh.

unwieldy *adj* trom.

unwise *adj* neo-ghlic.

unworthy adj neo-airidh.
unwrap v fuasgail.
up prep suas. • adv suas; a-nìos; shuas.
upbringing n togail f.
uphill adv ri bruthach.
uphold v cùm suas.
upland n aonach f.
upon prep air, air muin.
upper adj uachdrach.
upright adj dìreach; onorach.
uproar n gleadhar m.
upset n cur troimhe-chèile m.
upshot n co-dhùnadh m.
upside-down adj/adv bun os cionn.
upstairs adv shuas staidhre; suas staidhre.
upward adv suas.

urban adj cathaireil.
urge v spàrr.
urgency n dèine f.
urgent adj dian.
urinal n ionad-mùin m.
us pron sinn, sinne.
usage n àbhaist f.
use n feum m. • v gnàthaich, dèan feum de.
useful adj feumail.
usefulness n feumalachd f.
useless adj gun fheum.
usual adj gnàthach.
usurp v glèidh gun chòir.
uterus n machlag f.
utmost adj as motha
utter[1] v abair, labhair.
utter[2] adj coilionta; dearg.
utterly adv gu tur.

V

vacancy n beàrn m.
vacant adj falamh.
vaccinate v cuir breac-a-chruidh air.
vagabond n fear-fuadain m.
vagina n faighean f.
vague adj neo-dheimhinn.
vain adj dìomhain.
vale n srath m.
valid adj tàbhachdach.
valley n gleann, srath m.
valour n gaisge f.
valuable adj prìseil.

value n luach m.
value-added tax n cìs luach-leasaichte f.
valve n pìob-chòmhla f.
van n vana f.
vandal n creachadair, milltear m.
vanish v rach às an t-sealladh.
vapour n deatach f.
varied adj iomadh.
variegated adj breac.
variety n atharrachadh m.
various adj iomadh.
vary v caochail.

vase n vàsa f.

veal n laoigh-fheòil f.

vegetable n glasraich f.

vegetarian n feòil-sheachnair m.

vegetation n fàs m.

vehement adj dealasach.

vehicle n carbad m.

veil n sgàile f. • v còmhdaich.

vein n cuisle f.

velvet n meileabhaid f.

vengeance n dìoghaltas m.

venison n sitheann m.

venom n nimh m.

venture n tuaiream m.

venue n làthair m.

verdict n breith f.

verge n oir f.

verify v dearbh.

vermin npl mìolan.

vernacular n cainnt na dùthcha f.

verse n dànachd f; (stanza) rann m.

version n innse f.

vertical adj dìreach.

vertigo n tuaineal m.

very adv fìor, ceart.

vest n peitean m.

vestige n lorg f.

vet n veat m.

vex v buair.

viable adj so-obrachadh.

vibrate v crith, cuir air chrith.

vicarious adj ionadach.

vice n dubhailc f; (tool) teanchair m.

victim n ìobairteach m.

victor n buadhair m.

victory n buaidh f.

video recorder n chàradair bhidio m.

view n sealladh m; beachd m. • v gabh sealladh; beachdaich.

viewpoint n àite-seallaidh m; ionad-beachd m.

vigil n faire f.

vigour n spionnadh m.

vile adj gràineil.

village n baile-beag m.

villain n slaoightear m.

vindicate v fìreanaich.

vine n fìonan, crann-fìona m.

vintage n fìon-fhoghar m.

violence n fòirneart m.

violent adj fòirneartach.

violin n fidheall f.

violinist n fìdhleir m.

viper n nathair-nimhe f.

virgin n maighdeann, òigh f.

virginity n maighdeannas m.

virile adj fearail.

virility n fearachas m.

virtual adj dha-rìribh.

virtue n subhailc f.

virtuous adj beusach.

virus n vìoras m.

visibility n lèireas m.

visible adj faicsinneach.

vision n fradharc m; (mental) bruadar m, taibhs f.

visit v tadhail.

visitor n aoigh m.

visual adj fradharcach.

vital *adj* riatanach; beò.
vitality *n* beathalachd *f*.
vivacious *adj* aigeannach.
vocal *adj* guthach.
vocalist *n* òranaiche, seinneadair *m*.
vocation *n* gairm *f*.
voice *n* guth *m*.
void *adj* fàs. • *n* fàsalachd *f*.
voluble *adj* deas-chainnteach.

voluntary *adj* toileach.
vomit *n* sgeith *m*. • *v* sgeith.
vote *n* vòta *f*. • *v* thoir vòta.
voucher *n* fianais *f*.
vow *n* bòid *f*. • *v* bòidich.
voyage *n* turas-mara *m*.
voyager *n* taisdealaich *m*.
vulgar *adj* gràisgeil.
vulnerable *adj* so-leònte.

W

wade *v* siubhail troimh.
wafer *n* abhlan *m*.
wag *v* crath.
wager *n* geall *m*.
wagon *n* cairt *f*.
wagtail *n* breacan-buidhe *m*.
wail *v* dèan caoineadh.
waist *n* meadhan *m*.
wait *v* feith; fritheil.
waitress *n* caileag-fhrithealaidh *f*.
wake *n* taigh-fhaire *m*. • *v* dùisg.
waken *v* dùisg.
Wales *n* A' Chuimrigh *f*.
walk *n* cuairt *f*. • *v* coisich.
walking stick *n* bata *m*.
wall *n* balla *m*.
walrus *n* each-mara *m*.
wan *adj* glas-neulach.
wander *v* rach air seachran.
wanderer *n* seachranaiche *m*.

want *n* dìth *m*; bochdainn *f*. • *v* iarr; thig geàrr.
war *n* cogadh *m*.
warble *v* ceileirich.
wardrobe *n* preas-aodaich *m*.
warehouse *n* taigh-tasgaidh *m*.
warlike *adj* coganta.
warm *adj* blàth.
warmth *n* blàths *m*.
warn *v* thoir rabhadh.
warren *n* broclach *f*.
warship *n* long-chogaidh *f*.
wart *n* foinne *f*.
wary *adj* faicilleach.
wash *v* nigh.
washing *n* nigheadaireachd *f*.
wasp *n* speach *f*.
waste *n* ana-caitheamh *m*. • *v* cosg, caith.
watch *n* uaireadair; faire *m*. • *v* dèan faire.

watchdog *n* cù-faire *m*.

water *n* uisge *m*. • *v* uisgich.

water-power *n* neart-uisge *m*.

waterfall *n* eas *m*.

waterproof *adj* uisge-dhìonach.

watershed *n* uisge-dhruim *m*.

watertight *adj* dìonach.

waulk *v* luaidh.

waulking *n* luadhadh *m*.

wave *n* tonn *m*. • *v* smèid; crath.

wax *n* cèir *f*.

way *n* slighe *f*.

waylay *v* dèan feall-fhalach.

we *pron* sinn, sinne.

weak *adj* lag.

weaken *v* lagaich.

weave *v* figh.

weaver *n* breabadair *m*.

web *n* eige, lìon *f*. .

webbed *adj* eigeil.

wed *v* pòs.

wedding *n* banais *f*.

Wednesday *n* Diciadain *m*.

weed *n* luibh *m*. • *v* priog.

week *n* seachdain *f*.

weep *v* guil.

weigh *v* cothromaich.

weight *n* cudthrom *m*.

weir *n* cairidh *f*.

welcome *n* fàilte *f*. • *v* fàiltich.

well[1] *adj* math; faillain. • *adv* gu math.

well[2] *n* tobar *m*.

west *adj* siar. • *n* an iar *f*. • *adv* an iar.

westerly *adj* on iar.

westward *adv* chun na h'àirde an iar.

wet *adj* fliuch.

whale *n* muc-mhara *f*.

what *interr pron* de? • *rel pron* a.

wheat *n* cruineachd *m*.

wheel *n* cuibhle *f*.

wheeze *v* dèan plòchan.

whelk *n* faochag *f*.

when *conj* nuair. • *interr pron* cuin?

whence *adv* co às.

whenever *adv* gach uair.

where *conj* far. • *interr pron* càite?

whereas *adv* do chionn gu.

whereby *adv* leis, leis am bheil.

wherever *adv* ge be ar bith càite.

whereupon *adv* leis sin.

whether *adv* co-dhiù. • *pron* co aca.

which *rel pron* a, (*neg*) nach. • *interr pron* dè?, cò?

while *conj* fhad is a. • *n* tacan *m*, greis *f*.

whin *n* conasg *m*.

whip *n* cuip *f*. • *v* sgiùrs.

whirlpool *n* cuairt-shlugan *m*.

whiskers *npl* feusag *f*.

whisky *n* uisge-beatha *m*.

whisper *n* cagar *m*. • *v* cagair.

whistle *n* feadag *f*. • *v* dèan fead.

white *adj* geal, bàn, fionn.

who *rel pron* a, (*neg*) nach. • *interr pron* cò?

whoever *pron* cò air bith.

whole *adj* slàn, iomlan.
wholefood *adj* slàn-bhiadh.
wholesale *n* mòr-reic *m.*
whoop *n* glaodh *m.*
whose *interr pron* co leis?
why *adv* carson?
wick *n* siobhag *f.*
wicked *adj* olc.
wide *adj* leathann.
widow *n* banntrach *f.*
widower *n* banntrach *m.*
width *n* leud *m.*
wife *n* bean *f.*
wild *adj* fiadhaich.
wildcat *n* cat fiadhaich *m.*
wilderness *n* fàsach *m.*
will *n* toil *f;* (*last*) tiomnadh *m.*
willing *adj* toileach.
willow *n* seileach *m.*
willpower *n* neart toile *m.*
wily *adj* seòlta.
win *v* coisinn.
wind *n* gaoth *f.*
window *n* uinneag *f.*
windward *n* fuaradh *m.*
windy *adj* gaothach.
wine *n* fìon *m.*
wing *n* sgiath *f.*
wink *v* caog.
winter *n* geamhradh *m.* • *v* geamhraich.
wintry *adj* geamhrachail.
wipe *v* suath.
wire *n* uèir *m.*
wiry *adj* seang.
wisdom *n* gliocas *m.*

wise *adj* glic.
wish *n* miann *m.* • *v* miannaich.
wit *n* toinisg *f;* eirmse *f.*
witch *n* bana-bhuidseach *f.*
with *prep* le, còmhla ri.
wither *v* searg.
withered *adj* crìon.
within *adv* a-staigh.
without *adv* a-muigh. • *prep* gun.
witness *n* fianais *f,* fear-fianais *m.*
witty *adj* eirmseach.
wizard *n* draoidh *m.*
wolf *n* madadh-allaidh *m.*
woman *n* boireannach *f.*
womanly *adj* banail.
womb *n* machlag *f.*
wonder *n* iongnadh *m;* iongantas *m.* • *v* gabh iongantas.
woo *v* dèan suirghe.
wood *n* coille *f;* (*timber*) fiodh *f.*
woodland *n* fearann coillteach *m.*
woodlouse *n* reudan *m.*
woodwork *n* saoirsneachd *f.*
wool *n* clòimh *f.*
woollen *adj* de chlòimh.
word *n* facal *m;* (*bond*) gealladh *m.*
word processor *n* facladair *m.*
wordy *adj* briathrach.
work *n* obair *f.* • *v* oibrich.
worker *n* oibriche *m.*
workmanship *n* ealain *f.*
world *n* saoghal *m.*
worldly *adj* saoghalta.
world-wide web *n* lìonra domhanta *m.*

worm n cnuimh, durrag f.

worn adj caithte.

worry n dragh m. • v buair, dèan dragh do.

worse adj nas miosa.

worsen v fàs nas miosa.

worship n adhradh m.

worst adj as miosa.

worth n luach m. • adj fiù.

worthless adj gun fhiù.

worthy adj airidh.

wound n leòn m. • v leòn, lot.

wrangle n connsachadh m. • v connsaich.

wrap v paisg, fill.

wrapper n filleag f.

wrath n corraich f.

wrathful adj feargach.

wreath n blàth-fhleasg f.

wreck n long-bhriseadh m. • v sgrios.

wren n dreadhan-donn m.

wrench v spìon.

wrest v spìon.

wrestle v gleac.

wrestling n gleac m.

wring v fàisg.

wrinkle n preas m. • v preas.

wrist n caol an dùirn m.

wristwatch n uaireadair làimhe m.

write v sgrìobh.

writer n sgrìobhadair m.

writhe v snìomh.

writing n sgrìobhadh m.

wrong adj ceàrr; coireach. • n eucoir f; euceart m.

wry adj cam.

XYZ

xenophobe n gall-gamhlasaiche m.

xenophobia n gall-gamhlas m.

X-ray n x-ghath m.

yacht n sgoth-long f.

yard n gàrradh m; (length) slat f.

yarn n sgeulachd f; (thread) snàth f.

yarrow n eàrr-thalmhainn f.

yawl n geòla f.

yawn n mèanan m. • v dèan mèananaich.

year n bliadhna f.

yearly adj gach bliadhna.

yearn v iarr gu làidir.

yearning n iarraidh m/f.

yeast n beirm f.

yellow adj/n buidhe m.

yelp v dèan tathann.

yes adv (non-affirmative) seadh (affirmative replies repeat verb used in question).

yesterday adv an-dè.

yet adv fhathast. • conj gidheadh, an dèidh sin, ach.

yew n iubhar m.

yield *v* gèill.

yoke *n* cuing *f*. • *v* beartaich.

yolk *n* buidheagan *m*.

yon *adv* thall, ud, an siud.

you *pron* (*sing*) thu, thusa; (*pl*) sibh, sibhse.

young *adj* òg.

youngster *n* òganach *m*.

your *pron* (*sing*) do, d', t', agad; (*pl*) bhur, ur, agaibh.

yourself *pron* thu fhèin.

yourselves *pron* sibh fhèin.

youth *n* òigear *m*; (*state*) òige *m*.

youthful *adj* ògail.

zeal *n* eud *m*.

zealous *adj* eudmhor.

zebra *n* asal-stiallach *f*.

zenith *n* bàrr *m*.

zero *n* neoni *f*.

zest *n* smior *m*.

zigzag *adj* lùbach.

zip *n* sip *f*.

zodiac *n* grian-chrios *m*.

zoo *n* sutha *f*.

zoology *n* ainmh-eòlas *m*.